WHITE
NIGHTS

WHITE NIGHTS

The Story of a Prisoner in Russia

by

MENACHEM BEGIN
Prime Minister of Israel

Translated from the Hebrew by Katie Kaplan

HARPER & ROW, PUBLISHERS

New York, Hagerstown, San Francisco, London

This work was first published in Israel under the title *Be-lelot Levanim*.
This work is published by arrangement with Steimatzky's Agency, Ltd., Tel Aviv, Israel.

FIRST U.S. EDITION

Library of Congress Cataloging in Publication Data

Begin, Menahem, 1913-
    White nights.
    Translation of Be-lelot levanim.
    1. Begin, Menahem, 1913-   —Political career
before 1977. 2. Prime ministers—Israel—Biography.
3. Political prisoners—Russia—Biography.
4. Zionists—Poland—Biography. I. Title.
DS126.6.B33A313 1979   947.084'2'0924   78-69610
ISBN 0-06-010289-6

79 80 81 82 83 10 9 8 7 6 5 4 3 2 1

Dedicated to

The Unknown Martyr

CONTENTS

I

THE ARREST

" You are invited to call at the Municipality, Room No. 23, between the hours of 9 and 11 a.m. in connection with your application."

This personal invitation from the Vilna Municipality reached me on the first of September, 1940, a few months after the Soviet Union had extended its direct rule, military and political, over Lithuania and the neighbouring countries of Latvia and Esthonia. The three small Baltic countries were recognised as a Russian sphere of influence in the German-Russian Pact signed in August 1939 by Ribbentrop and Molotov, but in the period between the collapse of Poland and the fall of Paris, Russia contented herself with bases that were " loaned " to the army against an " agreed " sum by the Governments of Tallinn, Riga and Kovno. These Governments were anti-Communist through and through. Nevertheless, in the interim period the Russians observed the principle of non-intervention in their internal affairs with studied punctiliousness. What is more, Lithuania received a heartening national gift from the Kremlin.

For twenty years the Lithuanians had cast longing eyes on Vilna, ancient city of Gedimin, which they called Vilnius. Vilna-Vilnius—home-town of the Gaon,[1] and called the Jerusalem of Lithuania by the Jews—was conquered by the Poles after the First World War. Because of this, little Lithuania broke off diplomatic relations and cut off all communication with her larger neighbour. Kovno was declared the provisional capital, and the belief that Vilna would one day again be the " eternal capital " of Lithuania was inculcated in the youth and in the people through school books and by means of

---

[1] Elijah ben Solomon (b. 1720, d. 1797), known as the Vilna Gaon, sage and Talmudical authority. His works cover not only every aspect of Jewish learning but also include treatises on algebra, geometry and astronomy.

striking pictures which adorned every railway station and public building.

Who can fathom the vagaries of history? The aim of a tiny people, regarded as fantastic by every observer (whether he rejected it or endorsed it), was " realised " in a manner no less fantastic. Poland was razed by German tanks; Communist Russia signed a treaty of friendship with Nazi Germany, in accordance with which Poland was partitioned for the fourth time by her mighty neighbours. Vilna was included in Russia's territorial booty. And Lithuania, resurrected as a State in a war against Moscow, now received the city of its dreams at the hands of Moscow.

However, the recipients of the gift were not at all sure of the sincerity of the donors. In the winter of 1940, at the height of the celebrations over the return of Vilnius to the bosom of their country, the Lithuanians used to say with bitter irony: *Vilnius musu, a Lietuva rusu*—Vilna is ours but Lithuania belongs to the Russians. But that winter, the winter of the lull, a winter of anticipation and anxiety, the Lithuanians were still thrilled with the diplomatic wisdom of their Old Man, President Smetana; and the sight of their own policemen (whom the Jews called the " metre-eighties "), tall and resplendent in their colourful uniforms, now in evidence in Vilna as well as in Kovno, warmed their hearts.

That winter we also heard—this time not from the Lithuanians—words of enthusiasm at the superhuman wisdom of another Old Man. The political officers of the Red Army, who were attached to the Soviet bases, used to accept invitations to private homes with alacrity, and would expatiate on the methods of Russian politics with surprising frankness. On one occasion one of them drew for the assembled guests two equilateral triangles, marked them, and proceed to deliver a geometric-strategic lecture.

" You see," said the Russian officer, " Europe now resembles a triangle. It has three centres of power which constitute the corners of the triangle: Berlin, London and Moscow. Now what did Chamberlain and the ruling circles in England want? They wanted to bring about the situation indicated in the first triangle: Berlin stands opposite Moscow at the base, while London is on top. Berlin clashed with Moscow and, in a protracted, bloody conflict, the forces of both Russia and Germany are spent. And then—that's what Chamberlain reckoned, and hoped—London would step down from her heights and bring about order in Europe.

"But," the lecturer went on to explain, "there is an ancient building in Moscow called the Kremlin, and in one of its rooms sits the wisest of all men, the genius of mankind, and he is very far-seeing. He, Joseph Vissarionovitch Stalin, succeeded overnight in trumping the cards of that wily Chamberlain. Today, as you see, the situation in Europe is as illustrated in the second triangle. Berlin stands opposite London, while our Moscow is on top. The war, which supposedly broke out because of Poland, will probably go on for many years. The Germans are very strong, but at the same time the combined strength of England and France must not be lightly dismissed. When the day comes, when both sides have exhausted their strength, *we* will come and institute order in Europe. . . ."

That was the calculation. And in the winter of 1940 it seemed to be correct. But once again free men—and particularly those free to *think*—were able to see how foolish it is to assume that great rulers, equipped as they are with all secret information, always know what they are doing. In the summer and autumn of 1939 Stalin trumped Chamberlain's cards—so the Soviet officer at that party in the capital of Lithuania was taught. But within a year the cards of that "wisest of all men" were in their turn trumped.

The Anglo-French front, which held for years in the First World War, was smashed to smithereens in the course of a few weeks in the Second World War. The German tanks were withdrawn to "Operation Red Beard" (or Barbarossa) at a speed which astonished London and Moscow equally, and the heads of the Russian army suddenly realised that they maybe did not have before them a protracted period of merely watching the enemies wear down each other's strength. It was almost certain that what they did have before them was a brief period of preparation for a terrible war against—the Soviet Union! With the fall of Paris, the Governments of Tallinn, Riga and Kovno fell at one blow. The causative connection between the two conquests, although effected in different parts of Europe and by different forces, was obvious. While German Panzers advanced rapidly through France, Russian tanks ploughed through the Baltic countries. In place of governments that were " lending bases " there arose overnight Communist governments that hailed the " liberation " that had been brought about not as the result of an independent revolution but as the result of the advance of the Soviet Army ; which is characteristic of what happened in other countries as well. There were no longer Soviet bases in the Baltic countries : the Baltic countries had become bases of the Soviet Union. Thus the second part of the ironic remark that was prevalent among the Lithuanians during the Vilna rejoicings came true. Vilna was indeed given to the Lithuanians, but the whole of Lithuania was transferred to the Russians.

Immediately after this happened, a large number of people in Lithuania began to receive " invitations " of various kinds.

I was invited by . . . the Municipality of Vilna.

I had not submitted any application to the Vilna Municipality. I lived in a little village a few kilometres from the town and had no interest in or business with its management. In those days, circumstances being what they were, it was not difficult to understand the significance and purpose of the Municipal invitation.

On the other hand, one has to have no small degree of scepticism not to be surprised at the odd mistake, small but at the same time serious, that the officers of the Soviet Intelligence made in issuing, or giving orders to issue, so naïve an invitation. The Soviet Secret Police is a mighty machine, highly experienced, with tentacles that reach out over the world. Not only friends of the Soviet Union, but even its enemies, believe that the Russian secret police are all-powerful and superhumanly clever. There is an impression that the Ministry of the Interior in Moscow has today inherited the legend that prevailed for generations about the British Intelligence. But it is only a legend. I was destined to come very close to both secret services, and I can testify that there are no few blockheads in both. On the strength of my personal experience, my advice is not to believe in the mysterious cleverness of secret services, whether they be Russian, British or anything else. The ordinary laws of shrewdness and stupidity, of aptitude and ineptitude, apply equally to them. They are not invincible.

The N.K.V.D. had decided to arrest me, but for some reason or other they tried to avoid doing so openly and to trap me instead into disappearing quietly. Was what they did the action of experts ? They gave orders to invite me to the Municipality in connection with my application, without troubling to find out first whether I had in fact submitted any application to the City Fathers, past or present.

Instead of being trapped I was warned. I decided not to comply with the courteous invitation, and not to call at Room No. 23 where, as I learnt from indirect investigation, the technical department of the Vilna Municipality had its offices. Having read between the lines of the Cheka epistle, I could have decided to hide or tried to escape. There was no certainty at all that I would succeed in getting out of their net, but on the other hand there was no doubt that I could hide in the homes of friends, particularly in another town, for a not inconsiderable time. But I decided not to call at the Municipal Building, and not to try to hide nor to escape. The reason for the first part of my decision was simple. If the Soviet Government, I said to myself, wants to arrest me, let its agents put themselves out and come to my house. That is their job. Why should I disappear as if the earth had swallowed me up? The reason for the second part of my decision was not simple, but I will not go into it.

The N.K.V.D. finally did " succeed " in arresting me—although not according to plan.

I suppose the head of the technical department in the Municipality waited for me for several days with most commendable patience, but eventually notified his superiors in another building that the invitee had not displayed reciprocal courtesy, or was not bothering about his application, and had not presented himself. I may also be permitted to presume that the people in the mighty machine who were dealing with my arrest smiled at each other and said : " Don't worry. He'll still show up! " Meanwhile, as I had failed to appear before them as invited, they—or their emissaries—showed up at my place, uninvited. But again—not to arrest me, just to keep me under surveillance.

One fine day we noticed that three people, one of them a girl, were watching our small house. Sometimes they just stood and looked. Sometimes they moved about or strolled around, but they never took their eyes off the place. They too displayed no expertness. On the contrary, they gave themselves away as soon as they appeared, and their function was only too obvious. We decided to try them out, and they certainly did not stand up to the test very well. I asked my wife to go with me on the short railway journey to town. " If the detectives arrest me," I said, " on the way to town, or in the town itself, I'll manage to say good-bye to you, but if their job is just to spy on me, it is just as well that we should get to know them and their job." We set out. A procession promptly formed. Behind us came the N.K.V.D. " observers " who were, from their point of view, far too visible ; and behind them came our friends, who were visible only to us. We even climbed into the train in that formation : my wife and I in one coach, our shadowers in the next coach, and our friends who were shadowing our shadowers in the third coach.

When we got out of the train at Vilna we all saw my escorts signal to some people who were waiting at the entrance to the station by rolling their eyes in my direction. The job was so crude, the facial contortions so unconcealed, that we were convinced that the arrest would take place then and there. But it did not. Still escorted, but otherwise unmolested, we continued on our way into town, always in three separate groups. Towards evening we returned home, in the same formation.

For ten whole days the hunt continued. A man who actually sees his pursuers, constantly hears their footsteps, and is fully aware of their intentions can hardly feel happy although, in certain circumstances, and having made up his mind as to what he intends doing, he does not necessarily have to be wretched. But were the hunters happy ? Is there any occupation more despicable than that of hunting human beings ? One day I glanced at my hunters and there was absolute terror on their faces. That day I had given them the slip. I did it merely for the fun of it because, as I have already said, I had no intention of escaping, and I believe that a sense of humour is an asset that should be preserved in all circumstances ; but when it was over I felt sorry for the agents, who were answerable for me with their heads and had orders to stalk me like a hunter stalks his prey before the kill. I almost regretted that I had made fun of them ; they were so confounded, so afraid, so abject. I did not try that joke again.

And so the fateful day drew near. On the face of it, nothing had changed in our little home. We continued to get up early in the morning and go out to gather wood in the forest which was yellowing in the autumn, and carried on with other household chores. We read, argued, laughed at ourselves, played chess and watched our watchers. " Are they still there ? " we would ask each morning. " Are you still here ? " my friends would ask each evening. We waited. Nevertheless, there was something in the air that could not be defined.

That autumn we lived through an unpredictable nightmare. Paris fell. France surrendered. The British Army took consolation in a successful retreat. Millions of Jews fell into the hands of Hitler and Himmler. Their doom was sealed. It was the fall of Paris that indirectly decided their fate. Millions of other Jews, most of them dreamers of Zion, were trapped within the closed borders of the Russian regime which saw, in the Zionist aim, the "national deviation" among the Jews. The Soviet regime always needed this deviation in order to prove that it was not pro-Jewish, as its enemies (who harped on the tune of hatred for the Jewish people, with which the masses were well imbued) maintained. Russia needed it to prove that the sword of revolutionary justice came down on the heads of Jews just the same as it did on those of Russians, Ukrainians, Poles and Uzbeks. All men were equal before the N.K.V.D. . . . Of course, the difference between persecuting Jews *because* they were Jews, and the persecution of Jews among the rest of the "enemies of the Revolution", was a very important moral and psychological one ; but the fact is that at times the difference was only psychological. A clever Lithuanian middle-class Jew remarked to me at the time : "Hitler and Stalin! Neither of them bodes any good for us. But there is a difference between them. Stalin will take away my fur coat, but Hitler would deprive me of my soul. So I'm lucky that I'm here and not over there." Nevertheless, it was not for long that this Jew was able to console himself with the distinction so succinctly and simply expounded by him. In his case, as in many other cases, the soul went the way of the fur coat.

Catastrophe followed catastrophe. And in the midst of all these catastrophes, both private and national, that befell humanity at large, Ze'ev Jabotinsky[1] died. I am certain that if I filled whole pages I could not even attempt to explain what the death of Rosh Betar[2] meant to me. A stranger will not understand. The word " stranger " in this special instance also includes some of my own people. And so all I will say is this : I felt that the bearer of hope was gone, never to return ; and with him—perhaps never to return—hope itself. . . .

---

[1] Vladimir Jabotinsky (1880–1940), statesman, orator, poet, writer, soldier—the greatest Jewish political leader of modern times, after Herzl.

[2] Title applied to Vladimir Jabotinsky in his capacity as head of the Betar (short for Brit Trumpeldor), the Jewish national youth organisation, which he founded. Out of Jabotinsky's teachings and the Betar, the Irgun Zvai Leumi arose.

Wherever you looked, there was suffering. A sea of suffering, deep and wide as the ocean. The suffering was not the usual kind of suffering, it was not limited. It was not the suffering of living ; not the suffering of individuals who rise against oppression or poverty. It was the suffering of stark fear, the suffering of people trapped by those who seek to annihilate them, the suffering of millions of ordinary people the purpose of whose lives was just to live, and that their children should live.

In the face of such a sea of suffering, listening to the tumult of its waves, hearing the cry of the tortured, the groans of the imprisoned —and they were all (or most of them) ordinary people, " bread-eaters " ; not public figures, not leaders, not declared idealists—one cannot help thinking that there is no form of inequality more terrible, more likely to drive man to revolt, than the inequality of suffering.

No one will deny that suffering as such is not the purpose of life ; it is not even an aim of life. Usually, a man will ask himself : Why do I suffer ? Usually his aim is to avoid suffering, to eliminate it, to be spared from it. But in days of mass catastrophe, under conditions of general collapse, of destruction without end, it is then that man asks himself : Why do they suffer ? Indeed, the natural, primary impulse is to help, to save, to comfort. But if you can no longer comfort ; if you are unable to save ; then nothing remains but the spectre of inequality in suffering ; a fearsome phantom that almost takes away the very zest of living.

Therefore, I am telling nothing but the truth when I say that when the fateful day came and the agents of the Russian Intelligence arrived to take me on my long journey, I felt no anxiety. On the contrary, my principal emotion was one of intense relief.

They came on a clear autumn day. There were three of them : a man in charge of the operation and two assistants. The man in charge asked me, angrily :

" Why didn't you come to the Municipality ? Weren't you invited to come ? "

It was a foolish question ; the answer could only be " guileless ".

" I have not submitted any application to the Municipality, I have no business with it. If the Municipality has any business with me, let the official concerned be so kind as to come to me."

" You have to go to the Municipality just the same, because you were, after all, invited," said the second detective in a more conciliatory tone.

" No, I won't go."

" Oh yes, you will," said the man in charge, drily.

I lost patience with this game of hide and seek and said to my callers, in an angry voice : " Who are you, gentlemen ? Why are you hanging around my house ? Who gave you permission to enter my private home ? If you will not stop disturbing our peace I shall be compelled to complain to the police."

The face of the man in charge lit up.

" The police ? Please, do come with us to the police, now! "

" I won't go now. I'll go when I consider it necessary."

" If you won't go of your own free will, we will take you by force," he exploded.

" Oh! . . . So will you tell me who you are ? Do you represent the authorities ? Where are your identity papers ? If you do not show me some official identification I will not go with you."

The detectives exchanged glances. When they had finished their wordless consultation the first man took out some sort of card and held it out to me, giving me a penetrating look as he did so.

I looked at it. It certainly was a most official card—issued by the Intelligence Service of the State of Lithuania. What was clear right from the beginning was now clarified further.

" Well," I said in a most placatory tone of voice, " you have come to arrest me. So why did you try to hide it ? Why didn't you say so right away ? Have you a warrant of arrest ? "

. . . Have you a warrant of arrest ? The words were an echo from out of the distant past. In a flash I saw it again, in my mind's eye, a dreadful night twenty years before, in Brest-Litovsk. The army of Trotsky and Tukhatchevsky had withdrawn and the Polish army had entered the town. That night—I was still a little boy—Polish detectives came to arrest my father on a charge of having assisted the Bolsheviks. My father was a veteran Zionist and secretary of the Jewish Community and was always busy—often at grave personal risk—trying to save Jews who were condemned to hard labour or to death, not because they were Bolsheviks but because the anti-Semitic authorities accused them of pouring boiling water on the Polish army or giving information to the Red Army. In the eyes of the anti-Semites every Jew is a " Bolshevik ". It was therefore not surprising that they had come to take my father on the occasion of one of their official pogroms. But he was able to ward off arrest and eventually save his life when he put the question : Have you a warrant of arrest ? The wheel had turned full cycle. Here was I, twenty years later, asking Bolshevik detectives the same question : Have you a warrant of arrest ? I knew perfectly well that the question would not ward off my arrest, but I put it just the same. Perhaps in doing so I was fulfilling a juridical requirement ; or maybe it was just atavism.

" We have no warrant," said the chief detective, " but what you said is correct. We have come to arrest you. If you refuse to go with us we have the right to use force."

" Very well," I said. " Now I know that you have been sent to arrest me. Permit me to get ready."

During this exchange, my wife and Dr. Israel Scheib and his wife were standing by. We lived under the same roof together with my friend and brother-in-law the late Dr. Arnold, and my childhood friend Joel Krelman. Batya Scheib began to cry, and I asked her not to. My wife did not cry. She was prepared for it, no less than I was. Scheib and I exchanged a few observations on the interesting game of chess that our " guests " had interrupted.

After they had admitted why they were there, we changed our attitude to the detectives. My wife and I invited them to have some tea with us. Somewhat taken aback, they thanked us politely but declined the invitation on the grounds that they could not tarry any longer. So I hurried over my preparations. I asked for some bread to take with me. I polished my shoes. I did not take any belongings because the agents would not let me take any " bundles ", explaining, with a surprisingly kindly smile, that although I was in fact under arrest they were sure I would be released immediately and return home the same day. They did let me take with me two books to read. That was a concession and at the same time a sign that they trusted me, for the detectives were unable to examine the contents of the books which were, in fact, counter-revolutionary. One was written in English, a language which I had just begun to learn. It was Maurois's book on Disraeli, the man who expanded the British Empire. The other book was written in what an ardent Jewish Communist termed " the Fascist language ". It was the Bible.

I said good-bye to Dr. Scheib and Batya. My wife was given permission to accompany me to the car which was awaiting me and my escorts at a certain distance from the house. I took the first fateful step towards the unknown ; as a prisoner I crossed the threshold of the house. We went down into the courtyard. The owners of the house, Polish officials and devout Catholics, dropped their eyes when I bade them good-bye and wished them everything of the best. Perhaps they were afraid. They were certainly amazed to see the Communist Government arresting their Jewish tenant. The scene was so foreign to their conceptions, so very strange in their eyes.

On the way to the car I saw my friend, David Yutan, who had also been awaiting arrest for several weeks now. We looked at each other—that was our leave-taking. My wife and I exchanged a few brief words. There was not time to say much. What point is there in saying much at such a time? I told her I thought I would be back, but in any event she was not to let people be sorry for me. She answered me in one brief sentence : " Don't worry, everything will be all right."

" Don't forget to tell Scheib that I concede that last chess game to him. He was leading, anyway, when they interrupted us."

" I won't forget," said my wife.

She stood there, waving, until the elegant car that the N.K.V.D. had put at my disposal was out of sight.

2

THE INVESTIGATION BEGINS

AFTER a little while we arrived at the grey building in the centre of Vilna in which N.K.V.D. Headquarters are housed. Formerly, the long corridors of that building used to resound with the voices of lawyers, litigants and judges, prisoners and policemen. This was the District Court of Poland. In the autumn of 1940 the litigants and their lawyers disappeared from the murky passages. There remained —or again appeared—prisoners and their guards, and their judges. The setting had hardly changed at all, but the players in the human tragedy had changed. And this change-over symbolised, perhaps more than anything else, the revolutionary transformation that had occurred around us.

In my student days I used to hear the Communist students sing a song of many verses, each of which ended with the words : " And we will be the judges." In this song, which was a translation from the Russian, there was an echo of profound faith and a vengeful threat. I do not think that these impecunious idealists ever really intended that they themselves would be the judges of their judges, but they did believe in the solace of revenge : a day would come and their judges would be judged, those who imprisoned them would themselves be imprisoned, their persecutors would in their turn be persecuted. This was the plan of the revolution, even if it was not its aim. And now the day had come. In the place where Polish judges used to try Communists, Communists were trying Polish judges. But for many of my unhappy generation, ardent fighters for Communism, there was no consolation in their revenge. Their persecutors were indeed persecuted, their judges judged, but they themselves, believers in the " New World ", were not only not among the judges, they were among the judged. And of their tragedy, a special tragedy which has no parallel in the history of human striving, I shall yet tell. I saw them in their ardour, and I saw them in their wretchedness; I saw them at the peak of their happiness, and I saw them fall into the depths of despair. Never have I seen a more burning ardour, a blacker despair, or a harder fall than theirs.

I came in contact with one of the new judges that appeared on the shifting platform of justice a short while after I crossed the threshold of thresholds, the threshold of the N.K.V.D. building. I was sitting in an ordinary room, opposite an ordinary desk, reading about the period of Disraeli's youth. Suddenly I heard footsteps echoing down the long corridor, the door opened noiselessly, and in the doorway I saw two of the detectives who had arrested me, and another—a new one. It was not difficult to guess that the investigation was about to begin.

The third man, having greeted me with a loud *ʒdrastvoytye!*, sat down on the other side of the desk and asked me my name, which he already knew. I answered. His second question was—about the book which lay open between us. He did not content himself with the name of the book, but wanted to know who the author was and what it was about.

So it was not the interrogation that had begun, but a sort of friendly discussion. We looked at each other. He sat looking at me, blinking his small eyes, with the searching interest that is so characteristic of his profession. I was not the first prisoner with whom he was having a friendly chat in order to come at him suddenly, in the manner of Dostoievsky's investigating judge, with a question to the point. For me, he was the *first* N.K.V.D. interrogator I had come across in my life. A new world was opening up before me, full of unknown horrors. I knew that anyone who came to " study " this world, which is closed as soon as it is opened, must pay a high price for doing so, but I found a certain satisfaction in having the opportunity—thanks, it is true, to the fantastic topsy-turviness of the times—of observing at close quarters, from within, the methods, the secret workings and the rulers of the realm of the N.K.V.D. I am telling the truth when I say that as I sat opposite my interrogator I felt that I was, by inner recognition, a student observer, and a detainee only by some external decree. The power of curiosity! But if I am to tell the whole truth, I must admit that I did not succeed in maintaining my status as a student all the time I was in the N.K.V.D. world, and in the course of my detention only my status as prisoner would probably have remained, if anything remained of the prisoner.

Nevertheless, I can say, on the strength of my personal experience, that one should, in all circumstances, give free rein to the thirst for knowledge which is in every man. Even if you are brought down to the depths of humiliation, to the valley of the shadow of death—open your eyes wide, and learn! For as long as you are learning, your inquisitors will not succeed in establishing between you and them the relationship they desire ; they, the superior beings, and you, the degraded. As equal to equal you will talk with them ; they will interrogate you, but you will " study " them. You will not just be a " case ". And from the knowledge that around you are not only crudity and humiliation, but also material for study, you will draw strength to stand up to the test of degradation—and remain a man.

During our conversation, I therefore tried to fathom what nature of person my interrogator was :

Is this a Chekist ? Is this the Chekist type ? Is this a product of the school in which mysterious methods of breaking people were devised ? How will he interrogate me ? What will he want to get out of me ?

I could find nothing special nor typical either in the external appearance or the behaviour of the man with whom I was talking. He was dressed in civilian clothes, and a bourgeois tie adorned his grey suit. Judging by his features, I gained the impression that he was a Jew, but I was not sure. Naturally, I did not promise myself any advantage from the possibility that his mother lit candles on Friday nights, but I would have given a great deal to know if my impression was correct. Evidently my curiosity was somewhat excessive and my interrogator noticed it. He stopped the discussion suddenly, and asked me crossly : " Why are you looking at me like that ? "

I was compelled to deny, in an apologetic voice, that I had looked at him in any special way.

" Do you know why you were invited to come here ? " he asked, suddenly.

" Why I was invited ? " I repeated, amazed.

" Yes. I want to know if you know why you were invited here."

" I do not know the reason, but I do know that I was not invited but arrested."

This time I put the stress on the word arrested, just as, before, I had put it on the euphemistic word invited.

" Who told you you were arrested ? " asked the interrogator, reprovingly. "Nobody arrested you. I only wanted to talk to you. I have a few questions to ask you, and if you answer them sincerely, like an honest man, you will go home right away. By the way, have you a wife ? "

" Yes."

" How old is she ? "

" Twenty."

" She's young. She's no doubt waiting for you. But don't worry, you'll just answer my questions and you'll go back to her. You must regard yourself as a free man, not a prisoner. I'm telling you again : you were not arrested. You were invited here for a chat with me and it is entirely up to you when you return home."

I listened to the interrogator's warm words of persuasion and enjoyed myself. The N.K.V.D. representative, the know-all, was trying to outwit me and I, thanks to my previous " obstinacy ", was being given the opportunity of depriving him of that satisfaction.

With a perfectly natural laugh, I said : " Why are you trying to delude me ? I know I was arrested and I am quite prepared to answer your questions as a prisoner."

He was not yet prepared to give in, and asked, with mounting anger : " Who said you were arrested ? Where did you get that idea from ? "

" The people who brought me here told me I was under arrest."

He jumped up as if stung.

" What ? They told you you were under arrest ? "

He waited for no further confirmation from me and dashed into the corridor without bothering to close the door behind him. From where I was sitting I could see the detective officer who tried to invite me to the " Municipality ", and heard the thundering voice of the N.K.V.D. interrogator echoing through the empty passage. In a torrent of execration, there reached me distinctly a number of traditional Russian curses that have, as I learnt in the course of time, full citizenship rights in the realm of the N.K.V.D., although they are forbidden by Soviet law.

Apparently, even under an all-powerful regime there are rules that have to give way in the face of the laws of life ; and how can a Russian, even if he is himself responsible for seeing that the law is kept, give expression to his feelings, both good and bad, without a " mother " curse ? The unfortunate detective at whom the hard words were hurled answered something—only the echo of his words

23

reached me—and the interrogator came back into the room, the foam of his outburst still discernible on his lips.

Then it became clear to me why the N.K.V.D. needed the whole comedy of the invitation to the Municipality ; why its agents played hide-and-seek with me for ten days. They decided to arrest me and liquidate me in the usual way. They could have done that simply, openly, but they wanted to conceal their real purpose from me. In the course of time, when I met other prisoners, I learnt that I was not the only one whom the N.K.V.D. tried to trap by means of a civilian invitation, which does not arouse suspicion, instead of carrying out the arrest the direct way. In most cases people went to the various offices to which they were invited ; and if their hearts were heavy within them, they deluded themselves—Dante's warning about having to abandon hope is not inscribed over the entrance of any sub-office of the Soviet secret police—that if the matter was cleared up they would be allowed to return home. And this illusion —the first, but not the last to be nurtured in the bosom of the prisoner —is required by the soul-engineers of the Cheka. If a man is arrested and knows that he is arrested—particularly by the N.K.V.D. —he will seriously doubt the promise : If you tell the truth you will go home immediately. But a man who is invited for a chat, a man who is requested with every courtesy to reply to a number of questions—why should he not hope, or why should he not delude himself that he has prospects of getting out safely ? The urge to get out of any police station is very great. But what is there to compare with the urge to get off N.K.V.D. premises ? And those who invented the " science of the N.K.V.D." gave orders to begin the treatment by playing on this urge in the victim. The warrant of arrest, therefore, usually remains in the file. The arrest itself is denied. The first interrogation is merely a " chat ". And if you tell the truth—which means, if you tell not what you know but what the N.K.V.D. wants you to tell—you will go home, you will return to your family.

That is the method. No one can say what percentage of successes the N.K.V.D. can record to the credit of this system. And whoever has seen all the possibilities of the N.K.V.D., whoever has gone through the Soviet soul-engineering with all its instruments, might well be surprised that this mighty authority should resort to so simple, so primitive, a means of persuasion. Is a man who is required to confess to the most heinous crimes—from the point of view of the authority that arrested him, or even invited him—likely to confess merely because the interrogator or the person conducting the discussion promises to let him go free ; or rather, go on being free ? Is the N.K.V.D. noted for the rapidity with which it releases its prisoners, or those it invites ? When any particular man is invited for a chat, were not thousands invited before him ? And have they not disappeared ? When any particular man is arrested, were not thousands arrested before him ? And what was their fate ? Anyone who analyses the known facts is entitled to call all these invitations and promises of release primitive, childish. But there is method in this childishness. Because, where a man's hopes are concerned, he is not inclined to learn from the experience of others. He always regards himself as an exception : Perhaps *I* have a chance, all the same.

Only someone who has experienced this system can understand the paradoxical expression : reactionary progress. Once, before the " progress " of Socialism and Communism, certain rules were laid down governing the attitude of society, or of the State, towards the individual who had committed, or was suspected of having committed, an offence against them. " In the name of the law I hereby arrest you " the representative of the authorities would say, and place on the table a warrant of arrest signed by a judge. The prisoner, or the accused, or the suspect, was then taken to a place known to his family, would demand contact with them or with a lawyer for his defence, and thus the open legal processes began, which ended either with the charge being proved and the imposition of a penalty or with the prisoner's being acquitted and released. This procedure is the essence of simplicity. So simple, that those who are used to it are surprised that it should be described at all. But it was not granted to humanity gratis. For generations, for hundreds of years, mankind suffered because there were no such rules, and it is only constant revolt for freedom, at the price of suffering, blood and tears, that brought about their introduction, and established them as a safeguard for the individual, alleged criminal or actual criminal, lest he be pounded between the millstones of authority.

And here comes " progress " of the revolution of our day, and back we go to the pre-revolutionary days when the ruling powers were entitled to arrest secretly, to kidnap a citizen, and hold him in a dungeon. How they scoffed, my contemporaries the Communist students, at the prejudices that were connected with the guarantees for the freedom of the individual! With what dialectic logic they tried to prove that these safeguards were merely a fake " super-structure " erected on the real basic " structure " of a regime of exploitation, in order to deceive the exploited and give them the illusion of freedom. When I met them, or bigger and more important Communists than them, in the world of the N.K.V.D., I no longer heard from them words of scorn about our prejudices. When we used to discuss this subject, in between night interrogations, they longed for the days before " reactionary progress "; they hankered for the simple procedure of the " old " world, which seemed to them in their " new "—but actually older—world no less legendary than the myths of ancient Greece.

But the N.K.V.D. system has created another paradox. Its power over people subjected to its authority is almost unlimited. The N.K.V.D. can arrest them at any time; it also has the authority to sentence them, with or without a confession, with or without witnesses. Nevertheless the N.K.V.D. elects not to arrest, but to invite; not to act openly, but secretly. And if it is an accepted thing in our world that the ruling powers of one State resort to secrecy to outwit the powers of another State by devious means, it is strange, even in our world, to see a ruling power employ such methods against individuals who actually fall under their jurisdiction, against individuals who join the vast multitude of prisoners of the N.K.V.D. History tells us of underground movements that were formed by citizens against their powerful rulers; but in the Soviet Union the rulers have created a powerful underground against their citizens.

When the interrogation was resumed, I could not, of course, think of all these things. Only astonishment at the primitive childishness of the system and momentary satisfaction at having discovered it were mixed up together inside me.

The interrogator repeated his promise, although not quite so persuasively, that if I would tell the truth I would go home. But what was the " truth " that he wanted to hear from me, that he lied so deliberately to get, with a kindly smile playing over his lips?

" Are you active in politics ? " he asked.

" Yes."

" Which ? "

" Zionist."

" In which Zionist organisation were you active ? "

" In the Betar."

" Were you just an ordinary member, or did you hold office ? "

" I held office."

" Which ? "

" I was the head of our organisation in Poland."

" Did you have many members in Poland ? "

" Yes, tens of thousands."

" Very nice. . . . Now tell me everything—everything, mind!— about your activities in Vilna against the Soviet authorities."

" There were no such activities."

" You are lying! "

Up to now he had addressed me in the plural, the accepted form of polite address in Russian, but now he used the offensive singular " ti ". Possibly, in my situation at the time, it was hardly worth while paying attention to such trivialities, but my prejudices did not let me reconcile myself with this sudden change in the attitude of the interrogator.

" I have read," I told him, " that representatives of the Soviet authorities behave courteously to citizens, and so I would ask you not to say ' ti ' to me. Furthermore, I am not telling lies."

" I didn't mean to insult you," said the interrogator. " I see you are *gramotné*[1], but you needn't be so proud. The main thing is that you must tell the truth and you, apparently, do not want to tell the truth. You'd better think it over, because you are only harming yourself."

For a while this dialogue kept on being repeated in various forms and in different wordings. Actually, in what I had already told him —or, in his language, in what I had already " confessed "—I had given him, according to the laws of the N.K.V.D., enough material to have me liquidated. True, there was nothing in it that was new to him. Our work in Poland was public and above-board, and information about it had been furnished to him beforehand by Jewish informers, who were not lacking. It is true that I did not tell him of the all-night vigils that we held in Vilna, Kovno and other Lithuanian towns to pay homage to the memory of Ze'ev Jabotinsky.

---

[1] Literally, "know how to read and write", but when used by the Russians it is a compliment and a recognition of education.

Or the mourning-parade that we held for Rosh Betar, on the thirtieth day after his death, in the Vilna Cemetery, where tens of Betar members gathered, among them Joseph Glazman who later commanded the fighters of the Vilna Ghetto ; Israel Epstein who fell in Rome as one of the officers of the Irgun Zvai Leumi ; Abraham Amper who became one of Abraham Stern's lieutenants and was, like him, killed by British agents ; Nathan Friedman and Dr. Scheib, at one time heads of the Lechi (Fighters for the Freedom of Israel, or so-called Stern Group) ; David Yutan who succeeded, by some miracle, in evading Soviet arrest but was not so successful in keeping out of the British concentration camp in Eritrea ; Yerachmiel Virnik, now editor of the paper *Yizma* in Israel ; the poet Shlomo Skulsky, and others. To that parade we secretly brought our flag. We took up positions around the grave of a young Betar member who had frozen to death in a snow-storm while trying to get to Palestine by way of Vilna. We said a prayer and sang the song of Rosh Betar, *Migov Rikavon ve'Afar*, the song of songs of the Revolt, and of faith that out of the " decay and ashes " Israel would rise again. And, with the blue-white flag flying over the cemetery, we took an oath to keep faith with the behests of our teacher, with the idea of the rebirth of our nation, under all conditions and at all costs. " We will yet have the privilege of fighting for Zion," I said to the group of mourners. " But if we are prevented from doing so, it will also be good to suffer for Zion. Come what may, we will fulfil our pledge."

Of course, such activities were considered political crimes ; that is to say, the most serious of crimes, in the eyes of the Soviet authorities. But could *we* regard them as crimes ? In what way could these mourning gatherings harm the government in Moscow ? There is no denying that under a regime that rigorously tracks down any deviation, the question was very naïve. But it was genuine, and when the interrogator asked me about our activities in Vilna " against his Government ", I denied there having been any, convinced that I was speaking the truth. But as the investigation continued I learnt that he did not in fact mean these trifling things ; he meant espionage activities and preparing acts of sabotage. In return for that " truth " he promised me, with his mouth, my safe return, but in his heart—the grave.

This, as I learnt from the experience of other prisoners, is also part of the " scientific method ". A man who is arrested by the

N.K.V.D. as a political offender is not accused of something concrete which he may or may not have done, but is confronted at the beginning of the investigation with the gravest accusations ; espionage and sabotage are the routine charges. The prisoner, dumbfounded, denies it all. The interrogator insists that he make a full confession. The prisoner tries to convince him that he is speaking the truth, and sometimes, in order to get out of the frightful trumped-up charges, he confesses to lesser deeds that he did not do either.

Did my interrogator really believe the things he accused me of, or was he acting in accordance with the method of proceeding from the more serious to the less, where the weight of even the " less " is as heavy as a man's life ? It is difficult for me to answer that. The interrogation had already lasted several hours, and the interrogator, after assuring me once more that I was only harming myself by withholding the truth, suddenly put a stop to the exchange of words and said :

" I will leave you here alone. Here you have pen, paper and ink. Write—write everything concerning your life and your activities. But you had better write the truth. In any case we know . . . You still have a chance of returning to your wife. Think carefully, and write the truth."

I had not learnt to write Russian. At that time I understood the language, having picked it up by hearing it spoken, and I could, by throwing in a large number of Polonisms, answer questions in Russian. So I asked the interrogator whether he preferred me to write my life-story in Polish or in Yiddish.

" It's all the same," he replied. " We translate from many languages here, but from my own point of view it would be better if you wrote in Yiddish, because I am a Jew, too."

I blurted out : " Really ? "

" Yes," he said. " I am a Jew, and as a Jew you can trust me. You write the truth! "

3

THE WALL

As I sat writing my life-story, I remembered the *Curricula vitae* that we used to have to write before being accepted into a school or entering for an examination. Who would have thought, then, that a day would come when I would be writing " I was born in 1913 ... I began school ... I completed my studies ...." for the High School of suffering, for the University of the N.K.V.D.!

I have always had a nostalgia for my school days, but never have I experienced so heart-constricting a yearning for my bygone boyhood as I did while I wrote the story of my life by order of the truth-expert of the N.K.V.D.

At moments like these, a miracle occurs and reality ceases to exist ; and the products of a good and beneficent imagination become reality instead. But these are, indeed, moments of weakness. A man who faces the supreme test of suffering for the things he believes in and strives for must not hanker for his boyhood. He must know that a mother's loving hand will not comfort him any more by its mere touch, and the joys of youth will no longer be his portion. One's waking hours, not the dream, are the reality. There is no home, no mother, no sister, no friend. There is the N.K.V.D. There is an interrogator who demands the truth. He would like to get it in exchange for his promise of returning home ; but he will also be pleased to read it, written black on white, out of special trust in a common origin ...

Well, I must write a short life-story and prepare for a long journey. Before me are paper, pen and ink with which the Guardians of the Revolution were kind enough to supply me. Behind me is a soldier with a bayoneted rifle. Write!

The armed Soviet soldier had come on the scene a short while after I was left alone with the writing materials. He was let in by a short, quick-bodied sergeant, and from then on I was never alone again, not in the room where I was detained nor in any other place. My guard stood in the middle of the room with his hand on his rifle, his eyes following every movement I made. He said nothing. I wrote.

Having completed my composition in which I confirmed that since I was a boy, up to and including the time when I was head of the Betar movement in Poland, I had worked for the return of the people of Israel to their land, I picked up Maurois's book and began once more to read of the " pre-historic " period when dreamers of Zion did indeed exist, although it never entered their minds that a day would come when their dream would be declared a crime. The guard let me read undisturbed. I became absorbed and did not notice the time pass.

Suddenly the door opened and the interrogator entered the room with quick strides. To my amazement, he first went up to the soldier and showed him some sort of document. The soldier examined it very carefully, pronounced it in order, and left the room. Where-upon the N.K.V.D. officer sat down in front of me and asked, genially : " Well, have you finished writing ? I am interested to read what you have written."

I handed him my life-story. He picked up the page with my hieroglyphic handwriting, glanced at the square letters, and put it aside. He did not read it. He did not even try to read it. I wondered whether he could read his mother tongue at all. But, whether he could read the ancient lettering or not, he paid no attention to the composition that he had himself asked for, and came back to his old question.

" Are you ready to tell the truth ? "

I replied that I had written down what I had already told him, and that was the truth. And if I had to sit in jail because of it, I would.

" Don't you know that we have ways of compelling you to tell the whole truth ? "

There was nothing to reply to that.

" Why don't you say something ? " the interrogator burst out. " Do you think you'll put me off with this scrap paper ? I'll still read what you have written, but I advise you to think your position over again. You had better not be so stubborn."

A number of times—goodness only knows how many—the interrogator reiterated his demand, his warning, and his dark hints.

Hours had gone by since I first crossed the threshold of that gloomy room. I was arrested in the middle of the day, and when our second " chat " drew to a close darkness had already fallen. I was hungry and far more thirsty. I asked my interrogator whether I might get something to drink.

" Yes, of course. I'll organise some tea for you."

I did not understand why having tea brought required any special organising, but his promise fell pleasantly on my ears. I was beginning to suffer acutely from thirst. The interrogator left me again. As he went out, the soldier came in again. I sat and waited for my tea, and in the meantime resumed reading the life of Lord Beaconsfield.

The hands of the watch on my wrist crept round the dial several times. I went on reading, until the changing of the guard in the N.K.V.D. building. The little sergeant entered the room with a number of armed soldiers, ordered one of them to take up his position, and told my guard to come with him. I noticed my former guard whisper something to the sergeant.

" Is that so ? " said the sergeant aloud, turning to me immediately. " I hear you spend your time here reading books. Do you think this is the reading-room of a club ? Who said you could read ? "

" The interrogator allowed me to," I replied.

" The interrogator ? He has no say here. We are in charge of this room. The soldier that is standing here is responsible to me, and I to the man above me. The interrogator has no authority . . . From now on, no reading here. Please see to it ! "

The sergeant ordered me to take the chair in which I had been sitting facing the table, and put it in the corner of the room. The edge of the chair was almost touching the wall, and the arm-rest was opposite it. I had not quite grasped the full intention of the officer of the guard, and sat in a more or less human fashion, with my face to the door and my left side to the wall.

" No, you don't sit like that here," the sergeant hastened to correct me. " Turn your face to the wall. And you," he said, addressing the new guard, " your job is to see that he stays like that and doesn't read any more books."

Well, a radical change had occurred in my situation. Instead of a book—a wall. But I must admit that for the first few moments of my expulsion from the Garden of Eden—every man, in all circumstances, has his own private Paradise from which he falls—I did not think of the blank wall, nor of the things that it, instead of Maurois, would tell me. I kept on thinking principally of the rather odd, categorical statement of the sergeant: The interrogator has no authority . . . WE decide here. . . .

I recalled that the interrogator too had said to me: WE know everything. You had better tell US the truth. Who, then, did the interrogator's " we " signify, and who were the sergeant's " we " ? Was not the one an officer of the N.K.V.D. and the other a non-commissioned officer of the same institution ? Then I also remembered how the N.K.V.D. officer who was my judge-interrogator had to identify himself to the guard, a private in the army of the N.K.V.D., before he could set about carrying out his official job. Apparently, in the first stage of the arrest—perhaps the correct technical term is " detention "—there is in the N.K.V.D. a dual authority in relation to the prisoner, or detainee. The function of the interrogator is to extract a confession. Although he holds the rank of judge-interrogator he is authorised to do no more than conduct the " discussion " along the familiar lines. The direct control over the prisoner is vested in a different authority. And this duality no doubt disappears somewhere way up in one of the high ranks of the Command of the N.K.V.D. machine.

I did not succeed in finding out, either as a prisoner or as a free man in Russia, since when that unique duality had been in practice. It may have been introduced in the Cheka or the G.P.U. by Dzherzhinsky, but it is possible that it took form only with the coming of the Thermidor of the October Revolution.

If the ruling power arrests Bolshevik leaders who have the adoration of millions of people, it is logical that they will not put them in the charge of the officer who interrogates them, but in the charge of a *gardovoi*[1] or *strilok*[2] who knows no nonsense. The interrogating officer is also carrying out the wishes of the people above him when he demands, to the accompaniment of enticements, threats and invective, a full confession from the prisoner who only yesterday commanded their " hurrahs ". But the interrogating officer is *gramotné* and knows who is standing before him ; and so, apparently, there is a certain danger lest . . .

The *strilok*, on the other hand, knows nothing except automatic discipline. He is barely literate, and it is precisely because of this that he can be relied on. If his superior, the sergeant, orders him to

[1], [2] Russian names for " sentry ".

guard a prisoner, that is to say, a criminal, he will guard him from everyone, even the interrogating officer himself. If the prisoner is Yagoda, who was himself chief of the N.K.V.D.—what of it? If the criminal is Yezshov, who replaced Yagoda as head of the N.K.V.D.—what of it? If the criminal is a man who held the official position of President of the Soviet Union, that too means nothing to the *strilok* who knows only one thing: the man who put him there will relieve him. After the Revolution, a new intelligentsia developed in Russia, but the Revolution does not even rely on its own intelligentsia. If it has to rely on anyone, it prefers to rely on the *mala-gramotné*, those who barely know how to read and write.

We have before us another paradox of the Soviet regime, or the regime of the N.K.V.D. The power of the Government, or of its police force, is unusual, but putting this power into operation is accompanied by unusual caution, a caution which borders on a fear complex. The regime was set up for the masses, but it puts its trust in the N.K.V.D. And even this trust has its basis in their lack of trust. If we are to judge by the number of people who go through the hands of the N.K.V.D. we find that very many of them are enemies of the N.K.V.D. regime. But the regime distrusts not only its enemies, real or imagined, but even its friends, its servants, and its guardians . . . " WE decide here," the little sergeant said to me, and with my own eyes I had seen the judge—who apparently held my fate in his hands—ask the consent of a private before continuing the interrogation.

My interrogator had to prove his bona fides more than once to the constantly changing guard. For almost sixty hours I sat facing the wall. Night went by, then day. Then another night and another day. And when the third night was almost over, the extraordinary session came to an end and the ordinary sitting began. . . .

I imagine that the figure sixty hours makes little impression on the reader. I too write it lightly today, after the lapse of a dozen years. Actually, I was lucky. Others have sat facing the wall for eighty hours, a hundred hours, and more. But I suggest that my reader try a simple experiment: place a chair in the position in which the N.K.V.D. sergeant placed mine, and sit on it for two hours, your knees pressing against the wall and your eyes glued to one point. I am sure that if the reader will try this only partial experiment—and it is extremely partial, not only from the point of view of time—he will understand my wild joy when at the end of those sixty hours I was able to throw myself down on a mattress—in jail.

It is true that even a point on a wall can be an open book, that even a point on a wall can conjure up again pictures that one has forgotten and that help one to forget. Even a point on a wall can tell of home ; of the hot tears that fall from a child's eyes because of a bad mark he has received from the teacher, not because he had not learnt or did not know his lessons, but because he did not want to write in a Gentile school on the Sabbath, and wanted to say, in the face of the humiliation and the contempt for his people : " Yes, I am a Jew and I am proud of it." A point on a wall can show wonderful processions of the new, proud Hebrew youth that rose out of the " decay and ashes ", and the eyes of old men that fill with tears as they behold the miracle, while their lips murmur a prayer of thanksgiving for having reached this day. It can tell of the first meeting with Ze'ev Jabotinsky. The hall of the provincial theatre is not large, but it is filled to overflowing. For you, the boy, there is no room either in the hall or in the gallery, which looks as if it is going to collapse. With difficulty you squeeze into the orchestra pit, beneath the stage. You sit there, down below, and begin to feel in every fibre of your body that you are being lifted up, borne aloft, up, up . . . Have you been won over ? No, more than that. You have been consecrated to the ideal, forever. A point on a wall can tell of boyhood love and the heights of happiness to which only young love can raise a person. It can tell of student days of penury, and the wings that a student sprouts when he passes an examination in spite of his poverty, or perhaps because of it. It can tell of important missions that had to be carried out, they too under conditions of perpetual hunger—but it did not matter! It can tell of the first speech which ended in a complete fiasco, the words of consolation and the jibes, the first more difficult to bear than the second, and of other speeches that ended differently. It can tell of the first experience of sitting in jail because of an "unpeaceful" demonstration in front of the British Consulate against the closing of the gates of Eretz Israel. It can tell of the first meeting with Polish *Urki* criminals, which was a useful preparation for the subsequent encounter with Russian *Urki* ; of a type of veteran and experienced jail-bird ; of a wily, professional thief whose name among thieves was " Graf " and whose real name was Pototzki! A point on the wall can tell of the sparks of revolt against those who tried to turn Eretz Israel into

" Palestine " ; of a group of young Jews, members of the Betar, who boarded a small boat somewhere on the shores of the Mediterranean and under cover of night landed on the shores of the land of their fathers and paved the way, with all its trials and tribulations, for the so-called illegal immigration, for those who came after them before the Second World War, during the war, and after it ; and in that first group was Shalom Tabatchnik, from the squalid quarter of the Lutzk ghetto, who was accepted as suitable for immigration although he had nothing to cover the essential expenses of the journey, and whose name was unknown until it was exalted and revealed as Shlomo Ben Yosef.[1] A point on the wall can tell of conferences and conventions, of meetings and debates, of the ups and downs of nights of sorrows and days of joy ; of the love of friends that warmed one's heart, and the astonishing hatred of opponents. And a point on the wall can not only bring up from the depths of the forgotten that which has been, but also conjure up things that are going to happen in the future : the rapture of meeting someone you love after a long separation, the light of joy in the eyes of friends as they welcome you back, and the continuation of the battle for the ideal that has become your aim in life.

That one single point on the wall can take you out of the detention room and carry you beyond its narrow confines, away from the building of horrors and the lost world of the N.K.V.D., to the world of the living, into your world which was and will be again. As you sit and stare, a miracle occurs. By means of self-command, that magic creation of the human soul, the one reality departs and another comes in its place. The reality imposed upon you disappears entirely, and the reality for which your soul yearns, and upon which even the N.K.V.D. cannot impose its will, appears in all its splendour.

What I have written is not mere theory. I am not dabbling in mysticism. I have told the truth of what happened not only around me but within me during the sixty hours when I sat facing the wall. That is how the time went by. Goodness only knows how it would have passed otherwise.

But what about sleep ? In the Talmud it says that a man who does not close an eye for three days will die. But perhaps man is incapable of not closing an eye for seventy-two hours. Those who are lucky enough not to have experienced what many of my contemporaries went through, possibly do not know under what conditions man is

---

[1] Executed in Acre Fortress by the British in 1938.

capable of sleeping. It is possible to sleep standing. I saw that not only in Russia but in ordinary times when, for days and nights, I travelled in packed trains across the length of Czechoslovakia or the breadth of Poland. It is even possible to sleep while walking. I experienced that with Nathan Friedman when, with our young wives, we made our way on foot to the eastern district of Poland, while the German army was ploughing up the country with their tanks. We walked for weeks on end, sometimes under a rain of German bombs which the misleading pre-war propaganda had derisively called " ersatz " bombs ; and mercilessly they reaped their harvest of death among the hordes of refugees. It is no exaggeration : we walked, sleeping ; we slept as we walked.

In comparison with these conditions, I had " ideal " conditions for sleep in the detention room of the N.K.V.D. Headquarters. I was not standing, and I was not walking. I was seated. The sergeant of the N.K.V.D. was right—the detention room was no reading-room of a library, and had no easy chairs. My hard chair almost touched the wall, so that it was, at times, difficult to know what to do with my poor knees. All the same, I was seated, which was the best of the four possible positions, besides the horizontal. Therefore, more than once during the sixty hours, I fell asleep. I even dreamt. The trouble was that whenever I dozed off in the room, which was lit either by the sun's rays or the electric bulbs, the armed soldier would tap me on the shoulder, not particularly brutally, and in a low voice—lest he wake me ?—he would say :

" You are not allowed to sleep."

My eyes would open again, and fix themselves again on one point. And again the soul dreamt its dreams. This time, awake.

The voice of the soldier who, poor thing, was also deprived of his natural hours of sleep, was not the only one that broke the sequence of my various kinds of dreams. From time to time, by day or by night, the interrogator would appear in the detention room and ask :

" Well, are you ready to tell the truth ? "

The question was a routine one, and the reply could only be a routine one. There is no need to repeat them.

The interrogator did not get angry and did not threaten. He smiled. I did not complain to him about the sergeant's order, nor about sitting facing the wall. I maintain that in certain situations into which man is brought, sometimes of his own choosing, and sometimes against his will, he must be able to renounce all things; principally, he must be able to give up the idea of complaining. In general, nothing is gained by it; it only gives satisfaction to those who are not worthy of any additional satisfaction. Did not the "judge" see, when he came into the room, how and where I was sitting? Did he not leave me as he found me, after he had asked his question and smiled, and after he had received my answer and smiled? It was clear that he knew, and that there was no sense in complaining.

But I had one complaint against him, a just one, even a "legitimate" one. He had promised to organise some tea for me. Where was it? They did not give food in the detention room. Again the sergeant was right: it was no club reading-room so you could hardly expect someone to bring you sandwiches. It is a fact that under certain conditions food is not important; the body "forgets" to demand it. For me, in any event, the bit of bread that I had taken with me sufficed. It is not difficult to stand three days of fasting—in those conditions. But thirst is an altogether different matter. The body cannot forget that under any circumstances.

The interrogator promised me tea. Let him bring it! Whenever he came, I would remind him of his promise and ask him to carry it out, with the persistence of a moneylender who demands his interest. But the reply of the interrogator was always the same:

"Oh! Didn't you get it yet? Never mind, be patient, I'll organise the tea for you."

Again—"organise" it.

I waited for sixty hours, and the tea was not organised; or perhaps it was organised, but it was not brought to me. And one may assume that if my interrogator is still alive, if he did not fall into the hands of the Germans during the war and was not liquidated as a Jew, or if he was not demoted from the position of judge-interrogator to that of the interrogated and the judged, he is still busy organising the tea which I no longer need, and organising the teas that the souls of thirsty prisoners are crying out for.

Sixty hours passed. Even that passed. I had experienced on a small scale the special means of pressure, possibly the worst conceived by the ancient international inquisitorial science: depriving a man of sleep.

On that last sleepless night that I spent within the walls of Headquarters, my interrogator did not appear. In his stead came other

38

people, and one of them ordered me to get dressed and take my belongings. I was put into a car in which I found a few more people, whose origin I will never know. We travelled quickly and fairly comfortably. One of the passengers complained loudly and tearfully that they had arrested him for nothing, and that he had left a young wife and baby at home without means. The others kept silent. One of the guards cut short the effusions of the complainant, and said in flowery Russian :

" If you didn't do anything wrong you will be released immediately after the inquiry. In the Soviet Union people are not arrested like in the capitalistic countries—without cause. And as for your wife and child, even if you have to be in prison for a while, why are you worried ? Have you forgotten that they are in the land of the Soviets ? "

The prisoner fell silent. As for myself, I had only one desire—to sleep.

4

THE LAW OF REVENGE

REGIMES may come and go, but prison goes on for ever, although changes occur within its walls. When a revolution succeeds, the gates of the prisons are opened and the prisoners, victims of the regime that has just fallen, go free ; literally on their heels, the gates close on new prisoners, victims of the regime that has just been set up. Humanity is still waiting for the revolution of revolutions that will not exchange prisoners but will do away with prisons.

From the time when the Czarist Russian Government erected the central prison of Vilna called Lukishki, its sturdy walls have been dumb witnesses of many revolutions, of the fall of regimes and the rise of others, of changes of " population " in its gloomy cells, and changes of guards in its long corridors. Each revolution had its guards ; every war had its prisoners ; and every batch of prisoners had its inscriptions. Half a dozen languages were engraved on the thick walls, reminders of the revolutionary war against the Czarist regime ; of the strivings for national liberation of the Poles and Lithuanians ; of the war of the Communists against the Polish and Lithuanian regimes ; of the persecution of the Lithuanians by the Poles, and the Poles by the Lithuanians ; of the imprisonment of Poles and Lithuanians alike by the new Russian regime. I gave the Hebrew language, too, a place of honour on the concrete walls of Lukishki.

I spent my first day in Lukishki looking around, and getting acquainted with my cell-mates. Although the surroundings were new to me, they were not strange. What the point on the wall conjured up at N.K.V.D. headquarters, living reality renewed. The barred window that limited the prisoner's range of vision to parallel strips of sky—I had seen the same thing a few years previously, from inside the Warsaw prison. The peep-hole in the door which enabled the guard to spy on the prisoner's movements unobserved—

I was acquainted with that too. The Polish *Urki* used to call it "Judas", after Judas Iscariot, symbol of treachery in the eyes of all mankind. It was called that in Lukishki, too, though not particularly by the criminal prisoners. The attitude of the prisoners to the "watching-eye" can be gleaned from the name they gave it. Apparently men can hate not only their fellow-men, but even things; I have never seen a hatred as intense as that which fell on the dumb thing that bore the name of the man who sold Christ.

I found all the usual items in the human cage—a straw mattress, a shelf, an ordinary table, a rickety stool, a small bowl, and, of course, the pail.

Taken all in all, the prison in Vilna is like the one in Warsaw; and all the others built by man to cage his fellow-men are no doubt just like it. There is nothing new. And it is just as well not to be a novice in prison.

Nevertheless, there was something new in Lukishki, something intangible, something in the air that kept not the body but the mind of the prisoner preoccupied. In the atmosphere of every prison there is always the unspoken question: "When will I get out of here?" In the prison under the supervision of the N.K.V.D., the question is: "Will I get out?"

"When will I see my family?" every prisoner asks. The N.K.V.D. prisoner asks: "Will I ever see my family again?"

A man who is accused of violating a law will ask, with a greater or lesser degree of anxiety: "What will they question me about?" But a man accused by the N.K.V.D. of some unknown offence, asks: "How will they question me?"

What lawyer shall I take? Who will be the judges? What witnesses will my defence lawyer call? When will the trial take place? What is the punishment specified by the law? These are questions that every accused asks; a prisoner of the N.K.V.D. does not. He knows that they have nothing to do with the issue. In the "old" world they had some point; in the "new" world only one question is actual: Where will they take me? . . .

But the day the iron gates of Lukishki closed behind me, the day when I first began to breathe the air of complete isolation which I had not hitherto known, I did not ask questions. I was asked questions. I was asked innumerable questions and I felt I had to answer them. My cell-mate was hungry for news. He had been arrested six weeks before me. For forty days he had sat alone. It is no wonder that he longed for human intercourse. It is no wonder that he wanted to know everything that was happening in the world at large. I did my best to satisfy his very natural curiosity.

My first cell-mate owned a little farm and was an officer in the Polish reserve; he was accused of belonging to a secret organisation but he did not have to " go underground " in order to find himself behind bars, one bright day, under the Soviet regime. His main sin, which was in itself enough, was his social position. The man was a small *pomieszchik* or big *Kulak*, which meant that he was condemned to liquidation as such. To this " original sin " my companion added another crime, also an old one: twenty years before his arrest he had fought in the ranks of the Polish army against the Russians. After his arrest he was examined on all three charges, but what astonished him most was the third. He asked me the question he had asked his interrogator: " Can I be accused of serving in the army of my own country? Wasn't a peace treaty signed between the Soviet Union and Poland in 1920, when the war was over? Can a citizen be charged for carrying out his lawful duty? " The questions were correct from the point of view of accepted procedure. But how could my cell-mate know the accepted procedure in the realm of the N.K.V.D.? Only from experience did he learn, just as I did, that one of the basic laws of the N.K.V.D. is the law of revenge. Later on, I had a neighbour in jail who was seventy-eight years old. He was full of years and wrath, and his body was a wreck. His eyes were dim, his ears blocked, and his legs could no longer hold him up. We even had to carry him to the lavatory. What was this broken old man arrested for? He began his military career in the 1880's and reached the rank of battalion commander in the Czar's army. He was on pension for more than twenty years, but neither his age nor his disablement saved him from being punished by the N.K.V.D. for having served the Czar. He was sentenced to eight years in a correctional labour camp. But he cheated the N.K.V.D. and regained his freedom, not—as they had ordained—when he was eighty-six, but seven whole years before that. The old colonel (who used to say to his cell-mates: " Don't call me 'colonel'. Can't you see that I've been reduced to a son-of-a-bitch? ") died a year after he was arrested. The law of revenge knows no pity. And if it applies to so feeble an old man, on the point of death, why should it not hold good for people who still have half their lives before them?

My first cell-mate was a middle-aged man, well-mannered and highly educated. It was a pleasure to talk to him and eat with him. He used to observe the " ceremonial " as if we were sitting not in a locked, evil-smelling cell, but in some grand banqueting hall. If, in ordinary circumstances, ceremonial adds beauty to life, its importance is even greater under conditions that are fit—to use the expression of the old colonel—for sons-of-bitches. Ceremonial to a certain extent takes away the ugliness of these conditions of life, and preserves the link, over the concrete walls and the iron gate, with the world from which you have been cut off in the storm of events.

My neighbour was also not without a sense of humour—man's most important means of guarding himself against the blows of fortune. Although he was a very proud Pole—of the ten degrees of pride that came down to the world, the Poles took nine—he used to permit himself, from time to time, a certain light irony at the expense of his own people. He used to make particular fun of Polish army officers, even of the highest rank, who came from the Czarist army and had never learnt Polish properly. On one such occasion he related the following story: A famous general was making a fiery speech on Independence Day, and said in his broken Polish: " Three cruel conquerors divided our unhappy homeland. The cursed Germans took one part, the Austrians took the second part, and the main part—we took! . . ." Perhaps this amusing story is not entirely out-dated. In our time, with a textual change, Marshal Rokosovsky is liable to repeat it.

It was good to joke with my neighbour. Nevertheless, it was not easy to live with him. He had a positive obsession for orderliness. I have never in my life seen a pedant like him, who put order among things above orderly relations with people. Of course, a liking for order is an admirable attribute. It is precisely as a Jew that I had a respect for it, as the twist in our character in the Diaspora manifests itself, among other things, in the loss of a sense of order. If order is important in ordinary life, it is far more so in a narrow prison cell. We had to fix the times for our " walks "; together we could not promenade between the window and the wall, a distance of two and a half metres. We had to divide between us the job of polishing the shining cement floor, or of taking out the pail and cleaning it. We had to suffer a certain amount from each other; and indeed, if we were able to stand each other at all, the keeping of some sort of order was essential in the small cell we shared, thanks to the vagaries of the time. . . .

My neighbour was a bachelor and a pedant. I do not know whether he had remained a bachelor because he was a pedant, or became a pedant because he had remained a bachelor. I only know that he had an obsession for tidiness and would go into a silent sulk for days merely because, when "setting " the table, the day I made his acquaintance, I had unwittingly placed my wooden spoon on that part of the table which he picked as his.

The N.K.V.D. did us a good turn and put into our cell an arbitrator in the person of a third prisoner. He was a corporal in the Polish army, a tailor by trade, a young man, uneducated but intelligent. We were drawn together mainly because I began to give him lessons in a number of subjects, principally the history of his people and of other nations. He studied with remarkable diligence and used to prepare for his daily lesson by endless repetitions. " In prison," he used to say with a wry smile, " here am I trying to make up for what I missed at school." These courses which we conducted purely by memory used to shorten for all of us the infinite time of our sitting in jail. My first cell-mate used to act as a sort of assistant teacher and prepare the corporal for his lesson, but he often walked out on his job because of his love of order. In the course of time the corporal and I grew accustomed to his cross spells. Sometimes he would break off diplomatic relations with me, sometimes with the corporal, and sometimes he would boycott both of us. As a result of our both being the victims of his spells, there grew up between us a sort of solidarity, unexpressed but natural, of the " attacked ", in spite of the fact that they were both Poles, and I—a Jew.

One day this solidarity was broken. That day we had a discussion —one of those discussions that kept on cropping up inside the prison walls—about the war and the international situation. We opened the conversation with France and the Western Front. My cell-mate, the officer, told us that during the " phoney " war he had received a letter from a friend who had escaped to France, after the collapse of Poland, and was serving in Sikorski's army. The letter was full of optimism. " Our cavalry," his friend wrote, " could not stand up to the German tanks, but in France there are tanks and aeroplanes in plenty ; that is a real force and one can rely on it absolutely." " And now we see," my cell-mate continued, " that

44

this force which we all wanted to believe in succumbed more quickly than our army did. Does that not prove that we were all right, more so than we ourselves thought after the victory of the Swabians ? "[1] My other cell-mate, the corporal, sighed and said : " Ah, yes, if we had only had the tanks and aeroplanes that were there! " In the words of both of them I sensed a certain strange satisfaction at the defeat of France, their country's ally. It was, it is true, satisfaction mingled with regret, regret at the victory of their cruel, eternal enemy, and the extension of the war, but nevertheless —satisfaction. As time went by, I learnt that my neighbours were merely giving expression to the general feeling that prevailed in those days among the Polish people. There is, apparently, a good deal of truth in the theory that the principle of consolation of the disabled—whether an individual or a nation—lies in the fact that someone else's disability is more serious than one's own.

From the subject of France and Poland we went on to the relations between Russia and Germany. We had all seen, before our arrest, the oil trains and the goods that used to pass through Vilna on their way from Russia to Germany. We had all read the telegram of congratulation which Hitler had sent Stalin on his sixtieth birthday. We all remembered the reply of the Russian ruler, in which he said that the covenant between Russia and Germany was a blood covenant. . . . Nevertheless we all held the opinion that a clash between both parties to the " blood covenant " was inevitable. Sooner or later it would come. This view was, of course, not just the opinion of individuals. Almost everyone who lived in those days in the " Baltic Corridor " felt instinctively that one day the narrow corridor that separated the two giants would disappear. And no one had the slightest doubt that, when the corridor vanished, a clash between Russia and Germany would be imminent, in spite of all the statements of people officially in the know, in spite of the external protestations of good neighbourliness, and mutual assistance between Moscow and Berlin.

My neighbours spoke of the impending clash between the " Swabians " and the " Muscovites " with a satisfaction that they did not even try to conceal. For their hopes there were not only national reasons—they had, with their own eyes, witnessed the partition of their country by the " neighbours "—but also personal reasons. My neighbour, the officer, said:

---

[1] Derogatory name for the Germans.

" Whatever the future holds in store for us, there is no doubt that if war breaks out between Germany and Russia we'll get out of this stinking cage."

And the corporal added:

"I think the Swabians will beat the Muscovites, and if the Germans come here we have a chance of being set free. And you, Mr. Begin, don't you worry. We'll stand by you and help you."

My reply burst, as it were, from my very heart :

" Gentlemen, I can't share your delight. I also think that a trial of strength between Russia and Germany is inevitable. If Hitler beats England he will want to conquer Russia, and if he does not beat England he will be compelled to try to conquer Russia. But I will not attempt to hide the fact that as I make this analysis I am very much afraid. I can't forget that in the event of a Russo-German war, more millions of Jews are likely to fall into the hands of Hitler. And what will become of them ? You maintain that war between these two will give us prospects of getting out of Lukishki. Yes, I also want to get out, but when I think of them I tell myself that if I have to be released at such a price, I would rather remain in Lukishki, if that will prevent Jews from falling into the hands of the Gestapo. Of course, this discussion is only academic, for is the trend of events dependent on what we want ? But why should I hide it ? I am not praying for a war between Germany and Russia."

The reply of my neighbour, the officer, was like an explosion of wrath.

" What you have just said, sir, is most characteristic. With you people, everything is decided according to one criterion: what is good for Jews. Actually I was told long ago that there is solidarity among all Jews, but you have given me confirmation that you people guard your solidarity under all circumstances, even in prison."

My pupil, the corporal, was equally angry.

" Yes," he said, " the Jews always stick together. Don't try to deny it, Mr. Begin. Why, you yourself have just said that it is better that we should all rot in this stench, if only no harm will befall your people."

What was there for me to reply to their contentions ? They both spoke of Jewish solidarity as if it were a crime, as if they were talking about a conspiracy, something evil. For heaven's sake!—I thought to myself—what have the Jews not done to prove that they do *not* stick together? In every European war, except this last, the

Jews of one country fought against the Jews of another. The divisions among the Jews, the multiplicity of their parties and their trends, are proverbial! The Marxists of Jewish origin—who can be compared with them in their inspired war against the prejudices of "narrow, national solidarity", and for super-national inter-class solidarity? What blood-offerings the Jews have given on this altar, the altar of proof that Jewish solidarity does not exist, or is not desirable! And all to no purpose. The fictitious Jewish solidarity exists and will always exist—in the minds of others. And if this is the case—I asked myself—has the time not come to strip it of the slur of a crime, the accusation of a conspiracy? Is our fate not unique? And is it not common to all of us Jews? Has not the time come to convert Jewish solidarity from a Gentile myth into a Jewish reality?

There was no point, of course, in posing these questions to my neighbours. I also felt that I had committed a psychological error and hurt them unintentionally when I said that I was not with them in their silent prayers, the prayers of hope of all prisoners, the prayers of consolation of the wretched. One thing I said to them :
" Gentlemen, what you call Jewish solidarity—I wish it really existed."

They both smiled. And their smile was more bitter than their words. A shadow fell between us, between the estate-owner and the soldier on the one hand, and myself on the other. This shadow never completely disappeared, even though it did grow a bit fainter in the course of our stay together in prison.

One day, another change occurred in my pupil, the corporal. When we first met he declared that he was not religious, that he was even an atheist. He used to tell many stories about priests who did not observe the various laws of abstinence. He used to get particular enjoyment out of repeating the story of the priest who used to preach to his flock : " My children, listen to what I say, do not look at what I do." His blatant unbelief used to annoy our cell-mate, the officer, very much. He was a devout Catholic and prayed a great deal. Interesting, but strange, was the contrast between the uneducated son of Catholics who had drifted away from the faith of his fathers and the highly-educated man who diligently and ardently observed all the commandments of the Catholic Church, in so far as it was possible to observe them between the prison walls of Lukishki.

47

But one morning we were amazed, both the Polish officer and I, to see the corporal isolate himself in a corner, cross himself, and sink to his knees in silent prayer. When he had finished praying, he turned to us and said with a certain shy hesitancy: " I shall pray every day. I have begun to believe again." The officer, who had just been through one of his attacks of obsession for order, forgot his anger and the boycott and shook the two of us by the hand most warmly. Before our eyes the miracle of religious rebirth had occurred. And I can testify that the revived faith of the corporal helped him, as his imprisonment continued, to overcome the melancholy which is the portion of every prisoner of the N.K.V.D. And I can further testify that this uneducated soldier was not the only prisoner in Lukishki who converted from atheism to ardent belief. I met other prisoners, among them highly educated people, sceptical men of science who, as the days of internment multiplied and the nights of interrogation increased (particularly the latter), began to turn their eyes beyond the prison walls to the Hidden Power— perhaps He would be merciful. . . . It is a fact—and I saw it with my own eyes—that man in his downfall has nothing to lean on, nothing to solace him, except faith. The N.K.V.D. brought many back to the religious fold. . . . And Lukishki nights taught us that faith takes better care of man, when things go badly with him, than man does of his faith when things are well with him.

In the atmosphere that prevailed in our cell with the religious resurrection of the corporal, I naturally found my cell-mates most understanding when I informed them, one day, that I would do without my supper and my food for the whole of the next day. Were it not for that atmosphere, it is possible that my neighbours would have sneered at my " fanatical " decision. We had been in jail for quite a while already, and the menu of the N.K.V.D. was beginning to have its effect on us. We were no longer hungry. We were starving. And the difference between those two feelings can be appreciated only by someone who has experienced what it is to go to sleep hungry, to wake up hungry, and know with absolute certainty that when he lies down again and when he gets up again he will still be hungry. In such conditions man is liable to give substance to the frightening words : ". . . Man hath no pre-eminence above a beast ".[1] Many an inmate of Lukishki used to humiliate himself to the lowest depths to get a little more, an extra spoonful

[1] Ecclesiastes iii. 19.

48

of soup. Many a man avidly licked his bowl dry. Many an N.K.V.D. prisoner used to gather the breadcrumbs into a little ball and gaze at it like a man gazes at a precious pearl before gulping it down. And these people were once well-to-do, and lived in ease and luxury. Their standing was high and their hearts exalted until they felt the taste of perpetual hunger and began to count the grains of the half-teaspoonful of sugar which they were given to sweeten the brown liquid called coffee in the realm of the N.K.V.D.

My giving up the portion of soup in the evening, the coffee in the morning, and more soup at midday, under circumstances like these, would certainly have prompted cell-mates that had no faith to ask me if I had gone out of my mind. But my two neighbours, who found consolation in their faith, did not scoff and did not try to turn me away from my decision; and it was only with the greatest of difficulty that I succeeded in persuading them to share between them the food which I renounced on the Day of Atonement.

I was arrested on the threshold of the Jewish year 5691, and I had no difficulty—with the daily counting that is customary in all prisons—in establishing when the Day of Atonement fell. I knew, therefore, which evening not to pass my bowl through the hatch, and to ask the warder to add my portion to the bowls of my neighbours. The warder was surprised.

"What's up? Sick?"

"No, I'm not sick. But today is Judgment Day for me."

"Judgment Day? What's Judgment Day? And what's that got to do with food?"

"I am a Jew, and on Judgment Day Jews don't eat."

"Drop that nonsense. You can eat—on my responsibility!"

His tone of voice was pleasant, humane. I thanked him for his readiness to guarantee for me. He opened the door, turned on me an expression that almost resembled a smile, and said:

"Well, hand over your bowl. I'll pour it."

"No, no." I hastened to correct the wrong impression I had given by thanking him. "Pour it for my friends."

"Half-wit!" he murmured.

I said nothing.

The warder shrugged his shoulders and told my neighbours to give him their bowls for an extra portion, an extraordinary addition which they owed to the Jewish Day of Reckoning and Fasting which was not cancelled in Lukishki, although a Guardian of the

Revolution was ready to take upon himself the responsibility for dispensing with it. . . .

I wondered where I would be next Day of Atonement. My wife —who had remained " at liberty " under the rule of the N.K.V.D.— where would she be then ? Where would my old father and mother be, and my brother and my sister ? Where would all my people on both sides of the " frontier " be ?

And as the brain had no answer, the fearful heart replied with a prayer. As I recited the words sanctified from generation to generation, as I prayed silently, I felt the impenetrable barriers that separated me and those I loved fall away. Once again the " secret button " of the mind operated. The cell vanished, the walls disappeared, and there appeared in all its splendour the great illuminated synagogue and my father's humble dwelling, lit up by love, purity, faith, and the eyes of a loving Jewish mother. Kol Nidrei night in an N.K.V.D. prison. . . . The Day of Atonement in Lukishki —even such a night can be a night of solace, even such a day can be a day of identification with all that is good in man's life.

The night passed, the day came to an end—and immediately after the Day of Atonement the nights of interrogation began.

WHOSE NAME BEGINS WITH "B"?

I was summoned and taken for interrogation in accordance with all the rules of the system. A few hours after the bed-time whistle had sounded, the door of our cell opened with a grating noise. We all awoke from a deep sleep. The three of us were already veteran prisoners. We had learnt to doze off in the light, and sleep soundly, particularly the first few hours of the night, in spite of the lamp which burned until daylight so as to enable our guards to use the Judas window even when we were lying down. But the echo of familiar footsteps, the grating of the lock and the opening of the door would awaken the prisoner from even the sweetest of dreams. We awoke, therefore, immediately, and looked over to the doorway where, next to the duty warder, two other uniformed men stood.

" Who is on ' B ' ? " one of them asked in a low voice. That is a speciality of the N.K.V.D. It means : whose name begins with " B " ?

According to the security regulations of the " Government in the Underground " a prisoner must not be summoned for interrogation by his full name, lest the name be heard in the adjacent cells ; or in case it is the wrong cell, and the inmates hear the names of other prisoners. Furthermore, for safety reasons, warders are not allowed to enter the cells of the prisoners, " enemies of the people ", except in special cases. For all these reasons, the science of the N.K.V.D. has laid down that the warder will ask, in the doorway : " Who is on ' A ' ? " or " Who is on 'Z ' ? " and the prisoner concerned will reply from inside the cell. If the man they are looking for is there, only his cell-mates, if there are any, will hear his reply ; if there is a mistake in the list, the inmates of the cell will not know who, besides themselves, has been caught in the net.

In our cell I was the only one whose surname began with " B ". I gave my name. The warder checked his list.

" First name, and name of father," he went on to ask.

" Menachem Wolfovitch."

" Get dressed, you're wanted for interrogation."

I did as ordered. My cell-mates were silent but their eyes were eloquent. We went out of the cell. We walked down the winding staircase. Between it and the wall wire netting had been stretched, to guard against the likelihood of the prisoner's escaping to a place where even the N.K.V.D. can no longer interrogate him. . . . On the way, two or three gates opened before me. I crossed lengthy courtyards. The Lukishki prison is big. Suddenly I was ordered to halt and turn right. My guards and I stood still for a few minutes. I saw nothing except the wall, but I heard footsteps behind me. It was not difficult to guess that we had crossed the path of another person being led to interrogation, and it was forbidden, by N.K.V.D. regulations, that we should see each other's faces. In another courtyard I passed a prisoner standing with his face to the wall. Out of the corner of my eye I could see his back. There is no breach in the wall of conspiracy of the N.K.V.D.

Eventually I was led into a small, warm, well-lighted room, and was ordered to sit down facing the desk. My guards left me. I was alone, and I enjoyed, for a while, the sight of a decent room. Shortly afterwards, an officer, with the insignia of a captain and armed with a revolver, entered the room and sat down opposite me without a word.

" Your name is Begin, Menachem Wolfovitch Begin ? " he asked, eventually, after surveying my shaven head and my unshaven face.

I said it was.

" Well," he continued, " I am your judge-interrogator, and this is our first meeting. We will have further meetings. The time the interrogation takes will depend on you, on the replies you give to my questions. By the way, I read what you wrote for us, but it is worthless. It can be thrown into the waste-paper basket. You will have to tell me the truth. In your cell you no doubt learnt that it is better to tell the truth here."

I asked him to proceed with his questions, and added : " May I know how to address you ? "

At the first interrogation at N.K.V.D. Headquarters, I had to go through many linguistic manœuvres in order to get around the necessity for using a direct form of address, like "sir". I knew that this was considered an unsuitable form of address in the Soviets, but I was in doubt as to whether I had to call the interrogator "comrade", as is customary in Communist society. My cell-mate, the officer, in spite of his pride, had no such doubts and decided that with comrades one must be comradely. But when he called one of the warders "tovarich" he was answered, angrily: "A grey wolf is your comrade!" I had no desire to get a similar reply from my interrogator, and it would be difficult, I thought, to avoid addressing him personally for the duration of a protracted interrogation.

"You must call me Citizen Judge-Interrogator," the N.K.V.D. captain replied quietly. "And now tell me—since when are you a Zionist?"

"Since my childhood."

"Which organisation did you belong to?"

"From the age of ten to thirteen I was in the Shomer Hatsair[1], and from the age of fifteen onwards I was in the Betar."

"I see you began your criminal activities very early."

"Why criminal? I think my activities were right and proper."

"You 'think'? It is indeed very important what Menachem Wolfovitch Begin thinks! And I tell you you are a big, political criminal. You are worse than a man who has murdered ten people."

"But why? Why?"

"Because all your activities were anti-Soviet and anti-revolutionary."

"In what way were they anti-Soviet?"

"Stop asking questions! You came here to answer *my* questions, not I yours. Who put you into the Betar?"

"Nobody. I entered myself."

"That can't be. With us, when a young man wants to join the Komsomol, other members vouch for him. Who recommended you?"

"Nobody. I went to school, they knew me in my town, and they accepted me without any difficulty."

"So why did you join the Betar?"

"I liked its programme. I had read and heard Ze'ev Jabotinsky."

---

[1] A national Jewish Scout movement in the early 'twenties; from the early 'thirties onwards, the pro-Soviet party in Zionism.

"Jabotinsky? Oh, that's an old friend of ours! He's the leader of Jewish Fascism."

"That's not true. Jabotinsky was anti-Fascist, he was a true liberal."

"Stop talking nonsense! We know that Jabotinsky was a colonel in the British Intelligence."

"That's not true. Jabotinsky formed the Jewish Legion in the First World War, joined it as an ordinary soldier, and rose to the rank of lieutenant. He was not a colonel and he did not work for the British Intelligence. He worked for the Jewish people, and the British did not even let him enter Palestine because of his fight against their anti-Jewish policy."

"My, my! What rhetoric! You are pretending to be insulted by what I said about your leader."

"I am not pretending. Jabotinsky was my teacher. He gave me my faith and his memory is very dear to me. I am a prisoner and I know I have to answer questions, but I will defend the honour of my teacher as long as I am able to do so. Wouldn't you, Citizen Judge, do the same thing if someone were to offend the memory of Lenin?"

For the first time, the interrogator lost his temper. He banged his fist on the table and shouted:

"Again you are asking your silly questions! You compare that Jabotinsky of yours with Lenin? Don't you ever dare make such comparisons again! Lenin was a leader of the peoples, and the greatest genius of mankind, so don't you mention his name together with the name of that Jabotinsky of yours!"

"I made no comparisons. I only wanted you to understand, Citizen Judge, that you don't have to hurt my feelings even if I am a prisoner."

"Your feelings don't interest me at all," he said, more calmly. "Your replies are what interest me. Tell me, where is Jabotinsky now?"

I was amazed at his question. I had spoken clearly of the memory of Jabotinsky. Did the N.K.V.D. captain not have enough intelligence to grasp that I was speaking of a man no longer alive? And was it possible that he did not know that Jabotinsky had died? My interrogator was undoubtedly one of the experts on Zionism in the N.K.V.D. Was it possible that he had not received information of the death of Jabotinsky? But the question had been asked, and I had to reply.

" Jabotinsky is dead."

" Are you sure ? "

" I am sorry to say that I am."

" You see, no one is shedding any tears over him."

" Many people are."

" No one is shedding any tears over him, just as no one is crying over that international spy whose head they split open with an axe a little while ago."

For a moment I forgot my situation and my fate. Before me sat a disciple of the generation of the Revolution, a young man, certainly not more than thirty years of age. When Trotsky was one of the heads of the 1905 Revolution he, the interrogator, had not yet been born. When Trotsky, together with Lenin, stood at the head of the victorious 1917 Revolution, my interrogator was still a child. When Trotsky was the head of the Red Army and his name was spoken with admiration by millions he, the interrogator, was still a lad. And here tonight, a night in autumn 1940, the young Guardian of the Revolution was calling one of the great leaders of the Revolution an international spy, and was speaking with profound hatred and murderous enjoyment about his cruel liquidation. I shuddered, and like lightning a thought flashed through my mind : If there is revenge in history, and if history came to take revenge on Trotsky for his sins, was there ever a vengeance like this ?

The interrogator brought me back sharply to reality.

" Where did Jabotinsky die ? " he asked.

" In America."

" He lived in America ? "

" No. He went there after the outbreak of the war."

" What for ? "

" To try and form a Jewish Army."

" Is that so ? In order to help the imperialistic countries ? "

" In order to fight Hitler Germany."

" Tripe ! You can't destroy an idea by arms ; only arms-dealers and those who suck the blood of the working-classes are interested in the imperialistic war, and your Jabotinsky was, of course, helping them."

Pravda was speaking through him. I had no wish to annoy him, nor was I interested in doing so, but I could not restrain my feelings.

" Hitlerist Germany is not an idea. It is murder, and particularly murder of Jews."

"Now, now, don't you worry about the Jews! You and your like are enemies of the Jewish people, because if it were not so you would help the Revolution and not the imperialists. But this evening we are not speaking about Germany, we are speaking about you. Don't evade the issue."

He did not say "Hitler" Germany, he did not say "Nazi" or "Fascist" Germany, just Germany. The Blood Covenant was binding on the N.K.V.D. officer even while interrogating a prisoner in complete isolation.

"Well," he said, resuming the interrogation, "where did Jabotinsky live before he went to America?"

"Latterly in London."

"In London? But you said that the British exiled him from Palestine!"

"That's right, but they did not object to his living in England."

For the first time the interrogator burst out laughing. His laughter was genuine, gay and boisterous.

"You want to tell me yarns like that?" he said, after he had got over his mirth. "And you still want me to believe them? On the one hand the British did not let Jabotinsky live in Palestine, which was under their rule, and on the other hand they let him live in their own country?"

"But it's a fact," I tried to convince him. "Look, Citizen Judge, before the war the British hanged one of the Betar boys, Shlomo Ben Yosef. Jabotinsky was in London and tried to stay the execution. Actually, his efforts were in vain and Ben Yosef went to the gallows —he went to the gallows with a song on his lips—but it is a fact that Jabotinsky was received by the Colonial Minister in connection with this matter."

I was glad that I had been given the opportunity of telling the Soviet officer that Betar members are prepared to endanger their lives for their beliefs, and even death does not deter them. But at the same time I gave him an opportunity of asking why the British condemned Ben Yosef to death. I told him the story of the Arab attacks on Jews, organised with the assistance of British agents; I told him how our young people felt in the face of the attacks; and I told him the story of Ben Yosef in detail. He listened without stopping me.

When I had finished he said: "That Yosef wanted to chase the Arabs off their land. He was helping British imperialism."

" So why did the British hang him ? " I asked.

" Are you asking questions again ? Ah, Menachem Wolfovitch, one can see that you haven't learnt to think properly. You don't understand the difference between subjective service and objective service to the bourgeoisie and imperialism. Take, for example, the Social Democrats, those of the Second International, those who swear that they are fighting capitalism. In actual fact they are traitors to the working class. They are an arm of the bourgeoisie within the working class, they are worse than enemies of the workers. Lenin and Stalin unmasked them. We, the Communists, will unmask all who serve international bourgeoisie."

" But Lenin said that national liberation movements must be supported."

" You are not a national liberation movement. You are an agency of international bourgeoisie and an arm of imperialism. Jabotinsky, the colonel of the British Intelligence, was an emissary of imperialism consciously. And that Yosef, or whatever you call him, may have been serving imperialism unwittingly. . . . As for you, we'll still see. But don't you go telling me again that the British banished Jabotinsky from Palestine and permitted him to live in London."

" But it's true," I said, despondently.

" Stop your nonsense ! We know that kind of truth."

I had no more arguments left. I felt that on this point I had lost. Actually, what I had said was factual truth. But it was completely unacceptable to the N.K.V.D. officer. It was not just I against my interrogator ; it was world against world, conceptions against conceptions, and between them lay an abyss. Factual truth cannot bridge it; it is cast into the abyss.

The interrogator went on asking, ironically :

" After all, why are you so sure about Jabotinsky ? Maybe he has deceived you. Do you think he told you everything ? By the way, did you know Jabotinsky well ? "

" Yes, I think I knew him well."

" Did you meet him personally ? "

" Yes, the last few years before the war I met him personally too."

" Did you go to him whenever you liked ? "

" No, I came when he summoned me."

" How many times did you see Jabotinsky personally ? "

" I can't say exactly."

" Approximately ? "

" It's really difficult to say. I reckon that, in all, I spoke to him a few dozen times."

" What did you talk about ? "

" Various things, education of the Hebrew youth, organisational problems of the Betar, the situation in Palestine, British policy, immigration of youth into Palestine—various things."

" Did you discuss the Soviet Union ? "

" No."

" You are lying! "

He uttered the word " lying " with emphasis, with an accompanying flash of the eyes, but he did not say it like the Jewish Chekist at the N.K.V.D. Headquarters did ; he said it politely, using the plural form.

" Why should I lie ? " I answered. " Do I deny anything about my Zionist activities ? I simply do not recall Jabotinsky's ever having spoken to me about the Soviet Union."

" You'll still recall it ! In the cell you'll remember many things. And now tell me, of what sort of people was your movement composed in Poland ? "

" People of all classes, mostly young people."

" But most of them were bourgeois."

" No. On the contrary. The large majority were poor working people, and in Poland there was no future for them because of anti-Semitism."

" That means you snatched young people away from the Communist Party."

" We didn't snatch them away. They came of their own free will. It is self-understood that, to the extent that they came to the Betar, they did not go to the Communist Party."

" *Vot!* " (That's it!)

In his " Vot! " which he accompanied by raising his hand, there was a ring of victory.

I have given the essence of what my interrogator and I said in our first " discussion ", but it is possible that I have inserted things that were said on other nights of interrogation. This is not a stenographic report. The dialogue was very protracted. Sometimes I would speak for five to ten minutes, and the interrogator would listen without interrupting me ; sometimes he would hold forth at length, and tell with unmistakable pride of the achievements of the

Soviet Union. When I left the wing where my cell was situated, the clock on the wall showed 10 o'clock. When the interrogator uttered his " vot! " I saw on his large wrist watch that it was nearly 2 o'clock in the morning. I wondered. Where was the interrogation? This was a discussion, not an interrogation. A debate between Communism and Zionism, an argument (at times stormy) between two worlds brought together in a small room, the night work-room of an officer of the G.P.U., a State security officer of the Soviet Union.

My doubts were soon dispelled. At 2 o'clock in the morning, the officer, who had not written anything down throughout the whole dialogue, took a clean sheet of paper and began to cover it with his handwriting. He wrote for a while without saying anything to me, without asking me anything more. When he finished writing, he read through what he had written, re-read it, crossed out a few sentences and wrote in others above them, between the lines. After that, he filled half of a second sheet and afterwards made certain corrections there too. He re-copied his composition with great care, without erasures, on fresh sheets of paper, and when he had finished he read to me what he had put down in the form of questions and answers, in direct speech.

" *Tochno?* "—(Accurate?)—he asked.

It was more or less accurate. In his report was the question as to when I joined the Betar, and beneath it was the correct reply. There was the question concerning the duties I fulfilled in the movement, and beneath it my reply in full. There was, among others, the question about the number of meetings I had had with Jabotinsky, and in the reply he used the word " *nyadinokratno* ", which means " more than once " or, actually, " fairly often ".

" It is fairly accurate, Citizen Judge," I replied, " but I am sorry you did not put into your minutes a few things I told you which I would like you to add."

" I won't add anything," he said crossly. " Do you think I'll put into my report all the nonsense you told me? I don't have to fill these pages with your rhetoric. I am writing these minutes, not you."

" Yes, but the minutes should be complete," I tried to persuade him.

" I won't add a thing," he replied, stubbornly. " In court you will be able to say all the things I didn't put into the minutes."

" So there will be a trial ? " I asked, with mixed feelings of anxiety and delight.

" Of course there will be a trial. You are in the Soviet Union where every man is given the right to defend himself even if he is a criminal. And now—sign! "

I was still a little hesitant. I wondered whether it would not be to my benefit—*Oh, naïveté!*—if I could get him to write that I was poor and had to give lessons as a boy in order to pay for my studies and help my family, as I told him when I was speaking about the human material of our movement. But it was already quite clear to me that he would add nothing to his short, clean essay. I was not in disagreement with anything that he had written : I was prepared to say those things and put my signature to them at any time. And in my heart of hearts I did not dismiss as an empty promise his assurance that there would be a trial and that I would be given the possibility of defending myself. So I put out my hand to take the minutes. He passed me the first page, which was covered with his fine handwriting and I signed at the bottom. On the second page I wanted to put my signature some distance away from the last line which was about half-way down the page. The interrogator told me that I must sign immediately under the last line so that no one should be able to add anything to the signed protocol. What punctiliousness!

" Well," he said. " Now you can return to your cell. Have you any complaints ? "

" No, I have no complaints, but I would like to get back the two books that were taken away from me when I came to prison, together with the rest of my personal effects."

" I'll look into it, but I don't know if you are allowed to read in the cell." He got up and went to the door to call my escort.

Suddenly an idea entered my head.

" Citizen Judge," I said to him, when he was already standing up, " I would like to ask you to have an interpreter here tomorrow. I understand everything you say to me, but I don't know Russian very well and I have difficulty in finding the right words to express all I want to say in reply to your questions, or everything that I want to explain."

" For my part, you speak Russian quite well enough. And if you only wanted to you could give answers worthy of their name.

But, very well, I'll try to have an interpreter for our next conversation." That is exactly what he said : " conversation ".

I thanked him.

I did not know that I had made a mistake.

Hands behind my back, I was led back to my cell. I looked up at the heavens. How many stars there were in the sky, and what a mist around them !

At the sound of the opening of the cell door, my cell-mates awoke, and when it closed they asked in a whisper :

" Everything all right ? "

" Perfectly. We had a chat. . . . I want to sleep."

" Goodnight! We'll talk tomorrow."

But my night's rest was short. With the coming of the dawn, a whistle, sharp as a knife, pierced the air of Lukishki : Time to get up!

6

THE INTERPRETER HELPS

THE next night they again woke me from my first sleep. Again they ordered me to get dressed, put my hands behind my back and go to the interrogation.

At the table, in the same room as before, two people were sitting this time : my interrogator-judge and, next to him, a man in civilian clothes.

" This is our interpreter," said the interrogator after I had taken my seat opposite him. " You see, I carried out your request."

I thanked him.

" This evening," the interrogator began, " I want to hear about your programme, the programme of your movement—but *all* about it ! You can speak in your own language. The interpreter will translate."

I breathed more freely. I would no longer have to grope for words, or try to give Polish words a Russian sound and never be sure that they were hitting the mark.

" Well," I began calmly, " our programme is very simple. The Jewish people has no country of its own, and we want to give it back its Homeland. We want to turn Eretz Israel into a Jewish State, and settle in it millions of Jews who have no future whatsoever in the countries of the diaspora." I turned to the interpreter : " Would you please translate this exactly : We say ' to convert Eretz Israel into a Jewish State '. That is a very important definition, because the British wrote in the Balfour Declaration : ' the establishment in Palestine of a National Home for the Jewish people '—*in* Palestine ; and they have taken advantage of the many interpretations of this sentence in order to get out of their commitments to the Jewish people. That is fraud on their part."

The interpreter asked me to give him time to translate. After the first few sentences it was clear that although his Russian was better than mine, he was not at all fluent. When he finished translating, he turned to me and said, suddenly, in Russian :

" Why do you talk about British fraud and not about Zionist fraud ? "

" What fraud ? " I asked, also lapsing into Russian, unconsciously.

" May I answer him ? " he asked the interrogator, with an ingratiating smile.

" By all means, Comrade! Explain it to him, tell him about the fraud that he has been indulging in all his life."

Whereupon the interpreter proceeded to deliver a lecture—not in Yiddish but in Russian—on the subject of Zionist duplicity.

" Zionism—there is no need, for my present purposes, to differentiate between its various trends—is one big fraud. The Zionist leaders, Herzl, Nordau, Jabotinsky, Weizmann and others, never intended to establish a Jewish State in Palestine. They were, or are, too clever to believe that it is possible to set up a Jewish State in Palestine. How can it be ? Why, the majority of the population is Arab ! And what about the English ? Will they give you Palestine ? They need it for themselves for their imperialistic plans! In short, the Zionist leaders knew and know very well that the programme which they put out is not all practicable. What, then, was the idea ? They thought up the programme of a Jewish State, or National Home, or whatever you like to call it, in order to draw the Jews, and particularly the Jewish Youth, away from the ranks of the Revolution. It is self-evident that Zionism today is also a tool in the hands of British imperialism in that it gives the British an excuse for oppressing the Arab masses; but its principal service is to international bourgeoisie the world over, by diverting Jews, and among them good Jewish Youth, to a fraudulent slogan, with the express purpose of weakening the forces of the Revolution. In fact, one might say that Zionism is nothing but a farce, except that its results are so tragic."

" Exactly, exactly," the judge-interrogator broke in enthusiastically. " That's what I said. Zionism is nothing but a farce, a puppet show. One big fraud! "

For a while I forgot where I was. I no longer saw the uniform of the N.K.V.D. officer. I no longer thought of my defence. All I felt was a grievous hurt, a deep spiritual ache that was difficult to endure, which aroused in me one single desire : to fight back, hard.

Zionism a farce ? Herzl and Jabotinsky knew that it was impossible to create a Jewish State and were only bluffing in order to mislead the Hebrew Youth ? I had heard many theories—Communist, Bundist, Socialist—about our yearning for Zion, but never such a theory ! My reply to the so-called interpreter came from the bottom of my heart :

" What right have you to say that Zionism is a farce ? You are a Jew and I presume you learnt Jewish history. Don't you know that Zionism, in its historical and moral sense, existed before there was Communism in the world, before there was Socialism, even before there was such a thing as bourgeoisie ? In the days of feudalism Zionism existed, and even before that. Zionism is no farce ; it is possibly the most serious national liberation movement that history has ever known. For other peoples, under foreign yoke, the problem was to attain political independence for their countries. In our case, it is a problem that concerns our very existence. Zionism was, in fact, not *created*. It *arose*. It arose out of blood and tears, out of suffering, out of persecution and out of longing. This longing, the age-old longing to " go home ", passed from generation to generation. The false Messiahs gave it expression. Because of the yearning for Zion, people left comfortable, wealthy homes, and went to a desolate country. They were students, doctors, engineers, and went to work at hard labour, to swamp-draining and malaria, for the sake of Zion. In the name of Zion our forefathers went to the stake. Even in our day—you see—Ben Yosef gave his life for his belief in Zion, and many, many are ready to follow in his footsteps. Is all this called a farce ? Look: I was arrested for being a Zionist, a Betar member. I know my fate will be bitter, but all the same I don't complain. I am prepared to accept the suffering because these are the things I believe in, and I am not the only Jew to suffer for his beliefs. . . ."

I spoke for about ten minutes. My words grew more and more heated. At one point, in my excitement, I banged my right fist in the palm of my left hand. The interpreter did not stop me. But the interrogator asked : " What's he saying ? What's he saying ? It's very interesting."

The interpreter began to translate. To my surprise, he began in the middle, with the false Messiahs.

" He maintains," said the interpreter, choosing his words slowly, " that even in the Middle Ages there were Messiahs like these among the Jews—(and it is correct, in Jewish history they are called False Messiahs)—who called upon the Jews to go to Palestine, but it always ended in disappointment."

" That's it, that's it! " cried the N.K.V.D. officer. " He is merely confirming what we said. The Zionists are cheats, and the thing they call Zionism is a puppet-show and nothing more."

" The interpreter was not quite accurate," I said, addressing the interrogator directly. " I mentioned the false Messiahs of the Middle Ages as an example of my people's yearning, even in the distant past, for its country from which it had been exiled. And I also said other things which the interpreter does not seem keen on translating. Will you permit me to translate myself what I said ? "

The interpreter went red, and said : " I haven't finished yet. And I translate exactly."

But the interrogator turned to me and said, almost reprovingly : " So why did you need an interpreter ? Well, go ahead! "

In my Russian I more or less repeated what I had said in Yiddish. I noticed that as I went on speaking my interrogator's face grew more and more serious. He did not interrupt at all, but when I finished he got up from his chair, walked a few paces in the small room, and then began his reply, bending over me as he spoke. His words poured over me like a stream of lava. At times I had the impression that he had forgotten his function as interrogator, just as I, previously, forgot my rôle as prisoner, as the interrogated. He stood before me in all the awfulness of his dogmatic faith, representative of the school of thought that leaves no room for doubt, the school of thought armed not only with the rifle of the firing squad but with the weapon of dialectic analysis. He thundered:

" And I tell you again, Zionism is a puppet show ! All those fine words about Zionism arising out of suffering and persecution are wasted. The truth of the matter is that it was invented ; yes, Zionism was invented by the international bourgeoisie for one purpose : to side-track the Jewish masses away from their real duty, to a ridiculous thing, a non-existent State! What was the real function of the Jewish masses in Poland, or in the other capitalistic countries ? You maintain that the Jews are persecuted. That is true. But why are they persecuted ? Your thinking power was apparently not enough to give you the correct answer to this question. I will explain it to you. The Jews are persecuted in Poland because the Polish capitalists were interested in throwing dust in the eyes of the Polish proletariat. The capitalists egged the workers on to hate the Jews, to take their minds off their hatred for their own exploiters. But don't forget that the Jews were not the only ones who were persecuted in capitalistic Poland ; so were the Ukrainians, the Byelo-Russians and the Lithuanians. For national persecutions are an inseparable part of the capitalistic regime. They are a weapon in the hands of the exploiters, in the hands of the factory-owners and landowners. Only the Revolution can solve the national problem, and put an end to the hatred between peoples and the persecution of one people by another. That is what the geniuses of mankind, Marx, Engels, Lenin and Stalin, taught. And that is what we have achieved in the Soviet Union. In the Soviet Union we have many nationalities, but they all live in amity. All are freely developing their language, their culture, in accordance with the precept of Lenin and Stalin : National in form, socialist in content. Do you know that we also have an autonomous Jewish Republic ? Well, do you see how the Revolution solves the national problem ? And what you should have done in capitalistic Poland ? You should have fought for the success of the Revolution, all of you together : Poles, Jews, Ukrainians, Byelo-Russians. In that way a great revolutionary force would have arisen and when the day came you would have had in Poland what we brought about in Russia under the leadership of Lenin and Stalin : armed rising of the masses against the exploiters, and the wiping-out of the factory and landowner class. Instead of which, what did you do ? You deserted from the Revolution. You went to some non-existent state, to a non-existent State! Not only did you desert, you also organised desertion, mass desertion. You could not have served the bourgeoisie better if you had tried! Why, you sabotaged the Revolution ! You told us, here, that Jews always had a sentiment for Palestine. Let us suppose that that is true. It is, of course, the result of a certain education. But Zionism exploited this sentiment in order to make it easier for itself to carry out the mission assigned to it by the international bourgeoisie. This mission was diversionist in the fullest sense of the term. Its purpose was to take forces away from the Revolution in the whole world, and divert them to some puppet-show fraud, to a non-existent State. And you, Begin, were one of the diversionists. You and your like not only deserted from the Revolution, but organised the desertion of others. That is why you are in jail and for that you will be held responsible."

My interrogator's enthusiasm waxed greater and greater. He was not speaking, he was making a speech. He spoke with passion, faith and conviction. As you listened to his words, you could see, almost tangibly, an organised, united body called International Bourgeoisie, and at its head a Central Committee or General Headquarters staff which directs its various emissaries. One such emissary is Zionism, and Bourgeoisie Headquarters instructs it, saying : " Go among the Jews, exploit their difficult plight, use their sentiment for Palestine, and turn them in that direction. Trick them, persuade them that they should and can establish a Jewish State, and thus you will carry out your assignment : weaken the enemy—the Revolution—outflank it, carry out the diversion plan that has been worked out by Headquarters . . .! "

The structure that my interrogator had erected was astonishing in its logical completeness . . . on condition that you set about building it up from the point where *he* started to lay brick by brick. But everything depends on a small point called the starting-point, or " leaning-point ". Perhaps Archimedes, ancient discoverer of the laws of Nature, was referring to the processes of thought when he said : " Give me a leaning-point and I will shake the foundations of the earth." Accept my interrogator's basic assumption and you will be able to (or compelled to) agree with everything that he told me ; you will " shake the foundations of the earth ". Take it away, and his structure collapses and becomes a heap of lies, rooted in stupidity and darkness.

If I had been able to argue with the N.K.V.D. captain on equal ground, I could have told him that he was sinning against the laws of logic, that he was making an assumption and calling it a proven fact, while it still required proving and had not yet been proved. In the interrogation-room, under the conditions in which the " discussion " was being conducted, I could hardly tell the interrogator that his logic was faulty. But it was my faith against his faith ; my basic assumption was entirely different from his. I had something to fight for, even in the interrogation-room. When his fiery speech came to an end, I asked the interrogator :

" Citizen-Judge, may I explain something to you ? "

The question was not carefully worded. The interrogator, inflamed with his own words, replied angrily :

" You have nothing to explain to me, you have to explain yourself."

" May I, nevertheless, add something ? " I corrected myself.

" Speak. Today I'll let you speak, but before you do, listen to what I have to say on the subject of those doctors and engineers who go to work the land in Palestine. You told me that to prove, as it were, that Zionism is not a farce, that Zionism is a serious movement. Do you know what you proved? You proved the reactionary character of your movement! For, what are you doing? You are going backwards; you are putting ability into the ground. In the Soviet Union everyone works according to his profession; doctors cure and engineers build. And that is how it ought to be. That is progress. In Russia we say: ' You do not plough with a —— !' You understand what I mean ? "

" No, I don't," I said. He had used the rude Russian word with a smile, not as an insulting curse but as part of a popular saying.

" I meant a *socha*," he explained, hastily—" a wooden plough that they used on the land in Czarist times. We don't plough with it any more, now that we have machinery. In the Soviet Union we have modern machinery, and you need education for it. But what do you do? You take educated people and put them into the ground!

" By the way, what you told me today reminds me of another ' smart ' fellow like you. He is a member of the *Gashomer Gatsair*[1] and when he was free he was, perhaps, a worse saboteur than you because he pretended to be a socialist; this disguised servant of the bourgeoisie, this traitor against the working class! He told me that in Palestine you have Kolkhozes like in the Soviet Union. Stupid fool! He thinks he can tell us yarns like that. They took money from the American millionaires and put up Kolkhozes . . .! No, Begin. Rhetoric won't help you. Your movement is reactionary, it is against the Soviet Union, against the Revolution, against progress."

" Citizen Judge," I began, in Russian, dispensing with the interpreter, " you mentioned the autonomous Jewish Republic in the Soviet Union. Permit me to dwell on this point, on the matter of Biro-Bidjan, because it is very important in order to understand my point of view. The Soviet Government decided to allocate a special territory to the Jews in the Soviet Union. Why did they do it? The Jews in the Soviet Union have full equal rights, they are not persecuted any longer. One might claim that the Jewish

[1] i.e. Hashomer Hatsair—see footnote, page 53.

problem has been solved in the Soviet Union. If so, why special territory for the Jews ? The Soviet Government no doubt came to the conclusion that the situation of the Jews was exceptional and could not be compared with that of the Ukrainians or the Byelo-Russians. The Jews are a minority everywhere, whereas every people must have its own territory. From this, no doubt, the decision emerged to set up an autonomous Jewish area. Actually, the Biro-Bidjan experiment has not succeeded. . . ."

The interrogator suddenly interrupted me in the middle of a sentence : " What do you say ? The Biro-Bidjan experiment hasn't succeeded ? "

In the heat of the argumentation in support of my reasoning, I had said something which was not to my benefit, but it was too late to take it back. I continued :

" It is a fact that in the area of Biro-Bidjan—according to what I've read—there are today no more than thirty to forty thousand Jewish inhabitants, while, throughout the Soviet Union, there are nearly three million Jews. What is the reason for that ? I think the reason is that the Biro-Bidjan territory was never Jewish, never was our homeland ; and every people—particularly an ancient people—has its own homeland. But in my eyes, what is decisive is the very fact of the Soviet Government's decision to grant the Jews special territory of their own.

" By the way, in one of Jabotinsky's last speeches before the war, I heard him make the following statement : ' The Jews of Europe are sitting on a volcano, and everything that is done to save them is good in my eyes. Actually, I have not yet acquainted myself sufficiently with the Biro-Bidjan project, but in so far as it can save Jews this plan too is important in my eyes.' Now, Citizen-Judge, let us suppose that the Revolution is victorious in the whole world. . . ."

" What did you say ? " the interrogator interjected. " Let us suppose that the Revolution is victorious in the whole world ? Of course it will be ! And do you know why ? "

I said nothing.

" Because Marx, Engels, Lenin and Stalin said so," the interrogator thundered.

Whenever I recall that statement, I see before me the flashing eyes of the youthful captain, and hear his fist striking the desk. He appears before me again in all the awfulness of his utter, dogmatic faith. The Revolution will be victorious! It will be victorious not because of some qualitative reason or other, but " Because Marx, Engels, Lenin and Stalin said so. . . ."

Having made this observation, the interrogator let me continue.

" Well, let us suppose that the Revolution succeeds in the whole world and a Supreme World Council is set up. Let us suppose that a delegation of the Jewish people presents itself before this Council and requests that the ancient homeland of the Jews be given to them as their national territory. Wouldn't the Supreme Council grant such a request? Why, even the Soviet Union recognised the necessity for giving special territory to the Jews ; and the historical homeland of the Jews is Eretz Israel. Where does this sentiment come from? Eretz Israel was once a Jewish State ; there our culture originated ; there our language was born. So what was wrong with our wanting to get our country back for our people? You said the Citizen-Interpreter said, that there never were any real prospects of setting up a Jewish State in Eretz Israel, and that there are none now. But that is a question of faith. Every ideal has its believers and those who do not believe in it. Did many people in Russia believe in the prospect of victory of the Revolution? I, Citizen-Judge, am one of those who believe that a Jewish State will arise, even if it is possible that I will not see it."

" No, you won't see it," said the interrogator drily.

He did not answer my hypothetical question as to what the Supreme Soviet of All Countries would have resolved if a Jewish delegation had requested it to decide that the national territory of the Jewish People is Eretz Israel. He stubbornly repeated what he had said previous to that.

" Yes, the Revolution will solve the territorial problem of the Jews as well, but you people won't solve it. You deserted from the ranks of the Revolution instead of helping it. You helped its enemies—international bourgeoisie, British imperialism."

While this interchange of words went on between the interrogator and myself, the interpreter did not say a single word on his own initiative. His total preoccupation in the discussion was confined to nodding his head violently to denote enthusiastic agreement with whatever the N.K.V.D. officer said. While I spoke he sat motionless. From time to time I would enlist his aid in finding a suitable Russian expression ; he would try to help me, not always with success, and lapse again into silent listening. But at this stage of the discussion, the interpreter turned to the interrogator and began to tell him something in a whisper. Although I was sitting near them I could not catch what he was saying. The interrogator immediately let me into the secret.

"Something very interesting," he said, turning to me, "and you, of course, did not find it necessary to tell me about it. My comrade has reminded me of the letter sent by that Herzl of yours to Plehve, that Czarist hangman Plehve, asking the Czarist Government for support for the Zionist plan, and promising that Zionism would keep young Jews from joining the ranks of the Revolution. I remember seeing that extract, but it is good that the interpreter reminded me of it. Well, isn't it clear to you yet who that founder of Zionism was? We are now speaking of a written document, and there is a proverb which says : ' What the pen has written the axe cannot cut down.' It is clear that Herzl was an agent of international bourgeoisie. He himself confirmed it. He was sent by the bourgeoisie to weaken the fighting proletariat. What is there for you to say, when we have the proof in black and white?"

I had something to say, something that I very much wanted to say, but I could not. I went on speaking broken Russian to my interrogator but would have preferred, at that moment, to speak not to him, but to the interpreter, and in very *real* Russian. And that I could not do. After all, the interpreter was the interrogator's "Comrade". Silently I cursed the moment when I took it into my head to ask for an interpreter. There was an interpreter for you! A Jewish Communist, perhaps a former Zionist, who had read Herzl's writings and remembered them.

"I would ask you to understand," I said to the interrogator, "that Herzl felt that a catastrophe was about to befall his people, and we see now how right he was. He was a statesman but he had no power behind him. He wanted to speed up the rescue of his people and looked for help. What the interpreter said is not at all new. Herzl worked at a particular period. He went to the Sultan, too, to the German Kaiser as well, he even went to the Pope. He felt that the Jewish people could not wait. Jabotinsky also had this feeling. We all had it. May I give you an example, Citizen-Judge? A fire breaks out in a house, and you happen to pass by. What do you do? Naturally, you hasten to telephone the fire brigade, but if you hear the voice of a woman or a child screaming in the flames, will you wait for the fire brigade to get there? Of course you won't.

You will try immediately to save the woman or child from the burning house. That was exactly our situation. Do you know what anti-Semitism did to us ? Our house was on fire, and in it our brothers and our children were about to be burnt to death. Could we wait ? Let us suppose that the Revolution was a sort of fire brigade for the Jews who were being persecuted by anti-Semitism in Poland or in Germany, or in any other place; but we could not wait for it to come. What if it came too late, as often happened with fire brigades ? We had to try and save them, and that is what Herzl did, that is what Jabotinsky did, that is what we all did."

" That is Talmudism! " the interrogator interjected.

Talmudism! I heard that word for the first time in my life. So my interpreter was not an exception, he was not the only Jewish instructor of the N.K.V.D. interrogator. The Jewish Communists taught their Russian comrades, and taught them very well, giving them—among other things—a new term of sneering abuse in the form of a word linked with the centuries-old wisdom of our people. A new expression had been invented by the N.K.V.D. philologists and their Jewish agents : Talmudism.

The interpreter was a great help that night. Not to me, in his capacity as interpreter, but to the interrogator, in laying the blame and finding " proofs ". The interpreter was not a Soviet Communist ; he was a local Communist, from Vilna. His knowledge of Russian was limited ; his knowledge of Zionism veritably limitless. Were it the other way round, he would have been an excellent interpreter ; as it was, he was a special assistant to one of the N.K.V.D. " experts " on matters concerning Palestine, a great expert who asked me in all seriousness, as the interrogation went on, why we, the members of *Hatsohar*[1] and the Betar in Poland had not joined the Popular Front of the Communist and Socialist Parties ; while a comrade of his, a major in the N.K.V.D., he too an expert on Jewish affairs, asked a Bundist[2] prisoner :

" You Bundists were in the Second International together with the Revisionists, hey ? "

My interpreter was not only able to distinguish between Bundists and Revisionists, he not only knew that the Revisionists had never been in any International, he even knew that the Bund was not a member of the Second International. And what did he not know ?

---

[1] Zionist Revisionist Party, formed by Jabotinsky.
[2] Jewish Socialist (anti-Zionist) party in Poland.

He knew the writings of Herzl, he remembered Jabotinsky's speeches, he knew of Weizmann's meetings with Mussolini, he knew the difference between the two factions of the Left *Poalei Zion*.[1] I had the misfortune to have invited a Zionist—or anti-Zionist—Encyclopaedia in the shape of an interpreter who knew everything, including the first names of the leaders of the Zionist movement.

As the " discussion " in the interrogation-room continued, the dividing-lines grew hazier. The duet became a trio. The three of us talked in turn, and the interpreter, sometimes addressing me directly, with the permission of the interrogator, sometimes addressing the interrogator, laid all his material, so to speak, " on the table " ; contents of books, articles, speeches and writings, and names and dates. Of course, all this material would have reached my interrogator in any event, either directly or through the Jewish Department or Zionist Section of the N.K.V.D., whether through the N.K.V.D. agent who acted as interpreter at my request or through other Jewish agents. In retrospect, I also know that nothing that the Jewish Communist from Vilna said that night in any way influenced my fate. Even without him I would have got what I did : eight years in a Correctional Camp. The fact that I was head of the Betar in Poland was enough in itself to get me this sentence from the Special Advisory Commission of the N.K.V.D., with or without Herzl's letter to Plehve. But the interpreter did not make things any easier for me as I sat in the interrogation chamber opposite the Guardian of the Revolution, who had decided—and repeated it in almost every talk we had—that Zionism was nothing but a farce and a fraud.

That night—the night I fought in the isolated interrogation-room for the spirit of faith in Zion and for the honour of those who believed in it—was a long night. The stormy "conversation" came to an end at the break of dawn. That night no minutes were recorded.

And when I left the interrogation-room, as I walked, hands behind my back, from iron gate to iron gate, from courtyard to courtyard, I was still under the influence of the storm that had raged in the room and inside me. I felt as if I was returning from a conference where I had participated in a heated discussion on the future of my people, and was now on my way back to my hotel room. The storm had been so fierce, the battle had been so absorbing, the

[1] " Workers of Zion ", Leftist movement.

illusion was so realistic, that when I entered the long corridor of the building in which, on the third floor, my cell was situated, I turned to the duty officer and asked, as if he were the hotel manager : " Did anything come for me ? "

The officer gave me a peculiar look, cursed, and said : " What's got into you ? Is this a hotel ? Get back to your cell ! If any parcel is received for you it will be sent to your cell. Have you ever seen such a fellow ? "

And I was still on my way—from a conference to my hotel room. Lightly, I ran up the steps, until the warders began to whisper, hoarsely : " Sh . . . How are you walking ? " I entered—my cell ! The door was locked behind me. My cell-mates, as usual, asked : " How was it ? All right ? "

" It was a very interesting night," I replied. " I'll tell you about it tomorrow."

" Tomorrow ? Why, it's almost day already."

There was no sleep for me that night. I lay on my mattress, with open eyes, and said a silent prayer of thanksgiving. I got up when the whistle sounded.

The next evening I found only the interrogator in the room. At the opening of the conversation he said, without waiting for my question :

" I didn't ask the interpreter to come, nor will I invite him any more. Yesterday I saw that you managed nicely without the aid of an interpreter. We don't need him. We will talk alone."

The conversation dealt principally with my services to British Imperialism. When I explained to the interrogator that we, the disciples of Jabotinsky, were fighting to put an end to Britain's anti-Jewish policy in Palestine, and for the opening of the gates of Palestine, for a colonisation regime which would permit the mass-absorption of Jews, he seized on the last point :

" There ! You admit that you were in favour of a colonial regime in Palestine. Will you still try to deny that you and those like you were agents, even conscious agents, of British Imperialism ? "

" Citizen-Judge, we were not in favour of a colonial regime," I said; "we demanded a colonisation regime and those are two different conceptions entirely."

" What is the difference ? Are you trying to influence me by playing on words ? "

"No, it is not a play on words. A colonial regime means the rule of a foreign people over a country that is not theirs, and we are returning to our own country. A colonial regime means letting the desolation remain, preventing industry from developing; while a colonisation regime means agricultural reform, expansion of industry, in order to make it possible for the masses of immigrants to settle. The British want a colonial regime, while what we want is, in fact, anti-colonial."

"Talmudism! Colonial, colonisation, it's one and the same thing. You simply want to deprive the Arab farmers of their land. Do you know what that is? It is *zakhvatt*, robbery! The policy of the Soviet Union was always against domination over the lands of others. Immediately after the October Revolution we liberated the peoples that were subjugated by the Czarist regime and now, as you see, we have given Vilna back to the Lithuanian people, whereas Zionism is *zakhvatt* in the fullest sense of the term."

"We do not want to take away the land from the Arab farmers. There are, in Palestine, vast estates, like in ancient or in feudal times, and those have been divided among the Arab farmers and the Jewish farming settlers. In Roman times the eastern part of Palestine was called *Palaestine salutaris* because it was the granary for the countries of the Roman Empire. Now some three hundred thousand Bedouin live there. In the early days there were between seven and eight million people living in Palestine. There is room in Palestine, as Jabotinsky told the British, for the Arabs, for millions of Jews, and for peace."

"Whatever you've said is —— " The etymological source of the first part of the epithet he used was distinctly physiological. I was dumbfounded. The interrogator had, hitherto, observed a measure of decency. Of course, he was almost refined compared to other interrogators that I had heard about from other people.

"Why is it —— ?" I asked, repeating the epithet he had used.

For a moment he forgot himself completely and grabbed the water-bottle which was standing on the table—and, without lifting it, said in a threatening voice: "Na, Na! Mind! I have this 'grafinka' here!"

I said nothing.

The interrogator released the water-bottle and went back to the subject.

"I tell you, what you have been saying here is nonsense. Why

75

do you talk of ancient times? We have to speak of today. You really are making ' progress '. Yesterday evening you talked of the Middle Ages and those false Messiahs of yours, and now you've already jumped to ancient times, to the Roman days. Leave the past alone, speak to the point! Is it not clear to you that by sending people to Palestine and demanding the land that belonged to the Arabs you enabled British imperialism to tyrranise the Arab toilers, labourers and farmers, by pretending to defend them? Not only here did you help international bourgeoisie; there, too, in that non-existent State of yours, you were agents of British Imperialism, actual agents."

This contention he had already voiced more than once. Repetition is, apparently, one of the prerogatives of the interrogator. And perhaps it is one of the things he has to do, that is part of the 'system', the system of attrition.

This time my reply consisted mainly of questions.

" If we are British agents, why don't the British let us into Palestine? Why do they persecute us? Why did they say in their last White Paper that, in a few years' time, they will not let one more Jew enter Palestine? If we were indeed serving British interests, the logical thing would be for Britain to help us, not hinder us. But the fact of the matter is, they obstruct us at every step. It is a fact that before the war we had to break through the British blockade to bring people to the shores of Palestine, as Garibaldi did in his time in Italy."

" Now, now, don't you go making comparisons with Garibaldi. Do you know who Garibaldi was? He was a true fighter for freedom, his movement was a progressive one whereas your movement is thoroughly reactionary."

I learnt for the first time that the deeds of the liberator of Italy are praised in the political schools of the Soviet Union. Garibaldi was, therefore, the bearer of progress, and not the emissary of international bourgeoisie which had assigned him the diversionist task of diverting the attention of Italian workers and directing it to some non-existent State—a united and independent Italy. What luck! Garibaldi fought in the nineteenth century and managed to die before there was an N.K.V.D. Otherwise. . . .

Suddenly the interrogator changed the subject.

" Tell me exactly, but exactly, what your function was in your organisation," he said.

76

He had already asked this question. He had already received a full reply. And now : " Tell me exactly."

Somewhat astonished, I answered, this time using the common Polish expression which I adapted to my Russian :

" I was the Commandant of the Betar in Poland."

" What were you ? " asked the interrogator, in amazement and anger. " Why, you told me you were in charge of all the activities, you said you were a sort of General Secretary, and now you say that you were the ' Commandant '."

I did not understand a thing. I could not understand his sudden anger, nor his amazement, nor his questions. Were they not " Talmudism " ?

" I have no intention," I explained, " of changing anything that I told you about my functions, Citizen-Judge. I told you, and I tell you again now, that I was the man in charge of the activities of the Betar in Poland, I was its Commandant, I was the chairman of the movement in the whole of Poland."

" Then say so," said the interrogator, relieved. " You were the chairman of your organisation, and that is like a General Secretary—not a Commandant !"

Again I did not understand.

Only much later, on the banks of the greenish Pechora river, lying on the back-breaking bunks in one of the huts of the *Pechor-Lag*, did I at last understand what he meant. It appears that in the Soviet Union the official function of Commandant does indeed exist. The Commandant, like the French concièrge, is the caretaker of a residential building and is responsible for keeping it clean. The interrogator feared, for a moment, that I was trying to back out of my responsibility for my " crimes ", and, after I had already " confessed ", was making myself out to have been the janitor of our offices.

On the third night the discussion was not as lengthy as when the interpreter participated. When we had cleared up the matter of the Commandant, the interrogator, with his characteristic precision, carefully straightened the sheets of paper which he always had in front of him and began to write. Again I became a passive onlooker.

After a while the interrogator looked up and said :

" I am writing ' colonisation regime ', but I want you to know that colonial and colonisation are one and the same thing."

" Let it be so."

The interrogator went on writing, and when he had finished he read me the questions and answers. I listened very carefully and noticed, to my surprise, that he had given as one of the paragraphs of our programme, the following :

"The Biro-Bidjan experiment in the Soviet Union did not succeed. In the autonomous zone a mere thirty to forty thousand people are living. Nor can this experiment succeed, as Biro-Bidjan is not the Jewish Homeland."

"There was no such paragraph in the programme of our movement, Citizen-Judge," I said.

"What do you mean ? You said so yourself. The interpreter also heard it."

"It's true that I said it, but it was a view expressed by me in the course of a discussion, and you of course know, Citizen-Judge, the famous saying : *Gedanken sind ʒollfrei.*"

"That is German. I don't know what it means."

"There is no charge for what one thinks," I translated freely, being unable to find a Russian translation for "customs dues".

"With us," said the N.K.V.D. officer, quietly, but with emphasis, "you do pay for your thoughts, if they are anti-revolutionary. And we know all about those thoughts. . . ."

Naturally, it never entered my mind to deny the things I had said. True, I had said them in the course of a conversation, but I had said them. In my heart of hearts, I could hardly accuse the interrogator of distorting the facts if he put those things into the minutes. All I asked of him was that he should word my reply in the following manner : " *my* opinion was . . ." instead of " *our* opinion was. . . ." To this he agreed.

Once again : what I was given by the Advisory Commission of the N.K.V.D. I would have received in any event, with the Biro-Bidjan matter or without it. But that night, too, I learnt a great deal. What it amounted to was this : the " conversation " is not a conversation at all. The conversation—for all the courtesy with which it is conducted—is the actual interrogation. And " with us " —even for thoughts one pays. . . .

7

MORE NIGHTS OF INTERROGATION

THE nights of interrogation continued. Sometimes there were short intervals between them. Sometimes interrogation followed on the heels of interrogation without a break, continuously.

One day an idea crossed my mind and, in the course of one of the interrogations, I put it to my interrogator.

"Citizen-Judge," I said, "before I was arrested I read the Constitution of the Soviet Union and, if I am not mistaken, there is a clause in it in which the Soviet Union promises asylum to citizens of foreign countries persecuted because of their fight for national liberation. I think I belong in that category. I dedicated my life to the national liberation of my people, and I came to Vilna because I was hounded by our enemies. There is no doubt that I would have been one of the first to be executed had the Germans caught me in Warsaw. Being in the Soviet Union, I ought, according to the Constitution, to enjoy the right of sanctuary and not sit in prison."

The interrogator who, until now, had been quiet, courteous and well-mannered, listened to my contentions and my reasoning, and his face changed colour. He went red, and then white. The man forgot himself completely. I had never seen him so angry. The last remnants of his politeness deserted him. He banged his fist on the table and shouted at the top of his voice :

"What? You quote me the Stalin Constitution, you damned lawyer? Do you know how you are behaving? You are behaving just like that international spy, that mad dog, that enemy of humanity—Bukharin. Yes, yes, you are doing exactly what Bukharin used to do. He used to extract some sentence from Marx's writings and say : 'You see? I was right. That's what Marx wrote too.' But Stalin taught us not to base ourselves on fragmentary sentences taken out of their context. We have to see the thing in its entirety, otherwise we are not proving something

79

which is true, but putting across a fraud. Well, there is such a clause in the Stalin Constitution, but there are many other clauses in it and you have to see it as a whole. Have you ever heard of such a thing! A genius has been found in Vilna who quotes one of the paragraphs of the Constitution and wants to use it to convince me! . . ."

I was struck by this surprising outburst. I was quite unable to understand why I had angered him so, precisely on this point, and why he lost control of himself because of a question which was essentially naïve, perhaps too naïve. Could he not have answered, quietly : " This clause does not apply to you " ? But not only did he shout at the top of his voice and bang his fist on the table, to the danger of the *grafinka*; that night, for the first time, the interrogator came out with the well-known " mother " curses, which made the matter of the Constitution less important in my eyes. I told the interrogator that I had quoted a complete paragraph and not a mere extract, and that the clause in the Constitution which deals with the right of refuge of the persecuted has no connection whatsoever with the clauses that deal with, say, the election of the Supreme Soviet and the House of Nationalities. On the merits of the case I did not continue to argue. What was the use ? On the other hand, I was not prepared to put up with the curses any more than I put up with the " ti " form of address of the interrogator at N.K.V.D. Headquarters. I said :

" I also read, Citizen-Judge, that in the Soviet Union the use of swear-words is forbidden by law, and I would ask you not to use them when talking to me. It is true that I am a prisoner and my fate is in your hands, but you do not have to insult me."

" Don't be so proud," said the interrogator, repeating almost word for word what his comrade at N.K.V.D. Headquarters had said to me, but from then until the end of the interrogation I did not again hear that form of vilification from him. He had many more outbursts, even rude outbursts, but unaccompanied by those particular curses. At times, even prejudices serve some purpose.

On one occasion, I asked the interrogator another naïve, legalistic question.

" Citizen-Judge," I said, " you maintain that my Zionist activity in Poland was a crime according to the law of the Soviet Union, and for that you will bring me to trial. For the moment, I will not deal with the essence of the problem. As I said before, it is a matter of faith, and I believe that I was out for the good of my people, and worked to that end. But I would like to deal with the legal aspect of the problem. You are also a lawyer and I am sure you will understand me. What I did, I did in the State of Poland; and there my activities were absolutely legal. There was no law there forbidding what I did. The State did not ban our work which was public and known to everybody, and no other laws applied in the area where the Polish State existed. Now I am in the Soviet Union and its laws apply to me, but how can they apply to what I did in the past? There is a principle in jurisprudence which says that a man shall not be penalised for a deed which was not recognised as an offence at the time when, and in the place where, he did it. I imagine this rule also exists in Soviet Law. So how can I be punished for what I did in the past, within the law?"

This time I did not make the interrogator angry. On the contrary, my question put him in a good humour. He smiled and said:

"Your code of law is very amusing. Do you know, Menachem Wolfovitch, under what section of the Criminal Law you are charged?"

"No, I do not."

"You are charged under Section 58 of the Criminal Law of the Soviet Socialist Russian Republic. Do you know what that Section deals with? Do you know who wrote it?"

"No, I don't."

"It is good that you should know. Section 58, under which you will be brought to trial, deals with anti-revolutionary activity, treason and diversion; and it was written by Vladimir Ilyitch Lenin himself."

"But how can it apply to what I did in Poland?"

"Ach! You are a strange fellow, Menachem Wolfovitch. Section 58 applies to everyone in the world. Do you hear? *In the whole world.* It is only a question of when he will get to us, or we to him."

In spite of my situation, in spite of the fact that I had already " got to " the N.K.V.D. and it had already got to me, and imposed on me Section 58 (not just in theory but in actual fact)—I was shocked. For days I kept on thinking of that frank, surprising reply, which is a contradiction of all that is fundamental in civilised man's concept of law. So there exists a State which imposes its

Criminal Law, and particularly the anti-revolutionary section of that law, on every one of the two and a half billion human beings that inhabit the earth. And who does not dabble in counter-revolution? Perhaps Communists who work hard, sometimes at the risk of their own lives, to bring the Revolution and the N.K.V.D. to their countries, are exempt from this Section? No such thing! At Lukishki and in the concentration camp I met Communists from Poland who had fought underground; who were arrested nominally for interrogation every First of May, from year to year; who had sat for years in prison. And when the time came, Section 58 was applied to them. Their main defence was: " For Communism, for the victory of the Revolution, I sat for years in the prisons of capitalistic Poland. You can check that. I can bring witnesses. How can you accuse me of counter-revolution? "

The interrogator would laugh at them.

" You sat in jail, traitor? Tell me, how long did you sit? "

" Three years, five years, seven whole years . . ." the unhappy people would reply, as the case might be.

" And what happened to you after that? " the interrogators would ask the anti-revolutionary Communists.

They would answer with heart-breaking naïveté:

" Then I was released and went on working for the Revolution."

" So you were released from prison? " the interrogators roared.

" Yes, at the end of my term of imprisonment, according to my sentence, I was released from prison."

" Why, you fraud! You were a devout Communist and the capitalistic police released you from jail? Who are you trying to bluff? If you were a loyal Communist you would not have been let out of jail after a few years. You were released because you promised the Polish secret police that you would hand over to them devoted Communists. Do you think we don't know it? Now, tell the truth, everything! . . ."

What happened to these Communists also happened to their attorneys. Many lawyers, among them men of note, who defended accused Communists in the Polish or Lithuanian courts, were, under the Soviet Regime, charged under Section 58. Their main defence was:

" How can you accuse us of counter-revolution? We devoted the best of our efforts and our time to the defence of Communists, and getting them out of the hands of the police."

The N.K.V.D. interrogators laughed at them.

"You defended Communists? To whom are you telling these yarns? Had you not been in league with the secret police, would they have let you 'defend' Communists before the capitalistic courts? Your very appearance before these courts is proof that you were an agent of the secret police and denounced true Communists to them."

The protests of these unhappy people were silenced.

Perhaps the accusations themselves were not the most terrible thing in the case of the Communists and their defence attorneys who "got to" the N.K.V.D., with their "credentials" in their hands, credentials which the N.K.V.D. converted into proofs against them. The really terrible thing lay in the fact that the interrogators, in this case, were not lying. On the contrary, they were convinced that they had in their hands real proof. Not suppositions, but facts that could not be contradicted. Again, it was one world against another—with an abyss between them. In the world of the N.K.V.D. a political criminal who is "worse than a man who has murdered ten people" is not, as a rule, released when his prison term has run its course. In the world of the N.K.V.D. there is no attorney who would not be in collusion with his client's persecutors and accusers. How can the disciples of the N.K.V.D. believe that in another world (which they have been taught to regard as the "world of oppression") the accused—whether political or criminal—is given a sentence, that the sentence one day comes to an end and the prisoner goes free? How can they believe that "over there" there is a defence counsel who appears on behalf of his client against the secret police, against its reprehensible methods, against the counsel for the prosecution and the Government that appointed him? And all that is permitted?

Two worlds. The abyss that divides them is not deep, it is bottomless. And a ghost hovers over the abyss, the spirit of Section 58 of the Soviet Criminal Code, and calls to all who are affected by it: "Workers for freedom in all countries—Unite!" Lest . . .

One night the interrogator read me the following question:

"What connection was there between you and the Polish secret police?"

My reply was instinctive: "I refuse to answer such a question, Citizen-Judge."

" What do you mean ? " asked the interrogator. " You have to answer all my questions."

" You can write in the minutes, Citizen-Judge, that I refused to answer this question, and I shall give my reasons in court."

" You have no right to refuse to answer questions. But, actually, why do you refuse to answer such a simple question : ' What connection was there between you and the Polish Secret Police ? ' "

" It is an insulting question, Citizen-Judge, and I've already told you that if I have to suffer for my beliefs I shall do so uncomplainingly, but as long as I am able to do so, I shall not put up with insults. I worked for my people and I had nothing to do with secret-police forces. Not only did I sit in a Polish prison because of our struggle, but the head of the secret police threatened to send me to the concentration camp at Bereza-Kartuska if the demonstrations against the British—which were very frequent in the year 1939—did not stop. And after all that, I am asked what the connection was between me and the Polish police! "

The interrogator laughed.

" You see," he said, " you did have some connection with the Polish secret police. You yourself have just said that the secret police in Warsaw summoned you."

" Well, then, Citizen-Judge, will you kindly write in the reply : ' The head of the Warsaw secret police sent for me and threatened to send me to the ' Green Field ', as he expressed it—to Bereza-Kartuska.' "

The interrogator was still in a good mood. He said : " You are a funny person, Menachem Wolfovitch, the way you insist on playing the hero. I refuse to let my question go—you have to answer it. I'll write in the reply : ' I had no connection with the Polish secret police ', but if you think they will believe that in court you are only making a fool of yourself."

" Let it be so."

One night, in the course of the conversation, the interrogator said, without putting it in the form of a question : " It is clear to me that your organisation left you here to carry out anti-revolutionary work."

I replied: " Only a few days ago, I told you that I had received a *laissez-passer* from Kovno for my wife and myself, and also visas for Palestine. We were on the point of leaving, and it is only my arrest that prevented me from doing so. From these facts, which can be checked at any time, is it not clear that no one left me here, and that I had no intention of remaining here, but wanted to go to Palestine, my homeland ? "

" Well, then," the interrogator concluded, " you are guilty of planning to run away from the Soviet Union. Running away from the Soviet Union is an offence and you will be punished for it."

When I told my cell-mates about this conversation, the three of us gave free vent to our laughter. We laughed so loud that the sound reached the ears of the warder and disturbed his rest. He opened the hatch in our cell-door and said: " I see you are very gay here. Do you want me to add something to your gaiety ? "

We stopped. When the hatch was closed again, the officer said: " He was right. The N.K.V.D. is always right. If you stayed in the Soviet Union—you committed a crime. If you wanted to leave the Soviet Union—that's also a crime. If you don't want to commit a crime—don't get born! "

One night, when the discussion was over and the interrogator had finished writing, he said:

" Tomorrow you will meet a person close to you. There will be an *otchno-stavka*."[1]

" With whom ? " I asked quickly.

" That you will see tomorrow. You must get used to not asking unnecessary questions."

I spent an almost sleepless night and a disturbed day. I neglected my pupil in the cell. The corporal prepared his lesson with his usual diligence and I asked him a few questions, but I heard his answers abstractedly, and let the lecture go by the board entirely. The corporal did not object to the " holiday ". Both he and the officer understood how I felt and left me alone with my thoughts and my anxiety.

I was exceedingly anxious. With whom did they intend staging this confrontation ? And why didn't the interrogator want to tell me who the person " close to me " was, with whom he was about to confront me ? Had they arrested—my wife ? Once that thought had entered my mind I could not get rid of it. " No, it can't be," I said to myself, pacing from the door to the window. " It must be," dread whispered back, as I retraced my footsteps from the window

[1] Face-to-face meeting of prisoners under interrogation.

to the door. I tried to reconcile myself to the idea and calm down, telling myself that there was nothing that could be done about it ; that such were the times we were living in ; that we were not the only ones whose lives had been broken up in the tornado that was sweeping the world.

The wave of dread began to mount again. Why must she suffer because of me ? I had been arrested, but I, after all, had always exhorted the others to be ready to sacrifice, and had issued this call to service in all sincerity and in faith ; so now, when I myself was called upon to stand the test of suffering, I naturally would not complain, I would accept it willingly. But why should she be cast into this den ? Why ? And how would she, ill as she was, fare here in jail, without her medicines ? But perhaps she had not been arrested at all, and was among friends ? I was back again where I had started in my efforts at putting my mind at rest.

In the name of heaven, how long was this day going to be ? When would the time for interrogation come ? When would I know ?

And in the midst of my dread, I thought of the days gone by, days of happiness, days of hope, days of ardour. My heart rejoiced at the recollection of the day when I saw a seventeen-year-old girl, and said to myself : She will be my wife. Next day I left the town where I found her, the town where I was studying my profession, and I wrote her a letter of one line : " I saw you, my lady, for the first time, but I feel as if I have known you all my life." . . . Later, I told her life would be hard, I told her we would never have any money, but trouble there would be in plenty, and probably prison, too, for we would have to fight for Eretz Israel. She said she was not afraid of trouble.

After that I waited for her one winter night at the railway junction. She came from her home and I, as usual, from a public speech. I took her to my parents' home, and they loved her. I left her the very next day—for another speech. Afterwards a letter came from Vladimir Jabotinsky in which he wrote:

" I wish you what I would wish my own son. There have been bad days in my life, but I have known many good days too. Now that I have grown old, I know that the best of the good days was the day I put a ring on a girl's finger, and recited a verse of nine words to her . . ."

Then came our wedding day. . . . The old people were happy, our friends full of joy, and Ze'ev Jabotinsky was among the witnesses.

And afterwards—no leave; not a month, not a week, not even a day. Next day—to Warsaw, to the movement, to work, to organise the big migration to Palestine, the big break-through without British certificates. And again she remained alone, but she did not complain. I was keeping my promise—that there would be troubles to bear—and she was keeping hers, not to be afraid and not to tie my hands. After that, everything collapsed. The war broke out. We were compelled to leave Warsaw. We began our wanderings on foot, our knapsacks on our backs, under a rain of bombs. She stood up to every situation, but at one point, when we stopped to rest, her illness broke out, an illness which could kill her. After that I brought her to her parents' home and wanted to leave her in that good house for a while lest she come to harm on the way, when we would have to cross the border illegally. My efforts were in vain. She insisted : " Where you go, I go." So we set out again, together, and eventually arrived safely. We were about to leave for Eretz Israel, before the Baltic Corridor between Russia and Germany disappeared, but we had to surrender our places to a friend, and she did not complain. " Never mind," she said, " we'll go another time." And after that our hopes of getting away grew fainter and fainter ; as against that, the chances of my being arrested and our being separated for an indefinite length of time grew stronger. " Well," I said to her during these days of waiting, " I shall carry out my promise in full. There will be prison." Actually, I was thinking of prison under other conditions, in Eretz Israel, but Lukishki is also a prison. Again she did not complain, and did not try to influence me to hide or run away.

All these pictures came up, dissolved. They kept on returning. They made me happy, and they filled me with longing. But once more the dread within me increased. Had they arrested her, or had they left her in peace ? The silent, unspoken questions followed rapidly on one another. Perhaps this meeting was going to be with one of our friends who had been arrested ? Who the devil did the interrogator mean when he said: tomorrow you will meet someone close to you ?

The day eventually drew to an end. We were given our supper. My cell-mates pressed me to eat as, they urged, I would need strength for the night. I waited for the bed-time whistle, and even more anxiously for the whispered question : " Whose name begins with ' B ' ? " And when it came at last, I dressed with the speed of a fireman on hearing an alarm. If I could only have run to the interrogation room! But running was forbidden. You must walk with measured steps, not too slowly, not too quickly. I fervently hoped we would not encounter any other prisoners on the way, and have to lose time over a " left turn! " or " right turn! ". But that night the route was clear. The only time lost was in actual walking. I was led into the interrogation room and found there only the interrogator.

" Sit down," he said.

Bearing in mind what he had said the previous night, I did not ask any questions.

" You probably want to know who it is you are going to meet this evening, don't you ? "

" Of course I do, Citizen-Judge."

" Then wait a bit. You'll know right away."

I did not wait long. The door opened and, escorted by the interrogator's comrade, the Major, Dr. Jacob Shechter was brought into the room!

Dr. Shechter, one of the leaders of the Revisionist Party in Cracow, a famous speaker, was arrested in Vilna a few weeks before I refused to avail myself of the invitation from the Vilna Municipality. Before him, they arrested—one after the other—the engineer Sheskin and David Knoll, both of them leaders of the *Brit HaChayal*, the big mass organisation of Jewish ex-Servicemen who rallied to the flag of Jabotinsky.

I learnt subsequently that none of the active central figures of our movement in Vilna were arrested, and eventually they all succeeded in getting out, perfectly legally, by way of Moscow and Odessa, and reached Palestine. I suppose the hand of chance, which is sometimes decisive even in the N.K.V.D., had something to do with it. These people were, for the most part, known, and my friend David Yutan's father was summoned to the N.K.V.D.—before I was arrested—and told that his son had to wait at home, they would send for him. David Yutan actually did wait at home for a few days, but they never came and they never summoned him. . . .

The meeting in the interrogation room between Dr. Shechter and myself surprised him more than it did me. Although I still did not know why this face-to-face meeting had been arranged, I did know that he had been arrested. Shechter, on the other hand, knew nothing about my arrest, and here I appeared before him in the full glory of a prisoner of the N.K.V.D.

The two interrogators conducted the *otchno-stavka* with great formality. They cautioned us that we were not allowed to talk to each other and must answer only when addressed. But on the whole, and in spite of the considerable ceremonial, the personal meeting between the two prisoners gave the N.K.V.D. nothing.

They asked us each in turn who was in charge of the Palestinian visas that were received (some of them before the " revolution " in Lithuania, some after) for members of our movement. The handling of the exit of visa-holders passed to the Soviet authorities after the government had changed hands. It was done with their knowledge and their sanction. In fact, it was all absolutely legal—provided you were not arrested. When you were arrested, your crime was: Attempting to run away from the Soviet Union, and conniving at the escape of others.

To the interrogators' question I replied that I was responsible for getting the confirmation of the visas from the Palestine office in Kovno, which was in existence for some time under the Soviet regime, too, and that the confirmations used to arrive in my name, in my capacity as head of the Betar. Dr. Shechter replied that he had dealt with this matter. We both repeated our statements. Our replies were duly written down—the confrontation was over.

Why did they have it ? To this day, I am unable to say. Were they hoping that we would " accuse " each other of the deeds that were so bad in the eyes of the N.K.V.D. and so good in our own eyes ? Were the fellow-interrogators hoping to enjoy the self-debasement of the fellow-prisoners ?

If that was what they were hoping for, they were disappointed. But was it possible that they arranged the meeting merely to carry out one of the N.K.V.D. customs ? The face-to-face meeting is also part of the system of interrogation. Sometimes it has results ; one man testifies against the other. It always undoubtedly gives the N.K.V.D. interrogators considerable pleasure to watch the unfortunate creatures. . . .

The meeting with Shechter was over. We said goodbye to each other with glances more eloquent than words. *We'll meet again . . . The sun will shine again. . . .*

8

ADMIT OR CONFESS

ONE evening, before we had even put out our mattresses, I was summoned to the interrogation-room. It transpired that this was my last meeting with the interrogator.

" This evening," he said, " we will conclude the interrogation. This is where my job with you finishes. What we still have to do is to complete the minutes."

" And when will the trial be, Citizen-Judge ? " I asked.

This time he did not tell me not to ask unnecessary questions. He answered me with understanding and courtesy.

" That does not depend on me. My job is the interrogation. Others will fix the date of the trial." Having said this, he proceeded to write something and then read me the short text :

" *Priznaius vinovnim vtom chto bil . . .*"—" I admit I am guilty of having been the chairman of the Betar organisation in Poland, and being responsible for the Betar work, and calling upon the Jewish Youth to join the ranks of the Betar."

" Please sign," said the interrogator politely, " and you can then go back to your cell. With this, the interrogation is closed."

" Citizen-Judge," I said, " you wrote everything down very exactly and I will of course sign it, but I would ask you to make one change in the wording."

" What change ? Again a change! Why, it's all so straightforward! "

" That is true, and the change is only in the first sentence. Instead of *priznaius vinovnim vtom chto bil*, instead of ' I admit *my guilt* in being ' . . . would you please write : *priznaio chta bil . . .* ' I admit that I was . . .' The rest is perfectly all right and I will sign it readily."

At first the interrogator could not understand.

" What do you mean, not write *priznaius vinovnim* ? You yourself admitted that you were the head of your movement in Poland, you yourself said you were in charge of all its activities, you yourself said that you travelled a good deal through the towns of Poland, calling upon the Jewish Youth at public meetings to join your organisation. And what did I write? I wrote just what you said, so why do I need to make changes and copy it out again?"

"Citizen-Judge," I still tried to explain, "I made no complaint against the wording in its essence. I said I was head of the Betar in Poland and I say it again, and I am prepared to sign on that any time. But I cannot sign the statement that ' I am guilty of having been . . .' It is clear to me by now that in your eyes that is a serious charge, but in my eyes it is not an accusation at all. On the contrary, I know that I have carried out my duty to my people ; that was my aim in life. Before the court I shall try to explain that."

Still the interrogator did not understand. In view of his behaviour in the first part of our conversation, I felt that he was not pretending, but was genuinely unable to grasp my new " Talmudism ". The wording : " I admit I am guilty of having been . . ." was apparently his routine wording for rounding off the minutes in the interrogation-room. So why was I suddenly suggesting altering it?

"Tell me," said the interrogator, not angrily, " were you the head of Betar in Poland, or were you not? "

"Yes, I was."

"So what do you want of me now? You were—that means that you are guilty! "

"No, Citizen-Judge, not guilty. And that is the whole difference between us. To you, my having been a Zionist, a Betar member, is my guilt. To me, that was my service to my people. I understand that the court will judge me according to the laws of the Soviet Union, and it is possible that it will not take into account what I feel about it. I have reconciled myself to that possibility. But you want me, of my own accord, to sign that ' I was guilty '. That I cannot do because I do not recognise that I was guilty."

The interrogator began to get angry.

"Then don't sign!" he cried. "Do you think I need your signature? I can submit these minutes to the prosecution even without your signature."

I said nothing.

The interrogator changed his mind.

"But I always finish off the record like this, and I have to finish your minutes as well. Why don't you sign? I only wrote what you told me. Why don't you sign? "

I explained again. He repeated his story.

In vain I hunted in my poor Russian for new words, to express differently what I had already said before.

Then he began to threaten.

I shrank within me. " This is the hour of trial," I told myself. " Maybe, the decisive test. If I do not pass it, there will be no point in living. Confess to my guilt in having been head of the Betar ? No, no, under no circumstances! Let him do what he likes, I will not sign."

I prayed to God to help me in my hour of need. I was not aware that I had spoken the words out aloud.

" What did you say ? " shouted the interrogator.

" I didn't say anything, Citizen-Judge."

" What do you mean, you didn't ? Are you going to lie to my face ? Why, I heard you speak."

" I didn't say anything, I was talking to myself."

The interrogator burst into a roar of laughter.

" Look at him," he sneered. " He's already beginning to talk to himself! Have you ever seen a lawyer who talks to himself! Don't talk to yourself," he snapped. " You'd better listen to what I tell you. I tell you you must sign these minutes, otherwise it will be bad for you."

His mocking words hurt me, but I did not react to them. I was actually pleased that the atmosphere was lighter.

" Citizen-Judge," I said, " I am asking you to understand that I cannot submit to the word ' guilty '. After all, I am only asking you to change those two words in your summary. For me they are very important, but what is their importance from the point of view of the investigation ? In any event all the material will go to the court, and the judges are the people who will decide whether I am guilty or not."

" Don't you teach me what is important and what is not from the point of view of the investigation! I advise you again, reasonably: sign, and the interrogation is ended and you can sit in your cell in peace."

" I can't, Citizen-Judge. I am sure that if I were to sign I would lose a lot, even in your eyes. After all, you are also an idealist. . . ."

" I am not an idealist," the interrogator broke in, ironically, " I am a Communist and for me historical materialism is the thing that counts."

" No, no," I hastened to rectify the misunderstanding, " I was not referring to the philosophical problem of idealism and materialism. I wanted to say that you certainly understand what an ideal is, what it means to have a lofty aim. Wouldn't you be prepared to give your life for your ideals ? "

" Your questions are stupid. Of course, if I were required to do so I would at any moment give my life for the success of the revolution, for the Soviet country."

" Well, I am ready, too."

" Ready for what ? "

" To give my life for my ideals."

" What ideals have you got ? Is a puppet-show farce an ideal ? For what you call an ideal, it is not even worth giving a single hair, never mind your life. And who needs your life ? You are a young man and an educated one. You said you wanted to serve your people. Up to now it was not your people that you served, but the enemies of your people and the enemies of mankind. It is true that your crimes are very grave, I can't say what the court will decide, but if you behave as you should, it is possible that you may still be given an opportunity to work for the good of your people. Of course, you will first have to undergo a period of education and re-education."

" With the help of God," I said, half to myself, " I will perhaps still work for my people."

" God ? Do you believe in God ? "

Unintentionally, I had changed the subject. I was certainly pleased at the change.

" Yes, of course I believe in God."

" I see that in this sphere too you will need re-education. But I must say I didn't expect to hear such nonsense from you, Menachem Wolfovitch. After all, you are an educated man. How can you believe in a God ? "

" I have seen university professors who believe in God. There have been great scientists who believed in God."

" Nonsense! A scientist can't believe in God. Those that you are referring to only said they believe. They were in the pay of the bourgeoisie. Incidentally, can you tell me why you believe in God ? "

" It's very hard to explain, Citizen-Judge. Faith is not a thing that one can explain rationally."

" That's it. Belief in God is something that stands in contradiction to human intelligence, so how can you believe ? "

" Faith does not stand in contradiction to intelligence ; but man, in his intelligence, understands that there are things he cannot fathom by rationality, and so he believes in a Higher Power."

" Are there things that the mind cannot grasp ? There are no such things! An answer can be found to everything in science."

" All the same, science hasn't been able to solve the problem of life and death."

" Who told you that stuff ? Biology explains everything concerning life and death."

" I didn't mean the process of life, but the riddle of life. Where does life come from ? I was not referring to biological development, but what they call the ' primary cause '. And that science cannot explain. Perhaps I haven't studied enough to know the scientific explanation. In any event, I do know that science has done great things, but it cannot bring a dead fly back to life."

" What are you talking about ? There is nothing that science cannot explain. Of course, it is a question of development. Two hundred years ago man knew less than he knew, say, a hundred years ago. And we know more than those who lived a hundred years ago. Science is progressing. And a time will come when there will be no more mysteries in science. I believe in science, and that is why I don't believe there is a God. You spoke of the riddle of life. Do you know that in the Soviet Union medical science has succeeded in bringing back to life people who have died ? "

" No, I haven't read about it."

" Well, I tell you it is a fact. I myself have read of heart operations that brought people back to life. It is true they did not live long afterwards, but this is only a beginning. I am sure science will solve this problem, too. I really am interested that you should read about it ; I know in what a world of prejudices you have been living up to now. If I find the item I'll try to send it to you in your cell. Are you already allowed to read in the cell ? "

" No, we've not been given any books yet. Nor have I got back my own two books."

" Oh, yes. Prisoners are permitted to read only after the interrogation has been concluded."

His geniality left him with the same suddenness with which it had come. He went back to the subject.

94

" Enough philosophising," he said sharply. " When you finish the interrogation, you'll be able to get books. But you yourself are holding things up by refusing to sign."

" I want to sign, Citizen-Judge, but I am asking you just to change two words, only two words."

" Are you at it again ? Change what ? What must I change ? I wrote exactly what you said. You said you were the chairman of the Betar in Poland and that is what I wrote."

" Yes, but I am not guilty."

" Ah! ah! You are guilty all right! You don't even know how guilty you are."

And so the argument continued for hours, with various digressions, with threats and cajoling, with exhausting repetitions of the same reasons.

Suddenly, the door opened and the interrogator's comrade, the N.K.V.D. Major, entered.

" What do you say to this ? " said the interrogator to him. " He refuses to sign."

" Sign what ? " asked the Major, innocently.

" The minutes."

" What ? " The Major turned to me. " I see you want to play the hero. We've already seen that kind of hero. For your own good, I advise you to sign. In general, you are lucky to have such a judge-interrogator, but I see he is too good to you. Why don't you sign ? "

" Citizen-Major," I said, " I am not a hero and I am not playing the hero. It is a question of my belief. I cannot sign that I was guilty because I believed in my ideals."

" What is he talking about ? " the Major asked the interrogator.

The interrogator read him the text, adding : " And this he refuses to sign."

" You refuse to sign this ? " asked the Major, turning to me again. " Why, it is the truth. How can you refuse to sign something that is true ? "

I was about to repeat all over again the reasons I had given—goodness only knows how many times!—to my interrogator, but at that moment a new idea occurred to me and I jumped at it, not only because I was tired of going over my previous explanations, but because it was a properly juridical idea.

" Citizen-Major," I said, " I am ready at any moment to sign these minutes, but how can I sign that I am guilty ? I want to defend myself and I think I have the right to defend myself. When I come before the court I shall try to prove that I am not guilty. That will be my defence, my sole defence. But how can I defend myself at the trial if I admit in advance that I am guilty ? "

When he heard this, the Major said, not to me and not to his comrade, but as if to himself : " Trial ! Give him a platform, give him a platform for his rhetoric ! "

" Whom do you want to convince," he asked, addressing me again ; " us ? Veteran Chekists ? "

It was the first time since my arrest that I had heard the traditional word which had become a word of horror : Chekist ! With what pride he said it ! But the Chekist had said something more important. He did not repeat his comrade's promise that there would be a trial. " Trial ! Give him a platform ! " he said.

The Major thereupon left the room, and I said to my interrogator in a tone of undisguised disappointment : " Citizen-Judge, you told me several times that there would be a trial, and now I understand from the Major that there is not going to be one."

The interrogator replied hotly : " *I* am your interrogator. I told you there would be a trial, and so there will be ! But first we must conclude the interrogation. Sign the summary, and we've finished."

From now on, I no longer used ideological reasons. I repeated my juridical contention : If I sign that I am guilty, what is there left for me to say in court ?

For almost an entire night the argument about the two words in the summary went on. Finally, the interrogator said :

" You are doing yourself harm. You make me sick, you are like an ape, an African ape, and I never want to see you again. I'll take out the word *vinovnim* and write : *priznaius chto bil*, and so on . . ."

I was overjoyed. I no longer paid any heed to his abuses.

Because of the kinship of the Polish and Russian languages, I was able to understand the difference between *priznaio*, which means " admit ", " admit to a certain fact ", and *priznaius*, which means " confess ", " confess guilt ". So I asked the interrogator to write *priznaio*, and not *priznaius*. He did not even deign to answer me. He tore up what he had written and wrote it out again, as follows :

" *I admit* that I was the chairman of the Betar in Poland . . ."

I had not given in !

I signed. I was taken back to my cell.

9

THE RIDDLE OF THE CONFESSIONS

BEFORE I resume the story of my imprisonment I would like to contribute something out of my own experience towards solving the riddle that has puzzled the world for fifteen years and more, the riddle of the Soviet trials.

I hardly think the world is amazed at the revelations that keep on cropping up concerning " conspiracies " against one or other ruling group in Russia or in the countries annexed to it. We find in the history of many countries, not specifically Communist, instances of plots to overthrow governments which allow no criticism, other than " self-criticism " by order. According to the evidence of Edouard Beneš, late President of Czechoslovakia, there are grounds for thinking that Marshal Tukhachevski really intended some sort of " Buonapartist revolution " in the Soviet Union. If, on the other hand, one may presume that Zinoviev and Kamenev, Bukharin and Rykov, who were Lenin's friends and colleagues (and also critics), sinned only in that they knew Stalin of old and had more confidence in their own opinions than in his, it must not be forgotten that there are, in history, also instances of imaginary plots, concocted by the rulers themselves and " uncovered " by them in order to liquidate their rivals. As Fouché, Napoleon's Minister of Police, said: " Every self-respecting Minister of Police must have in his knapsack at least a few conspiracies against the State . . ."

The trials in Moscow and Sofia, or Budapest and Prague, arouse amazement not because of the accusations but because of the accused. Observers who stand outside the circle of Communist influence, tangible or otherwise, can either believe in the accusations of Prosecutor Vishinsky and his disciples, or regard their charge-sheet as one of Fouché's " conspiracies ". There is no third possibility. In both these instances, the observers—free men—stand and wonder, and want to know : What happened to the accused ?

97

If they indeed rose against the rulers, if they believed that their rulers had deviated from the right path, if they were disappointed in the Communist regime and decided to fight for some other regime, or if, still being Communists, they rose to fight for " *true* Communism ", as they had pictured it in the days of their youth, as they dreamt it would be, all their lives ; why, then, did they not admit their beliefs, what they were striving for, what they were fighting for ? Most of the Soviet accused were veteran revolutionaries. Prison and the dock, torture, even the shadow of impending death, were nothing new to them. They were experienced people. They had learnt the ways of revolutionary war, not at " evening classes " but in the " universities " of the underground, of persecution and suffering. They had stood before interrogators, judges, even hangmen, more than once, and they were not afraid, they did not bow their heads, they did not beg for mercy, but they fought for their ideals. What, then, happened to these same people when they stood before a Cheka interrogator, before a Soviet prosecutor, before a Red hangman ? Why did they not accompany their admissions with a clear, proud statement, as becomes fighting men with a mission, men whose characters have been moulded : " The truth is with us, not with the rulers ".

If, on the other hand, the accused were but victims of a " plot-to-order ", if they had done nothing against their governments, what happened to their instinct of self-preservation ? Why did they not behave as every man behaves in the face of danger ? Why did they not shout, to the very last moment : " We are innocent. The world will still see that we were right " ?

In the annals of revolutions, whether scientific, social or national, there are instances of people who sacrificed their lives for the sake of their faith, and people who renounced their faith to save their lives. But the accused in Soviet trials sacrifice their beliefs in order to give up their lives. And the world is astounded. What brought them to this double renunciation, unprecedented in the history of revolution?

Of course, this is not the only question, nor the last, that occurs to us in the face of the startling phenomena which we witnessed in the 'thirties in Moscow, in the 'forties in Sofia, and in the 'fifties in Prague. And which we shall yet witness in . . . ? One might ask, further : What is the political purpose of the " soul-engineers " who demand of those about to die that they cease to exist even before the merciful bullet has pierced the back of their skulls ? There is no difficulty in answering this question. The rulers in Moscow also graduated from the " university " of revolutionary war. They had learnt that one of the decisive factors in war between the " weak ", the idealists, and the " strong ", the rulers, is the " blood-witness " of the persecuted who give their lives for the ideal. Because of this martyrology, powerless Jewry was able to stand up to its persecutors ; because of it, Christianity, the faith of a sect, became a world religion ; because of martyrology, the concept of freedom prevailed over the spears of tyrants in all continents, and in all eras ; thanks to it, the Hebrew rebels in Eretz Israel, in our time, triumphed over the British occupying power and its mighty army. It is a golden rule of history : The blood of believers is the life of faith. The rulers in Moscow know this rule not only in theory but in fact, from their own personal experience. Therefore, they will not permit any heroics, any martyrology on the public platform of the trial. On the contrary, the platform of the trial, in so far as it can be used, has to destroy the ideological blood-witness of the accused. The N.K.V.D. Major had scoffed at me in the interrogation room : " Trial ! Give him a platform ! " With these sneering words the interrogator's comrade had explained the principal factor in the system of investigation and judging of the N.K.V.D. There is no platform. The choice before the accused is : Either a trial with ideological annihilation, or physical destruction without a trial.

One may also ask : What is the spiritual source from which the rulers of the Kremlin derive their decision to impose on the accused the confession of repentance ? This question too is easy to answer. Every despotism is by nature " paternal ". There is in it a father-complex, either positive or negative. The ruler is the father, and his subjects are the children. The father-ruler looks after his children-subjects if they are good, and chastises them if they are bad. That father-complex has reached its climax in the Soviet regime, since its discipline is absolute not only in the political sphere but also in the economic sphere. The ruler is the father who provides their sustenance, and the subjects get their bread from the ruler like children dependent on their father's table. As is well known, a father does not content himself merely with punishing his son who has sinned, but demands of him that he admit that he has done wrong, that he repent, that he beg forgiveness. In the past chastising fathers even used to demand that their sons kiss the chastising hand.

Perhaps one may therefore contend that if the father-complex of the rulers has reached its climax in the Soviet Union, the complementary complex, the child-complex, of the inhabitants of the Soviet Union has also reached its climax, and so the " bad children " kiss the " father's " hand even if it chastises, tortures, strangles. There is no doubt that there is some truth in this contention, but it still does not explain the phenomenon of the " confessions " of people who were themselves once rulers, sometimes very cruel rulers, and not merely revolutionaries who knew what suffering was.

One must admit that the phenomenon which is revealed from time to time in the Soviet trials is far beyond the bounds of accepted human thought. It is not surprising, therefore, that inexperienced observers who try to solve the riddle and probe what goes on in the minds of the accused tend to take refuge in the realm of mystery and come out with the idea that drugs are used which are known only to the science of the N.K.V.D. That, of course, is something for scientists to judge. But even a layman may ask : Is there a drug that will activate a person's memory and cause him to give figures and mention names, and talk for hours saying precisely the opposite of what he really thinks is the truth, but which has been relegated to his subconscious mind? There are drugs that weaken a person's will ; some people call them truth drugs. Are there lie drugs? I think it is sufficient to pose the question, in order to come to the conclusion that although there is horror in the story of the confessions of those interrogated by the N.K.V.D. there is no mystery in it.

My contention that " usual " pressure—usual in the inquisition chambers—such as torture by beating, or torture without beating, is not the decisive factor in the confessions, will no doubt be received with the counter-contention that my personal experience during the nights of interrogation was not complete. It is a just contention. I was not tortured and I was not beaten. Although I was threatened with " other means " which would make me accept the interrogator's opinion both at N.K.V.D. Headquarters and at Lukishki, the threats were never carried out, even though they failed to achieve their purpose. I can also give further evidence " in favour " of the N.K.V.D. In the prison cells and in the Correctional Camp huts I came into personal contact with hundreds of other prisoners of that period. Not one of them had been beaten up or tortured. A few of them told me that they had heard that some Polish officers had been thrashed by their interrogators. A Polish captain who sat in one of the cells with me told me that one night the interrogator put a revolver under his nose and said : " Smell! And know what is in store for you." The cold metal touched the captain's upper lip. He did not feel too comfortable. But the interrogator did not hit him, neither with the revolver nor with his hand. It is possible that luck was with the Lukishki inmates of that period. We were brought to the cells in a wave of mass arrests. The N.K.V.D. was not at that time conducting a " special " purge, but one of its " usual " purges. For twenty years Lithuania had been outside the Soviet sphere of influence. Then the Red Army staged the " June Revolution ". And on the heels of the Red Army and the Revolution, came the Avengers and Guardians and carried out a sort of " social hair-cutting " operation. No " trials for the education of the people " were held at that time. The purpose of the arrests was to liquidate the stratum of " suspects " of all nationalities, of all classes. Intelligentsia, army people, scientists, political figures especially, were collectively doomed to disappear, quietly, without public trials . . . simply by the decision of an " Advisory Commission " that operates somewhere in Moscow.

I too was lucky. I, too, was one of the tens of thousands of the grey hordes of prisoners who were condemned in advance to disappear, with or without an investigation. My interrogator did not for one moment doubt that I was guilty. In all sincerity he said : " You were (chairman of the Betar) ?—That means that you are (guilty)! " Similarly, I did not for one moment doubt that I was in the right. And in all sincerity I said : " I was—and I am not guilty! " Of course, it never entered my mind to deny that " I was ", and this admission in itself was perfectly sufficient for both my interrogator and his principals. However, my interrogator wanted me not only to admit that " I was ", but to confess that " I was guilty ". He was not lying when he asserted that others had done so. Army officers signed confessions that they were guilty of having been . . . a colonel or a lieutenant-colonel in the Polish Army. High officials signed admissions that they were guilty of having been section heads, or departmental directors, in the Lithuanian Ministry of the Interior. They signed the summary of the minutes without being tortured, without being beaten up ; not out of inattentiveness, but out of lack of sleep, out of an overwhelming desire to finish, to bring the mental torture to an end.

One of my cell-mates, an elderly major with whom I became particularly friendly, told me that he had paid attention to the wording of the summary. He too asked that it be changed. He, too, heard threats and abuse, but he persisted in his demand. He, too, signed only when the interrogator had struck out the word *vinovnim*. It is possible that the N.K.V.D. attached no special importance to the fine distinction between " I hereby admit that I was . . ." and " I hereby confess that I am guilty of having been . . .". The principal admission, " I was "—of which I and the other prisoners were so proud—was given into their hands. And that was what they needed.

Of course my experience was not complete. I did not " admit ", I did not " confess ", I was not brought to trial. But let us suppose that the N.K.V.D. interrogators do beat the *special* detainees, and torture them. There is no doubt that the interrogator can use means of breaking a man physically. There is no law in the Soviet Union that forbids the use of beatings or torture during the interrogation. And the interrogation-room is isolated. . . . One of the Communist prisoners, of whom I shall tell later, told me what he went through in the interrogation dungeon of the Tomsk prison. He told me how the interrogating " expert " jumped up suddenly and with a swift movement wrenched out the leg of a chair, and with it proceeded to belabour him, accompanying his blows with the monotonous cry : " Will you confess or not, will you confess or not ? " The prisoner, who was a very important Soviet leader, begged only one thing of his assailant : not to hit him over the heart, because he was already then suffering from a heart disease.

But can one explain the phenomenon of the admissions and con-fessions by putting them down to blows and physical torture ? Do not other police forces beat up their prisoners ? Do they not use torture in the interrogation-rooms of both civil and military police in other countries, outside the Soviet Union ? In most countries laws have been passed prohibiting the infliction of bodily harm on prisoners, but who can in all honesty deny that interrogators of various kinds deliberately disregard the prohibition ? Who will deny that in most cases the barbaric behaviour of the guardians of the law does not even reach public knowledge ? Which truth-loving person will deny that the *official* criminals very seldom get punished ? Nevertheless, there is no police force in the world that can boast of what the Soviet secret police boasts, together with its branches in the annexed countries. For, although the history of the Inquisition, in its various forms and various epochs, tells that those who did not stand up to torture were far more numerous than those who did, it is a fact that the will of the tortured is not always broken. As a matter of fact, among those who " confessed " on the Soviet platform of annihilation, were people who had been put through the tortures of hell by other police forces—and had not been broken!

Where, then, lies the solution to the greatest riddle of our day ?

I think I learnt from close up, from inside, what the decisive factors are that make those who are about to die admit and confess before their hangmen. The first in importance is—isolation.

I do not mean physical isolation, which is known in the law as incommunicado. That does, of course, exist in the realm of the N.K.V.D., where it is absolute. When you are arrested by the N.K.V.D. no relative will visit you except to say goodbye before you set out on the long road to re-education. No lawyer will visit you, to undertake your defence. You will see no one except your fellow-prisoners and your interrogator. When you have crossed the threshold of the N.K.V.D. you have disappeared. The members of your family will be permitted to know just one thing—and sometimes not even that : that you are in a " secure " place and in " secure " hands. The wall of isolation cannot be estimated, either in height or in thickness. It is doubtful if there ever was anything like it.

But over the wall of physical isolation another wall is placed. It is imperceptible to the human eye. But it is more solid, more impenetrable than the other, which is built of iron, cement and watch-towers. The second wall, the upper one, signifies not a regime of isolation but the isolation of a regime. Such isolation is unprecedented in history.

In every other regime there will be a paper that will print the words of the prisoner, or the man being investigated, or the man judged. If the prisoner is a fighter, whose ideal and activities have been placed outside the formal law, there will appear, in every other regime, a printed, duplicated or handwritten leaflet which will make known to a circle of citizens, large or small, what the man was arrested for, what he was required to say, and what he actually said. The knowledge that his words will reach someone, that his very silence will be heard of, that his stand will be recorded—these are the things that give strength to the revolutionary and fighter. It is not a craving for publicity. It is a noble urge to serve, it is the identification of man with the ideal for which he is prepared to give his life. The man who is prepared to suffer abuse, tribulation, hunger, torture, the dread of death and the destruction of his life, in order to serve his ideal, is a fighter, whether he is armed or defenceless, whether he has religious faith in his heart, a scientific idea in his brain, or the striving for freedom in his soul. But whether he be one of many, or one alone, he will be prepared to suffer, to be tortured, even to die for his ideal, if he knows that his sacrifice is worth while, that it serves some purpose, at least for the ideal, which requires other adherents, more fighters, and others who will learn from his example and also be prepared to choose suffering in preference to a life of ease. Otherwise how will the cause triumph? How will the weak overcome the strong? How will tyranny fall? How will freedom rise? From this point of view the fighter resembles a mother who suppresses the primary and most natural of instincts, the instinct of self-preservation, for a nobler instinct, for the identification of her soul with that of her beloved son. Like a mother who endangers her own life to save the one she loves from danger, so is the fighter ready to sacrifice his life in order to ensure life to the fruits of his love, that which he believes in, his spiritual son : his ideal.

That is the spirit of the fighter. That is his mission. But if the fighter knows that his service is rendered worthless, that no one will hear what he says, no one will learn of his stand, no one will receive his sacrifice from his hands, and no one will learn from him how to sacrifice ; then the thread between him and the ideal is likely to be severed ; it is then that his inner recognition of his mission is completely eradicated, and his tortured soul asks : Who will know? Who will follow after me? Who will come in my place? What point is there in my suffering, what purpose in the tortures I undergo ?

Behind the double wall erected by the Soviet regime around the special prisoner, these questions give him no rest. Perhaps not every prisoner will ask these questions, but most of them will. Perhaps they will not ask them immediately ; but one day, or one night, they will ask : What is the point? And answer : There is no point. When that happens the prisoner is doomed, not to physical annihilation—that he is assured of in any event—but to serve the ideal of his hangman. Without any mysterious drugs, without even any of the " known " tortures, but by natural means, the double isolation achieves its double purpose : there is no evidence of self-sacrifice for an ideal opposed by the rulers ; there is evidence of self-annihilation for the supremacy of the rulers.

If Bukharin could have assumed that *Pravda* (" The Truth ") would print what he said to his interrogator, or wanted to say to his judges; if he could at least have assumed that somewhere, secretly, a leaflet would appear under the name of " The Real Truth " and publish what he said; if he could have assumed that his words would reach that youthful interrogator, disciple of the revolution, who cursed him in my presence, dubbing him " international spy " ; if he could have believed that it would be distributed among the citizens in the capital, or in the cities, towns or villages, it is possible that he would have accused the authorities of anti-revolutionary policies (if he really rose against them), or would have rejected, courageously, the accusations of the authorities (if he had not risen against them). But Bukharin knew that *Pravda* would write daily that he was an enemy of humanity, an international spy, a mad dog, a contemptible traitor, even before he was brought to trial, even before he was sentenced. Bukharin knew that all the newspapers and all the broadcasting stations in the country would repeat what *Pravda* wrote, with the addition of vilification, abuses, oaths and curses. He also knew that no " Real Truth " would appear in the Soviet Union and make known *his* truth. Bukharin knew, therefore, that not one of his fellow-countrymen would hear or read his words, but all would be persuaded, and actually believe, that he was nothing but an agent of the international bourgeoisie and an enemy of the proletarian revolution. Knowing all this, he must have asked himself one night : What is the use ? And come to the conclusion that : " To sign or not to sign, NOT that is the question. . . ."

My young interrogator who believed without any doubt that Bukharin was a spy when he stood at the head of the Comintern, and that Trotsky was an agent of the bourgeoisie when he was at the head of the Workers' and Peasants' Army, held in his hands one key to the weary souls of the accused who go to their death, not singing a song of defiance, but justifying the sentence. The second key was held by the veteran Chekist, my interrogator's comrade, who said to himself: " Trial ! Give him a platform! " These keys open the gate to the world of double isolation in which the great riddle is solved, where there is horror but no mystery.

In the world of isolation threats concerning the prisoner's family also have special persuasive power. There is no doubt that the N.K.V.D. utilises these threats. And there is certainly nothing worse. The true fighter will readily accept suffering of his own for his ideals, but everything in him will revolt against inflicting suffering on those near and dear to him. Even in conditions entirely different from those of an N.K.V.D. interrogation, it is possible to reduce a fighter to despair and abnegation by means of threats to persecute his wife or his children. Nevertheless, there have been fighters who stood firm even in the face of this threat, and did not give in. There were such cases during our revolt in Eretz Israel, just as there were in the days of the revolutionary opposition to the Czarist regime.

It is said that Felix Dzherzhinsky, who was head of the Cheka after the Bolshevik victory, experienced a frightful personal tragedy during the period of the underground. The gendarmes of the Czarist Okhrana not only interrogated him to the accompaniment of fiendish tortures, but deliberately, and before his very eyes, assaulted and maltreated his fiancée. It is possible that because he was the victim of such cruelty, he treated his own victims with such cruelty when his day came. But it is a fact that Dzherzhinsky was not broken in the Okhrana interrogation. He stood up to the tortures and did not renounce his beliefs in order to save the woman he loved.

Yagoda, who was also for a time head of the Cheka, was broken by those who did his bidding in the past, and " confessed everything ". One cannot know if they threatened him, or other cruel people like him, with the annihilation of their families. But if they were threatened with this, it is not difficult to estimate the extent of its influence. Prisoners of the N.K.V.D. were not as lucky as its founder, Felix Dzherzhinsky. He was interrogated by the Okhrana. He fought for an ideal and believed that his fortitude would be made known to his friends, and would contribute towards the ultimate success of their common ideal. Whereas the others had the recognition of their mission torn from within them, night after night, and in its place came the recognition of its futility. And if there was no point in their suffering, why make their families suffer ? There is no doubt that the threat of harming a prisoner's family—just like the promise *not* to harm them—is one of the factors that cause him to break down.

The same, naturally, applies to the merciful " promises " of forgiveness, remission of their sins, of a period of education and re-education : after which the criminal will be permitted to return to society, to work for his people. Let no one say that these are but empty promises, and the N.K.V.D. prisoners know it and will not believe in them. They *will* believe, because they will want to believe. For the hope of living does not desert a man until the last moment. Did not our unhappy brothers believe, even when they stood beside the pits which they had dug with their own hands, that they would still be saved from the German murderers? It is a true saying: *Dum spiro, spero*—While I breath, I hope. There is, therefore, no doubt that the enticing promises also helped to get the " signature ", from which there is no return.

But all these are but subsidiary to the decisive factor in the breaking-down process, that of isolation.

The second factor is—depriving the prisoner of sleep. This was familiar to me both from " Headquarters " and from Lukishki. It is an inseparable concomitant of every interrogation in Russia. The N.K.V.D. works mainly at night. Practically all the interrogations are conducted between the first and third watches of the night. By day, sleeping is prohibited, even a light nap is forbidden. Regulations to this effect have been brought out in the Soviet jails. The warder is responsible for enforcing them. In order to prevent the prisoner from falling asleep (and not just to prevent him from committing suicide), a Judas window has been installed in the cell-door. And if, through the peep-hole, or Judas window, the warder sees you doze, seated on the rickety stool, he will open the door or pick up the hatch and caution you: " Don't you know you are not allowed to sleep? If you sleep you'll go to *carcer* " (solitary confinement). It is preferable not to sleep in the cell rather than to sleep in *carcer*. That too I learnt in Lukishki.

This, therefore, is the procedure, as I described it in the course of the story of my nights of interrogation: The prisoner is taken out of his first, deep sleep. The interrogation goes on until almost daybreak. The interrogator is fresh. It is true he works at night, but in the daytime he enjoys a white, comfortable bed. If, nevertheless, the interrogator does get tired, another takes his place. The N.K.V.D. is not short of interrogators, just as it is not short of people to interrogate. After a night of interrogation, the prisoner is taken back to his cell and lays his dizzy head on the mattress. He falls asleep, but in a very short time the reveille whistle startles him out of his sleep. A new day has come ; three meals come, that bring in their wake perpetual hunger ; night comes, bringing the darkness of the renewed interrogation. And again, and again. . . . Night after night for weeks, for months, for time without end. In the head of the interrogated prisoner a haze begins to form. His spirit is wearied to death, his legs are unsteady, and he has one sole desire : to sleep, to sleep just a little, not to get up, to lie, to rest, to forget. " To sleep, to die, to sleep . . . no more." Anyone who has experienced this desire knows that not even hunger or thirst are comparable with it. I came across prisoners who signed what they were ordered to sign, only to get what the interrogator promised them. He did not promise them their liberty ; he did not promise them food to sate themselves. He promised them—if they signed—uninterrupted sleep! And they signed. For there was no purpose in continuing to suffer, and they wanted to sleep, sleep. . . . And, having signed, there was nothing in the world that could move them to risk again such nights and such days. . . . The main thing was—to sleep.

The third factor is peculiar to the devotees of Communism, to its leaders, its active members and its servants, who cross the thre hold of the interrogation-room. Their world has been destroyeu for them and they have no other world—not on earth, not within themselves, and not above. They were big men ; the lives and deaths of thousands had been held in their hands. Now they were like dogs. And worse still, they had become " mad dogs ". The fall itself, which is as far as any fall can be, is enough to break the bones of opposition to the interrogator, and the interrogator is still ready to go on breaking. The unhappy people claim that they are true to the Communist ideal, but they are immediately compelled to admit that there is someone who decides what the Communist ideal is and how it is to be achieved. They not only said so, but wrote that it was so ; they believed it, and in fact still believe it. But the man who " decides " is far away and his authorised representative is sitting before them, and demands of them, for the sake of the Communist ideal, a " full confession " of their mistakes, their sins, their crimes. What should they answer ? What should they fight for ? Why should they suffer ? What is the use ? Who will follow in their footsteps ? Who will take their place ? How can they not give a " confession "—for the sake of the Party, for the sake of the Revolution ? This system, which was invented by the N.K.V.D., and perfected by experts in the light of experience, is intended principally for Communist leaders who, for some reason or other, have fallen out with the ruling body, or fallen victims to its " educational " programme.

And there are none who lend themselves more easily to the application of the N.K.V.D. system of breaking the spirit of a man without harming him physically than Communists and Communist leaders.

10

ON THE THRESHOLD

When the interrogation was over, the decision to give my wife a conditional divorce took shape in my mind. The idea first entered my head during the twenty-four hours that preceded the face-to-face meeting with the " person close to me ". That night and all the following day I was almost certain that the person to whom the interrogator had smilingly referred was my wife. The anxiety of those hours gave birth to the thought of a divorce, but when I took the decision I did not delude myself that I would thereby save my wife from arrest or deportation. What prompted me to take this decision was something else.

The end of the interrogation brought relief from the tension that had accompanied me day and night. I no longer thought about what the interrogator said to me, and what I answered, on the previous night; or what he would say and I would answer the following night. I thought of my future. I thought about it, fully reconciled to whatever it might hold for me. That was my portion, so why should I complain ? Although the heart wanted life and freedom and looked forward to the day of release, and refused to ask, in the midst of its happy anticipation : " Will it come ? When will it come ? " the brain could not forget what the interrogator had said : " There will be a trial. There will be a period of education and re-education." I could not help asking myself : " Will I live to see the end of the period of re-education, will I live through it ? Will I complete it and return ? "

" Then again," I went on arguing with myself, " the separation will be a long one, and maybe . . . maybe, after a number of years, no one will even know where my bones lie. About that too I must not complain. Did I not take an oath, did I not say with all my heart : I dedicate my life ? Am I the only one ? But if my future is doubtful, why should I destroy the future of my wife who would be hoping for my return—in vain? She is only twenty. She still has her whole life in front of her. Can I condemn her to waiting until her hair grows grey, to endless solitude? Is it not my duty to tell her that if I do not return by a certain date she should no longer wait for me? Is it not my duty to prevent her life from being ruined as well?"

In a prison cell all privacy, both physical and mental, disappears. The prisoner's soul seeks compensation for its isolation. And to the extent that the distance between the prisoner and his relatives increases, so the closeness between him and strangers increases. The prisoner is prepared to talk to his cell-mates about everything. He is prepared to consult with them on everything. He wants to ask their opinion on everything. In our small cell sat three isolated people. They did not have much in common. Each came from a different world, and wanted to return to a different world. But loneliness drew the three strangers together. It opened the hearts of my companions to me and mine to them.

I told my cell-mates about my idea concerning the divorce, and asked them what they thought of it.

At first they were angry with me. They said that with my thoughts and my question I had brought into the cell an atmosphere of concern for our families. They did not want such an atmosphere. The officer once said that in jail, and particularly in a Bolshevik jail, there was no point in wearying one's brain and chastising one's spirit with worrying about relatives who had remained outside. "We won't be able to help them, in any way," he used to say with irrefutable logic, "so what is the point of letting ourselves get consumed with worry over them?" The corporal was in full agreement with this viewpoint, and it was decided by majority opinion, with me abstaining, not to worry about our families and not to talk about them. The second part of the decision was strictly observed in the cell. For days and weeks we chatted about shooting birds, good drinking, priests and generals, singing and opera, history and politics. We spoke of many things; we did not mention our families. But as for the first part of the decision. . . .

One morning, having said his prayers and drunk his coffee, the corporal began to tell us, as he often did, about a dream he had had that night. "All night," he said, "I dreamt of my old mother." He told us how his mother was dressed in the dream, how she asked him if his new top-boots were not too tight for him, how she stroked his hair, how she promised him (calling him " little son ") that they would be together again, how he begged her to tell him when it would be and she did not, how she smiled, so sadly. . . . The corporal stopped abruptly and began to mumble to himself : " Mother, my Mummy, my good old lady." His eyes glistened with tears. He got up suddenly from the stool and went over to the corner where he used to pray after returning to the faith. He was a man, a soldier, and he was ashamed of his tears. The officer and I said nothing. A son was crying for his mother. A grown man who will always be her " little son ". The mother no doubt cried very much; the son, the soldier, the man, is usually dry-eyed. But sometimes. . . . And then her tears meet his, and flow into one channel, the great river of human misery which has no explanation, and at times no purpose. . . . The corporal stood in his corner for a while. It was quiet in the cell. Neither of us pointed out to him that he had gone against the decision and " worried ".

But both of them, both the officer and the corporal, accused me of openly and perpetually breaking the agreement. No, it was not a renewal of their solidarity against mine. They were right. The officer declared that he now understood why I had been so silent the last few days ; why I seemed to be absent from the general discussions. The corporal said he knew now what I was thinking about during my " excursions ", and why, at times, he had to repeat his questions to get an answer from me. " We all decided to help each other in this stench," they complained, " and not shut ourselves up in our thoughts. We see now that you have been worrying for days already. You will admit that we have the same rights as you. From now on we will also begin to worry about our families, and if each of us will be busy thinking of them, how can we help each other ? "

They were right, and the important thing was that they were speaking out of kindness. Their " egoism " was for the purpose of helping me. I apologised and thanked them. They did not repeat their complaints, but insisted that we consider my decision briefly so that, after taking a final decision, I should be able to stop worrying and resume listening to the officer's hunting tales, or the corporal's stories of the front. The discussion was indeed short. My companions weighed my decision—in accordance with the rules of caution—from both angles. Of course, they rejected the possibility of my not returning, just as I, when they were depressed, would have rejected the possibility that they would not return to their homes and their families. Nevertheless, to my surprise and to my strange joy, they confirmed my decision. The officer said: " I am sure your wife will not accept your ' gift ', but that is precisely why you can send it. God willing, the two of you will still laugh together at this ' divorce ' ." I shook him by the hand.

Our opinions were divided as to how long to allow before releasing my wife from her marriage vows. I suggested writing in the document that if I were not back within three years, " divorce is hereby granted to my wife, and she is free ". The officer suggested that we fix the final date at five years hence. The corporal supported him. I accepted their suggestion. They both agreed to witness the document, if necessary. To marry a girl according to the Mosaic law, two competent witnesses are required, but to give a bill of conditional divorcement, in Lukishki prison, to someone you love with all your heart, two " non-competent " witnesses will also do, both of them bachelors.

I set about carrying out my decision, bitter and cruel though it was, but for such a purpose paper and ink are required, and they are not easy to get in a prison under the control of the N.K.V.D. In order to draw up and send a document a permit must be obtained from the interrogator, but my interrogation was already over and my interrogator was no longer there. It was necessary, therefore, to apply to the interrogator in writing and request him to give me a permit to draw up the document. But in order to write a request to the interrogator a permit is required from the superintendent of the prison. And in order to draw up a petition to the superintendent a permit is required from the officer of the prison wing. How in the name of heaven does one get to write a " divorce " ? Days went by. Meanwhile, the year 1940 came to an end.

In the early hours of January 1st, 1941, we held a New Year's Eve party in our cell. Actually, the day which separated one year from the next was not any different in Lukishki from any other day. On the eve of the New Year we were given the same coffee in the morning, the same soups at noon and at nightfall. The bed-time whistle sounded at the usual time. At the usual hour we spread out our mattresses. We heard the usual footsteps outside the door of our cell and could guess that the sentry was peeping at us through the Judas window. My cell-mates went to sleep, after secretly deciding to get up a few hours later, in spite of the Judas window, and drink a toast to the New Year, when the city clock, whose chimes used to reach our cell, struck midnight. They invited me to the party and I accepted their invitation.

During the day we made the necessary preparations so that there should be something to drink at night. We drank only half our coffee in the morning. That is no trifling matter for prisoners of the N.K.V.D., who are hungry when they get up and when they go to bed, day and night, in their sleep and in their waking hours, who are replete only in their dreams.

One of the hardest things for N.K.V.D. prisoners is to leave over part of the food portion, to cut off a bit of the bread for later. There were many prisoners who could not, under any circumstances, control their hunger, and gobbled up their whole bread ration in the morning without leaving a crumb, and went hungry till next morning. With what envy they regarded their neighbours who were able to divide their bread into three, for the morning, for the midday meal, and for the evening! Time and time again they promised themselves that they would do the same. How many times did they say to themselves: " Only one tiny piece more and I'll keep the rest " ? How many times did they break that promise ? Just as a drunkard promises himself that each sip will be the last, and takes another sip and yet another, so did these unfortunate people, starved and hungry as they were, nibble away piece after piece until there was nothing left but the waiting for the next bread ration, waiting that devours one's insides.

In every prison cell that I passed through and in every concentration camp hut that I lived in it was possible to divide the prisoners into two categories, as far as the bread was concerned : the wasteful gobblers and the thrifty eaters, but all were hungry. In our small cell, too, we fell into these two categories. The corporal was a waster. He used to promise himself that he would save, but very seldom kept his promise. The officer and I were thrifty. He even broke a record in saving, and I followed his example. We both divided the bread ration not into three, but four (!) portions. We used to leave ourselves a small piece of bread for next day, for the many long hours of the morning between the reveille whistle and the new bread distribution. I am not ashamed to admit that there were many days when my first waking glance was directed upwards, to the shelf on which lay a piece of bread the size of an olive.

How great was my joy at finding it in its place! And how tasty it was ! What do those who eat delicacies know of taste ?

It was not a simple matter to leave off sipping the coffee in the morning, to see the brown liquid still half filling the mug and not drink. It was not an easy thing—especially for the waster—to see a half-empty cup, covered with a bowl, standing on the shelf all day and not touch it. But even the waster held out, for that night a year would come to an end, and another year would begin, and one must, according to tradition, " wet " the New Year. There is no vodka, let us at least drink " coffee " !

I would no doubt have been prevented from participating in the Sylvester Night carousals in the Soviet prison had the officer not aroused me from my sleep, he himself having awakened with the help of his " internal clock " which echoed the three-quarter chime of the city clock. I was sleeping after the long period of interrogation, and there is no deeper sleep than that. The officer was the host. He rose quietly from his mattress and brought us our mugs. We sat on the mattresses and waited, a vast silence all around us. Suddenly the silence was shattered. The clock began to strike : *one, two, three, four, five.* . . . There it is, *twelve* ! We wished each other a " Happy New Year " and raised our " glasses ". We clinked mugs and drank to the new year.

We did not know that we were entering not just a new year but a new epoch. The year 1940 was over, the year of the victory of Germany over France, the year of Dunkirk, the year of the exchange of greetings between Hitler and Stalin, the year of the Blood Covenant between Berlin and Moscow. The year 1941 had begun, the year of the German attack on Russia, the year of the Japanese attack on America, the year when the flames of war were to spread from one end of the world to the other, and—for us—a year of wandering to the distant north. . . .

We did not know. But we drank, draining our glasses to the bottom.

A few days after the New Year's Eve " party", the door of our cell opened and we heard the whispered question : " Whose name begins with ' B ' ? "

The question surprised me. Was the interrogation being re-opened ? And if so, was a revolution beginning in the realm of the N.K.V.D.? It was daytime, not night. Why that question in the middle of the day? But when the cell door is open at a narrow angle and the N.K.V.D. emissary stands there holding a list, and waits for an answer, there is no time to ask why and how. One must answer.

"With your belongings," said the warder after I had given my name, my father's name and my surname.

This is another of the refrains of the N.K.V.D. that echo within the walls of the prison, sometimes by day, sometimes at night. Instead of "Take your belongings and come with us", the elliptical phrase : "with your belongings". There are occasions when this summons arouses hope ; in general it arouses profound dread. The instances of releases from the prisons of the N.K.V.D. are few and far between, but the command "with your belongings" does sometimes arouse in the heart of the prisoner the hope that maybe he is one in a thousand, one in tens of thousands, and the order means— Home! But the order also has another meaning : To the unknown!

That is why the dread it arouses in the heart of the prisoner is always greater than the hope.

After what I had heard from my interrogator, I had no illusions as to the meaning of the words : "with your belongings".

"You are being transferred to another cell," said my neighbour, the corporal.

That was what I thought, too.

"It's a pity," added the corporal. "There was still a lot for us to learn."

I, too, was sorry.

In this small cell I had sat for more than three months ; which means, in prison, a hundred whole days, a hundred nights. I had grown used to my cell-mates and they to me. There were barriers between us. We even quarrelled. But we managed to get to know each other, we learnt to understand and to forgive. We had already become a small "community", with its unwritten laws and its customs. Here I had taught a little, and learnt a lot. Here I had gone through the interrogation; here I had made a heart-breaking decision. . . . It *was* a pity. . . . I wondered who my next cell-mates would be.

But in prison there is no time for pouring out your heart. From the mouth of the warder came the shout which is heard from one end of the Soviet Union to the other, in all the prisons, in all the transit stations, in all the concentration camps : "*Davai! Paskareya!*"—

" Hurry ! Hurry up! " I had to make haste and assemble my belongings and say goodbye to my cell-mates.

The corporal took my bowl, mug and wooden spoon down from the shelf. This is equipment from which the prisoner does not let himself be separated. I gathered my clothes together. There was not much. During this time I had received only small parcels of linen. In one of them a treasure was concealed, but it was also small. It was a toothbrush. Those meagre little parcels! We always searched them, and I am sure that our searches were more thorough than any that were made by officials of the N.K.V.D. and the prison guards. We searched for a sign, a thread; perhaps there would be some embroidery on the inside of a sleeve, under a collar. We found nothing. But even without that, the little parcels were like long letters to us. You are not alone, there is someone who remembers you, there is someone who is concerned about you, who thinks of you. . . .

" Davai paskareya," says the warder. Yes, you must pack your bundle and say goodbye.

My pupil the corporal went on helping me, but my other neighbour stood by, silently. As luck would have it, he had just had an attack of orderliness, one of his severe attacks, and had not spoken either to me or to the corporal for the past twenty-four hours. How could I take leave of him ? But there was no time left to think, there was no time to wait for the " appeasement " which would come, as it always did, of its own accord. I put out my hand. He forgot all about being cross, and shook my hand warmly.

" Au revoir, all the best! "

My pupil handed me my bundle. We embraced.

" Au revoir, all the best! "

" I suggest you think that matter over again, all the same," the officer managed to add, almost shouting.

" Thanks, many thanks. Au revoir, all the best! "

I understood what he meant. I had not yet managed to send the bill of divorcement.

The cell door closed behind me, in the face of my companions. I never saw them again.

11

HUNGER STRIKE

THE cell in which they put me was a large, communal cell. Twelve iron bedsteads were attached to the walls, but the cell buzzed with almost thirty people. Where there is no room there is equality. The beds in the communal cell were not let down, just as the solitary bed in our small cell was not let down. We all slept on the floor.

The prisoners were, for the most part, Polish army men. Among them was the officer who had " smelt " his interrogator's revolver. I talked to him, but it was impossible to break through his reserve. He was a cavalry officer, limited like every professional cavalryman, as proud as a thoroughbred horse.

There is not much to tell about that cell. I was there for a few days only. From there, I was taken, together with a number of other prisoners, to another communal cell. But before I managed to acclimatise myself to the new cell I was again transferred—no one knows the purpose of all those transfers—to a third communal cell, where I remained until I left the precincts of Lukishki.

The day I came to my " permanent " lodgings, I solved one of the small riddles which had puzzled me from the time of the interrogation. One night, in the course of a theoretical discussion on Marxism, Communism and Zionism, the interrogator had asked me : " Do you know Bernstein ? "

" Yes," I replied. " I read about him. He was the founder of revisionism in socialism."

" What are you talking about ? " asked the interrogator in amazement.

" About Bernstein, about the big argument that went on between him and Kautski."

" Oh you, and your burblings! " the interrogator exclaimed and went over to the main subject.

I did not understand. I did not understand my interrogator's amazement, nor his derision, until I got to know the inmates of my fourth cell. As was customary, I told them all my name, and they told me theirs. One of them said in a loud, emphatic voice: Bernstein.

Mordecai Bernstein was one of the leaders of the Jewish anti-Zionist socialist party in Poland, the Bund. His interrogator in Lukishki was the Major, my interrogator's comrade. Both interrogators no doubt exchanged views about their "clients". The interrogator's incidental question, casual as it was, was not unnatural. But it did reveal an astounding fact. An N.K.V.D. officer, pupil of the school of Marxism, disciple of the Revolution, who could quote by heart whole extracts from the *Abridged Course of History of the Bolshevik Party*, had never heard of Edouard Bernstein, just as I, in my many transgressions, had not heard of Mordecai Bernstein. The education of the Soviet Marxists of the younger generation was very one-sided, even as far as the history of Marxism was concerned.

Bernstein had a good laugh when I told him about the misunderstanding that had arisen about his name. And I laughed at his learned interrogator's question about the Bundist-Revisionist composition of the Second International. The ideological differences of opinion between us could not be bridged, not even in Lukishki. But the man was good-hearted, knew Hebrew, and was able to laugh even when things looked black. We became very good friends.

I found another Bund leader in the communal cell. He was a Dr. Lifshitz, a well-known dental surgeon from Warsaw. He was arrested as an enemy of the people, an emissary of the bourgeoisie among the working class, and as a "collaborator with the Polish police against the Communist Party". He, too, like his friend, told his interrogator that it was the Communist Party in Poland that was swarming with police agents, and quoted as proof the fact that the Comintern disbanded it because it was riddled with agents provocateurs. So, in any event, the heads of the Comintern maintained. His argument did not help him either. He, too, heard curses as counter-arguments, and he, too, took exception to them. But he suffered very much in the cell, mainly because of hunger. Unlike his colleague and myself, he was by nature a pessimist. But in one respect he expressed an optimistic opinion: "If Hitler is beaten," he said, stressing the "if", "you Zionists will enjoy the fruits of victory because England will certainly give you a State." Actually, England did not "give" us a State, but it nevertheless did arise. One cannot demand too much exactitude from prophets.

In the communal cell, which had sixteen beds although its inmates numbered close on sixty, I found another Jew. He was not a Bundist and not a Zionist. He was not a "leader" and not a "political" at all. He was a Warsaw thief, a veteran and an expert in his line. How did he get into prison without having managed to steal in Vilna? How did he come to be in the "political" cell, in which sat public figures, high army officers, judges, professors, police officers, and one Deputy Cabinet Minister? The N.K.V.D. experts can hardly be suspected of having selected the thief, of all people, as their emissary, to hear and not be heard. He was actually shy, perhaps by nature or perhaps because of the society in which he found himself, but in his profession he was not at all bashful. And it was because of his "profession" that most of the prisoners were careful of him and avoided coming in contact with him, except when it came to the game of draughts. The thief was an expert and used to beat all the "intellectuals", and they wanted to learn from him not, God forbid, thieving, but various combinations. Had he been put into our cell so that the prisoners should beware of him and so forget to beware of another prisoner—an intellectual, this time—who mixed with the prisoners and knew how to talk and make others talk? The assumption of double-bluff, particularly where secret police are concerned, always seems logical. But, having had many conversations with the thief, I think the matter was much more simple in his case. He had tried to get to Vilna, and had with him goods he had appropriated during the bombing of Warsaw. (Dr. Lifshitz, who heard his story, reprimanded him severely for exploiting the misfortunes of others. The thief replied, quietly: "If I had not taken, others would have, so what's the difference?") When crossing the frontier he was caught by a Soviet patrol and accused not of robbery and smuggling, but of espionage! "What sort of spy am I?" the poor fellow used to ask. He had been used to prison since he was a boy, but he failed to understand why he had to sit in jail if not for a "professional" offence. There was no reply to his question, but in the meantime he had been promoted to a political criminal, and sat as a spy among the "spies of the bourgeoisie and agents of imperialism".

The big cell where I found, among the inmates, the seventy-eight-year-old colonel and my friend, the elderly major, was like a beehive. Discussions went on throughout the day. As a rule, these discussions were confined to separate groups. In every society man seeks out those closest to him or those who seem closest to him. In prison as well there are " exclusive clubs " of a sort. But in our cell there were prisoners who tried to preserve a general good spirit. On their initiative, courses were organised in languages, literature and history. We held general debates. Among other things, we heard a lecture on the life of the bee from an uneducated man who had never heard of Maeterlinck but had an amazing knowledge of the habits of bees because he had worked with them. We could have listened to him for hours while he lectured on the tiny " kingdoms ", and we were of the unanimous opinion that his lecture was more interesting than those of the learned.

To help ourselves forget we arranged draught and chess tournaments. The " pieces " were made out of donated bread, and some of them were amazingly beautiful. When they were confiscated by the warders, in the frequent night searches, we went on playing with substitutes. Man is a social animal in all conditions ; which leads one to the conclusion that a communal cell is better than a single one.

There were prisoners who tried to exploit the advantages of our communal cell to a very practical purpose. They were the wasters, who suffered more from hunger than their companions did, starved as they were. When the soup came, at noon or in the evening, they used to try to get theirs first. Bowl in hand, they would go over to the window corner and gulp down their portion at an incredible speed. Then they would dash to the door, rinse out their bowls with a few drops of water—washing water was very precious in our cell—dry them with the rag called a towel, and take up positions again at the end of the queue which was still lined up before the dixie. They would succeed in getting another bowl of soup if the warder failed to count the portions, or if we managed to mix him up in his counting at which the warder did not generally excel. But in most cases they did not get more soup, but a portion of Russian curses. " Why, you damned cheat ! " the warder would shout. " Didn't you get yours ? " The wasters would retreat, shamefaced, with their empty bowls. They could not react to the insults. Next day, they would try again. *Hunger* . . . Hunger, which can drive a man out of his mind and deprive him of his self respect.

As the prisoners increased in number, the percentage of " double queuers " rose, and they were compelled to fix among themselves a queue within the queue. They took it in turns, each day, to try their luck. The wasters would, on occasion, suggest that all the cell inmates join in their strategy, but there were prisoners who declined. For them the ordinary ration " sufficed ". Even on the few occasions when our provider announced with positively revolutionary solemnity : " More today ", they would give their extra portion to their suffering companions. Hunger is hunger, but ultimately it is a man's will-power that counts.

It is an interesting fact that the thief never pushed into the double queue. He used his profession only outside. It was a principle with him, and he observed it not only in this connection. Once, one of his neighbours complained that something had disappeared from his bundle. It was a rare occurrence, and, as I remember, happened only that once in our cell. Of course, it never entered the mind of the man affected to complain to the authorities. It was an internal matter and the autonomous authorities of the cell had to clear it up. Suspicion automatically fell on the thief. But after a discreet search had been carried out among the effects of a number of prisoners at a suitable opportunity, namely, during the general procession to the lavatories, the lost item was found with one of the " society people ", as it happens.

In the course of our imprisonment we came across another unnatural phenomenon. Among the prisoners, particularly among the policemen, there were people with healthy, sturdy bodies ; and there were intellectuals with thin, puny bodies. But it was the healthy ones who broke down physically, and who were always complaining to the doctor (a woman), who usually dismissed them with an aspirin, which she regarded as a panacea for all ills, and the caustic reminder that " This is not a boarding-house ! " The " weaklings " did not fall sick and did not complain. Their spirit seemed to uphold them, and serve as armour to their bodies.

From among the brawny men who were susceptible to every ache and pain came the " telephonists ". The telephonists were prisoners who would stand for hours on end with their ears applied to the cell-doors, with the concentration of a doctor carrying out a medical examination. They were listeners. Now and then, they would urgently appeal to the people walking about the cell and chatting to be a little quieter. Sometimes we did as requested, but in most cases we did not pay any attention. We could not. The performance was repeated daily and would go on for hours. The telephonists did not despair and continued to stand guard. Suddenly they would give a shout : " It's coming! " But their telephone service was not always accurate. " It " did come, but not to us. When that happened the operators were crestfallen, but they did not lose heart. After a short interval they would go back to the door, apply an ear to it—like to a stethoscope—and resume listening . . . until it eventually came. " It " was the dixie! Of course, we treated them with understanding. The poor devils had a feeling that by listening with bated breath for the characteristic rattle of the big ladle in the soup dixie, and for the echo of the food distributors' footsteps, they were speeding up the coming of the long-awaited soup that only made them hungrier. Hunger, hunger. . . .

We also had " telegraphists ". These were genuine public servants, liked and respected by all. They did not see to nourishment for the body, but for the soul. Thanks to them, the N.K.V.D. wall of isolation was breached (although only in one direction) in spite of everything. They provided the prisoners with news, news from the big wide world far away for which they all yearned.

In one of Vilna's large squares, at some distance from Lukishki, a loud-speaker had been erected. This is an instrument that accompanies the Soviet regime in every country, in every district, town and hamlet, in every isolated village. From morning to night, sometimes from one morning to the next, the loudspeaker incessantly blares forth speeches, music, articles, songs, news, announcements, decisions and proclamations. Of course, the perpetual, mechanical, disciplined spokesman of the " Party and the Government " does not address itself to the " enemies of the people ", but to loyal citizens who have a right to see the sun, and to learn from the mouth of the loudspeaker how well off they are, how happy they are. But in the " loudspeaker regime " internal inadvertences occur, one of which results from the wind, which Soviet science has not yet succeeded in getting the better of, even with the aid of the N.K.V.D. Sometimes it happens that the wind carries the words of the loudspeaker in an undesired direction, to the prison walls and over them, And the " enemies of the people " hear not only speeches, but also what it is absolutely forbidden that they should hear : what is happening in the world.

Our telegraphists were indeed dependent on the favours of the wind, like the sailors of old. If there was a favourable wind, the important, though fragmentary, news reached the headquarters of our " telegraphic service ", two cells on the top floor whose windows faced the far-off square. If the wind was unfavourable, nothing was of any avail ; not all the efforts of the experienced telegraphists, nor the deadly silence that was observed in the cell. The news was not received and could not be transmitted.

But when the news *was* received, it was transmitted " lengthwise " and " breadthwise " to every communal cell : " lengthwise ", with the aid of the waterpipe, and " breadthwise ", by means of the walls.

The technique of the news transmission is simple. One tap stands for a " dot ". Two successive taps mean a " dash ". All the letters of the alphabet are, according to an agreed key, dots or dashes or a combination of both. In short : Morse. It is a general rule that there is an internal " telegraph " in every prison. It is characteristic that even in the N.K.V.D. prison the spirit of Morse prevails, alive and unconquered.

But our brave telegraphists worked in perpetual danger. When the time came for receiving the news or transmitting it, one man would be placed on guard, crouching next to the door, and a few paces away, upright, a second guard would be placed, to forestall a surprise attack on the part of the warder and to obscure the accursed Judas window. But the precautionary measures did not always help. Sometimes the duty officer, who purposely wore rubber-soled shoes, would manage to steal up slowly to the door, open it suddenly and catch the telegraphists, if not in the act of tapping, at least in a significant position in the neighbourhood of the wall. Sometimes we began to receive " telegrams " just at the moment when the Prison Superintendent or one of the frequently changed officers decided to visit our cell. Then we became " deaf ", just as our neighbours undoubtedly were " deaf " if we began to communicate with them when the official in charge of re-education happened to be present in their cell. But *he* was not deaf. And again there would be surprise raids, which were liable to end in the solitary confinement cell.

With the aid of the internal telegraph we not only received and transmitted news about the war fronts, but also exchanged introductions between cell and cell. There was a fixed rule in our communal

cell : whenever new prisoners arrived, the telegraphists used to
" introduce " them immediately to the inmates of the neighbouring
cell, and through it, to all the other prisoners. The N.K.V.D.
emissaries went on asking : " Whose name begins with ' A ' ?
Whose name begins with ' Z ' ? ", and we used to answer them with
secret satisfaction. The secrecy did not help them ; we knew the
names of our fellow-prisoners from A to Z. There is no doubt that
the N.K.V.D. also knew that we knew, but there was nothing they
could do, in spite of it all, to change the position. The Prison
Superintendent's warnings were of no avail ; threats did not frighten
us ; solitary confinement did not deter us. Man's hunger for news is
sometimes greater than the hunger for bread, like an inveterate
smoker's craving for a cigarette. It is stronger than the fear of
punishment.

Through the telegraph service I learnt, one day, that my friend,
Meir Sheskin, had arrived in the next cell. I had not yet learnt the
art of the dots and dashes. Bernstein, who was one of the best
telegraphists, brought me the news and flashed my greeting in reply.
Sheskin, also speaking through an expert, asked me how Ze'ev
Jabotinsky was. I did not answer immediately. It was impossible
to lie, and difficult to tell him the truth. But Sheskin plied me with
telegrams, all of them repeating the question. " Did you understand?
How is Ze'ev Jabotinsky ? " I had no alternative. I asked Bernstein
to transmit the truth to my friend, and add that I believed that we
would be carrying out the wishes of Rosh Betar if we did not allow
despair to get the better of us. For a while, no reply came from the
next cell. After that, we heard the call-sign. Sheskin confirmed the
receipt of the terrible news. He informed me that he would say
Kaddish, the prayer for the dead. He, too, sent words of consolation.
Once again the wave of grief rolled over.

One day I told Bernstein about my decision concerning my wife.
He revealed that he had also thought of sending his wife a divorce,
but he had not done it, nor would he do it. First of all, because of
his small daughter. Secondly, because one should not instil any
doubts in the wife's mind regarding the day of return and reunion
at the end of the separation. He maintained that the second reason
applied in my case as well. In any event, he reckoned, it was better
not to be in a hurry to take this serious step, to add grief to suffering.
He spoke very persuasively, for he had gone through an inner
struggle similar to my own. I could not but admit the soundness of

his reasoning. I promised to weigh my decision again, and post-
poned its execution.

Meanwhile, I earned myself seven days' solitary confinement. I
told one of my neighbours a joke, and the warder, a Jew in the
service of the N.K.V.D., thought that it was at his expense. He
complained to the Prison Superintendent and demanded that I
be punished for insulting him. Without conducting any inquiry
into the matter, the Superintendent sentenced me to seven days'
solitary confinement. There was no appeal against this sentence.

The announcement of the severe punishment inflicted on me
surprised both me and my cell-mates, who had heard me tell what
was only a harmless joke. It aroused great anger among all the
inmates of the cell, most of whom were my pupils in various courses.
They wanted to react to the Superintendent's arbitrariness which
they considered to be an offence not only against a prisoner but
also against their sense of justice. Some of them suggested staging a
hunger-strike as a demonstration. This gratifying solidarity cut
across national frontiers in our communal cell. I thanked my cell-
mates, not without emotion, for their stand, but asked them not
to take superfluous suffering on themselves because of me. " The
seven days will pass," I said, " and when I get back we will resume
the classes. Never mind. One has to experience the solitary confinement cell, too, I suppose."

The seven days and the seven nights went by. The solitary
confinement weakened me considerably, but taught me much. I
learnt from the stifling heat by day and the freezing cold by night,
from the filth and the stench of the windowless cage, without any
covering, from the chill, dirty cement floor which served as a bed
for me and promenade for the rats—from all these things I learnt
that there is a worse place than the prison cell, just as I learnt later
that there is a worse place even than the solitary confinement cell.
Man's imagination did not invent degrees in Paradise. It did create
them in Hell. Happiness is indivisible, suffering is graded. When
I returned, when I went up to my cell, I was the happiest prisoner
in the world.

Nevertheless, a hunger strike was proclaimed in our cell, though
not because of me. Nor was it because of the frightful overcrowding
that kept on growing worse as the number of prisoners increased ;
nor because we had no contact with our families ; nor in order to

get more time allocated to our " excursions " in the closed courtyard, the rare outings which lasted only ten minutes. It was not even because of hunger that we proclaimed the hunger-strike. The fact of the matter is that we did not proclaim a hunger-strike at all. It happened to us of its own accord, it arose from within us, it burst forth from our nostrils!

When we read this passage in the Book of Numbers :[1] " ... *therefore the Lord will give you flesh, and ye shall eat. Ye shall not eat one day, nor two days, nor five days, neither ten days, nor twenty days; but even a whole month, until it come out at your nostrils, and it be loathsome unto you ... "*—we certainly all thought that the words "come out at your nostrils " were just a figure of speech. In Lukishki, in the communal cell, I learnt for the first time in my life that they constituted an exact description of a physical sensation. It is not a metaphor, but a fact.

The N.K.V.D. fed us neither *mannah* nor meat. It fed us *kasha*[2]. Actually, from the time I was arrested, the Lukishki inmates went through a number of dietary phases. At the beginning, *kasha* was the main food, but not the only one ; the " soups " were varied. But at the time that I am writing of, cereal-soup held sole sway in the dixie for which the " telephonists " waited with bated breath. *Kasha*, nothing but *kasha*. *Kasha* every day.

In the text it was written that for " a whole month " we would eat it. To that we could have added : " more than a month, more than two months, ye shall eat (*kasha*)." And it verily came out of our nostrils, just as it is written. In its tangible sense, in the physical sense of the words. And the *kasha* was loathsome to us. We could not bear it any more. So we proclaimed a hunger-strike.

In the Soviet prisons, going on hunger-strike is no joke. N.K.V.D. prisoners have, to all intents and purposes, been practically deprived of this weapon, which prisoners use in gaols all over the world. Perhaps the perpetual hunger that makes the food unimaginably more precious in the eyes of the prisoner also helps to weaken the will-power required for doing without food, although— or because—the food is so meagre. There is no doubt that the isolation, the double isolation, is also a decisive factor in this matter. Prisoners who decide to undergo a protracted fast do so on the assumption that even if it does not immediately influence the prison authorities, it *will* set the influential wheels of public opinion turning,

[1] Numbers xi, 18–20.   [2] Cereal.

when it becomes known from the legitimate Press, or from illegal publications, what is happening within the prison walls. Prisoners of Zion, in the British prison camps in Eretz Israel and in Africa, resorted to this weapon more than once in order to insist on their rights as prisoners, as Jews, as human beings. Communist prisoners resorted to it often, in every country where their party operated in the underground. But the situation of N.K.V.D. prisoners is entirely different. Very rarely will they delude themselves that their abstention from food will soften the hearts of their gaolers. They know with absolute certainty that their hunger-strike will remain a hidden secret, like everything else that happens to them within the walls. Hunger is a weapon in the hands of the N.K.V.D. against the prisoners. It is not the prisoners' weapon against the N.K.V.D.

Nevertheless, our hunger strike ended in victory. Not only did they not punish us for our mutinous announcement that we would not accept the *kasha* any more, but, after a few days had gone by during which we made do with bread and coffee only, we succeeded in getting—for the first time in two months—a soup made of rotten cabbage leaves. The authorities of the Lukishki prison evidently took into account the fact that we had rejected the *kasha* because of the basic requirements of a person's body, which apply in every regime, and not because of some fanciful counter-revolutionary demands, such as getting newspapers, or letters from families.

The N.K.V.D. is very experienced in taking people through the " desert ". It is no wonder that it understands the meaning of the words : until it come out at your nostrils. They are not Talmudism ; they are reality. And in the reality of the N.K.V.D. even rotten cabbage smells good, and can be tasty to the palate, and enable the " wanderers in the desert " to return—to the *kasha*.

After the hunger-strike in Lukishki we had cabbage-soup two days a week and cereal-soup five days a week.

We had won!

12

THE TRIAL

THAT is how we lived, with the *kasha* and the cabbage, with the " telephonists " and the " telegraphists ", with the lectures and the courses, with the discussions and the arguments, with parcels of clothing bearing silent greetings from home—until the 1st of April. That day the N.K.V.D. gave us a " surprise ".

On the last night of March, 1941, our telegraphists were very busy. " Telegrams " flashed down from upstairs, and were passed on horizontally. In the cell the excitement mounted. " What is it ? What is it ? " many clamoured to know. Many of them refused to believe their ears. But the telegrams continued to arrive. The contents kept on being repeated. There was no longer any doubt of their authenticity. The telegrams were short. They gave the names of prisoners, and next to them—the number of years to which they had been sentenced. In most cases the figures eight years or five years appeared. Only occasionally was the figure three years mentioned.

" When did the trials take place ? " we asked the central bureau by way of the water-pipe, with the aid of dots and dashes.

" There were no trials, these are the sentences," came the reply.

For a while we were unable to continue with the exchange of telegrams. The news of the sentences arrived only in the evening. The bedtime whistle put a stop, as usual, to the operation of the telegraph service. We lay on our mattresses, still trying to explain, to understand the latest news. Each remembered his interrogator's promise that there would be a trial, so where was it ? Some thought that the prisoners who were sentenced without trial must be exceptions. They said : " We will certainly come before a court, and in any event we won't get eight years. . . ." It was impossible to continue even this whispered conversation. The warder opened th door and ordered us to stop all talking. That was the rule.

Next day our doubts were dispelled.

" Everyone into the passage, walk in single file! Keep in line! "
That was the command that rang out in our cell at dusk on April
1st, 1941.

We did as ordered. We were conducted along a route that we
knew, to a place that we knew, to the widening of the corridor from
which we used to go to night-interrogation. There two men in
civilian clothes were seated behind a small table. While one prisoner
went up to the table, all the others stood some distance away and
could not hear what was being said. They could only see that a
small piece of paper was handed to the prisoner, which he signed.

My turn came.

" Your name ? " asked the man sitting in the centre seat at the
table.

I replied as I was by now used to replying, giving my patronymic
between my first name and my surname.

The man seated at the end of the table began to flick through one
of the bundles of papers in front of him. He did it rapidly, as if he
were counting bank-notes. Without any difficulty he found the
slip bearing my name and handed it to his companion, who read me
the text which is engraved in my memory, word for word :

" The special Advisory Commission to the People's Commissariat
for Internal Affairs finds that Menachem Wolfovitch Begin is an
element dangerous to society, and orders that he be imprisoned in a
Correctional Labour Camp for a period of eight years."

" Sign, please," said the emissary of the Special Advisory Commission politely.

" This is a pleasant April Fool's Day," I said, picking up the pen
to sign the " receipt ". The N.K.V.D. man glanced at me sharply,
but said nothing.

I signed, and was taken back to the cell.

Soon all the others returned. The noise in the cell was deafening.
Each one shouted to the other : " How much ? How much ? "
Some raised a hand with outspread fingers and called out : " Five! "
The " important " prisoners, those who were given eight years, dis-
pensed with the gesture and contented themselves with merely giving
the figure. None of the inhabitants of our cell received the insulting
sentence (called " childish " in Russian) of three years' imprisonment. The thief got five years.

We exchanged information about the sentences we had received like students comparing their report-cards and marks. Nobody showed any anxiety. Many waxed sarcastic. " There's Soviet justice for you! " they said. " There was no trial, those who sentenced us have never seen us, have never heard what we have to say. But just so, wholesale, they fling eight years at us, five years. . . ." But on the whole an odd gaiety prevailed in our cell that evening. No one was impressed with the number of years he had got from the Advisory Commission. Those who had been given " only " five years did not rejoice at their advantage. On the contrary, they felt that they ranked lower, like pupils with a low mark. " Five years, or eight years, it's actually one and the same thing," they said. " We'll either all get out, or none of us will be able to hold out even for a few years." With this view there was general agreement in the cell. The sentenced men knew that far away from the walls of Lukishki a war was being waged. None of them knew how it would influence their fate, but deep down inside them they all hoped it would somehow break the bolts of the gates that closed them in. Of course, there were pessimists in the cell, too, but they were in the minority. Their voices were almost not heard. And the " telegraph " worked unceasingly. *Eight years, five years, eight years . . .*

I called to mind the words of the veteran Chekist, the N.K.V.D. major, who said : " Trial! Give him a platform! " and the words of his comrade, my interrogator, who said : " I told you there will be a trial, and so there will be! "

They both spoke the truth, the truth of the N.K.V.D.

This was the trial.

One of the achievements of the people who fought at the barricades in order to eradicate wrongs and make justice rule, to overthrow tyranny and cause freedom to reign was : a heap of little bits of paper, bundles of " receipts ", an underground factory for turning out sentences. There is no judge, and no accused ; no witness, and no attorney ; no defence, and no appeal. The man disappears, and there is no possibility of a mistake. The " Commission " passes sentence : eight years, five years, three years, eight years. . . .

A few days after we had signed the receipt for our sentences, our warders, in spite of our protests, took away the spittoons which stood in two corners of the cell. From the next-door cell, we received by telegraph the dry information : " Today they took away the spittoons."

13

THE LEAVE-TAKING

CLOTHING parcels continued to arrive and warm our hearts. I sensed that it was my wife who was sending the parcels, but I knew that my friends were providing them. My wife had no money. My friends were looking after her and me, and—as I learnt subsequently —my old parents. It is worth while recording this for the cynics of our generation, who put on an air of superior wisdom and, claiming to have no illusions, ask : " Friendship ? Is there such a thing as real friendship ? "

From the precious parcels which we received we learnt that " outside " they were preparing us for a long journey, to a cold place. Through the grating spring burst into the cell ; through the door came warm underwear for us : thick coats, top-boots, gloves. There was rejoicing at the " wealth ", but sadness at what the people outside appeared to know.

In one of the parcels I found something at last! On some of the handkerchiefs I found three embroidered Latin letters. The letters were a bit shaky, but they were unmistakably O—L—A. I was delighted with the inscription, but also surprised. Why O-L-A ? What made my wife change the " A ", the first letter of the abbreviated form of her name (Ala) into an " O " ? Was it dangerous to send handkerchiefs with monograms ? And if so, was not " Ola " also embroidery, a name ? I did not succeed in solving the riddle ; Bernstein solved it. He turned to me one day with a shout that could have been " Eureka! " " I know," he cried, " you have to read it as ' Olá ' and not ' Óla ', and everything will be clear. She is *going to Palestine*."[1]

It was all clear to me now.

Bernstein, the good fellow, had cudgelled his brains for days to solve my riddle for me. He added : " You see ? It's a good thing

[1] OLA is the Hebrew (feminine) word for " going to (settle in) the land of Israel."

you weren't in a hurry to send her the divorce. She is going in the conviction that you will both meet again."

It was the best day I had had in prison—and the hardest. I had learnt that my wife was leaving for Eretz Israel. . . .

She was going. I did not know then of the fights there had been between my wife and my friends before they could persuade her that she must not remain near me ; that by staying in Vilna she would not be near me at all ; and that only from Eretz Israel would she be able to help me, so that it was her duty to go with the others who were leaving.

It was the fault of the N.K.V.D. that I had left my wife in the first place, and it was their " fault " that I had not managed to send her a divorce. Thanks to friends and friendship we both lived to see the day when we could laugh at the divorce that was never written, never sent, and never happened at all.

A few days after we deciphered the secret writing the composition of our cell was broken up. A large number of prisoners were taken out, " with their belongings ", and transferred—as we soon learnt through the telegraph service—to other cells. Among those who went were Bernstein and Lifshitz. When we took silent leave of one another, all the barriers between us fell. In the eyes of each of us was the question : Is this forever ? Will we ever see each other again ?

The prisoners who left were replaced by others. Among the new-comers was my friend Meir Sheskin. Sheskin and I celebrated the Feast of Passover together in the cell. We held the " *Seder* ", observing the rites in so far as our situation permitted. For the four glasses of wine we substituted N.K.V.D. coffee. " This is the bread of affliction, " we intoned. What affliction it was ! " Let all who are hungry come in and eat." No, no ! For heaven's sake, do not come in, do not come to us, do not eat with us ! . . . We lifted our voices in prayer, in supplication : " This year we are slaves, next year may we be free men. This year we are here, may we next year be in Jerusalem."

After the Passover Festival one word began to run through every " telegram ", the word " *Kotlas* ". A rumour, the origin of which no one knew, started inside the prison, and spread from cell to cell, from prisoner to prisoner. According to this rumour, we were going to a place called Kotlas for the re-education period, for eight years, for five years. Prisoners of my generation, and even older people, had no idea where the mysterious place, Kotlas, was. Who ever heard of Kotlas? The old colonel knew. "If I remember anything at all," he said, with his ever-present self-mockery, "Kotlas is the railway station beyond Vyatka."

"Vyatka is called Kirov now," said one of the prisoners.

"I don't know what it's called now," the colonel replied, over-hearing the remark, "but I remember that they used to deport the revolutionaries to Vyatka. And that's where the princes used to go hunting."

Outside it was spring. In the cell it was hot. But a chill entered our very bones.

But we soon changed our opinion of Kotlas. We almost fell in love with the place where the princes used to go hunting. We wanted to go there. We plied our warders with questions every day: "Till when must we sit here? When are we going to Kotlas?"

"You'll go, you'll go," the warders would say, soothingly.

It was the prison barbers, principally, who shaped our revised opinion of Kotlas and the TIL in general. (TIL is an abbreviation, composed of the initial letters of the Russian words for Correctional Labour Camp.)

There were two barbers, and they used to visit us at odd intervals. One of them was a Jew. The Christian prisoners in the communal cell who, like my companions in the little cell, believed in Jewish solidarity, used to ask their Jewish cell-mates to try and draw the Jewish barber into conversation. I did not even try. I knew only too well what "solidarity" there was between a Jewish agent of the N.K.V.D. and a Jewish prisoner of the N.K.V.D. Bernstein tried, but without success. Nor did the Christian prisoners succeed in getting "their" barber to open his mouth. The barbers' mouths were sealed tight. We discovered another wonder of the world in Lukishki—silent barbers!

But after Passover the mouths of the two barbers suddenly opened. The Christian prisoners did not need to use Jewish solidarity in order to get our barbers talking, they spoke even without being asked. To each and every prisoner they gave lavish details about life in a labour camp.

"There you will have a life!" they said. "There you will not be shut up in a cell, like here. There you will be almost free. Work? Of course there will be work, but what of it? It's good to work a bit, isn't it? How many hours a day do they work there? Like all over the Soviet Union: eight hours a day. What is the work? All sorts. But each of you will work according to your profession. For your work you get paid. Is there a day of rest? What a question! Every week there is one day of rest. Are there newspapers, books? Every camp has a library and you can get books, papers, magazines to your heart's desire. Besides the library, each camp has a cinema. Do they show often? We don't know exactly, but they do show fairly often. You will be able to see many films. Sometimes mobile theatres also visit the camps. The cultural life there is on a very high level. How's the food? If you work well you get excellent food. Every camp has a canteen where you can buy good things."

Parts of their story were confirmed by the warders whom we questioned during the processions to the lavatories.

The duty officer, too, warmed up a little towards the prisoners just then. When he was asked, on his daily round, whether there was really a library in the camp, he would reply with disarming courtesy: "Of course there is a library! And isn't there a cinema? In the camp you will be much better off than here."

And we believed it all!

One fine day in May we were informed that we would be permitted to see our families. "Yes," said the duty officer, frankly, "it will be a farewell visit before you leave for the labour camp. In this questionnaire, fill in the paragraphs: 'Name of relative invited' and 'Address'. You may invite one relative."

I invited my wife. I thought that she might not have left yet.

The days in Lukishki, especially in the communal cell, were, as a rule, short. We were occupied from morning to night. We chatted, studied, played, thought, prayed—and waited. We were always waiting, waiting for something that would be out of the usual; and we also waited for the routine things that happen every day. In prison every meal is an event, taking out the pail is an event. Our requirements were primitive but that increased, rather than diminished, the habit of expectancy, which was greatest in the "telephonists".

Days in jail are not as long as people who are free imagine. The first half year of our arrest was already over, and we had hardly felt it. But the days that followed our filling in the brief questionnaire, the days after the invitations had been despatched to our families, were long, very long. Most expectations had been taken away from us, but this sole expectation was left us. Many expectations help to kill time ; one expectation lengthens it interminably. We counted the hours.

At last the visits began. I was among the last to be summoned to the office. I was led to the grille that divided the reception room. Next to me stood the Jewish warder who was responsible for my getting seven days' solitary confinement. On the other side of the grille—Paula Daiches stood smiling at me.

I knew the girl from her work in the Betar in Vilna. She resembled my wife a little. Perhaps it just seemed so to me as I looked at her through the grille. In any event, she had come in my wife's place, on the invitation that I had sent to Alisa Begin.

" You may speak either Russian or Polish. Go ahead! " said the warder.

We spoke Polish.

" Everything is all right," Paula began, speaking very rapidly. Aunt Ala is with Uncle Shimshon. I've already had a letter from her."

I said nothing. I understood. " Uncle Shimshon " was Dr. Shimshon Yunitchman, who was head of the Betar in Eretz Israel. My wife had arrived in Eretz Israel.

" Did you hear ? Aunt Ala is with . . ." Paula began to repeat.

" Yes, yes. I understood. What else ? "

" There are also letters from the parents. They are in good health, don't worry about them. They are being helped."

Again I remained silent.

" Your brothers are also well. They are all well. They are also with Aunt Ala."

I understood. I had only one brother. " Brothers " meant " friends ". They too had reached Eretz Israel.

" Do you hear ? Your brothers are with Aunt Ala . . ." Paula began again.

" Thanks, thanks. What else ? "

" Yes, I also brought you regards from Aunt (up to here she spoke Polish) Iggeret-besabon (she finished in Hebrew). (The Hebrew words *iggeret besabon* mean " note-in-soap ".)

I too went over to Hebrew.

" How are you, my child ? How is Uncle Joseph and how are you all ? " I was referring to Joseph Glazman.

" Everyone is all right, all are well. They all send their regards. Don't worry," the girl replied in Hebrew.

" Didn't I tell you to speak Russian or Polish ? " the warder broke in suddenly. " What language are you speaking ? "

" What is the matter ? " I asked. " Can't we speak ' *pa-yevrey-skye* ? ' "[1]

" If that was *pa-yevreyskye*, I would have understood. You spoke some other language."

"We were speaking *pa-yevreyskye*," I insisted stubbornly. "I am a *yevrei* and I am allowed to use my own language."

" Don't try to be clever. Speak Russian or Polish or I'll stop the conversation."

We went back to Polish. Paula, apparently afraid that I had not grasped the significance of the " regards ", repeated :

" I have regards for you from Aunt (in Polish) *Iggaret-besabon* (in Hebrew)."

" Yes, thank you. I understood."

The girl's face lit up.

" You have to finish off now," said the warder.

" Just a few more words," I requested. " We're just finishing."

" What should I write to Aunt Ala ? " Paula asked.

" Write that I am proud of her. Write that I am proud of them all. Write that I am strong and healthy, and I will come back."

" I will," replied Paula.

" That's enough! Finished! " cried the warder.

He passed through the grille-gate to the other side of the room and took from Paula the parcel that " my wife " had brought me as a gift for the road. He tipped everything that was in the package out on to the table. There was warm underwear, some things to eat, and two pieces of laundry soap. The warder handed the foodstuffs back to Paula. They were not allowed. I was out of luck. My companions who had their meetings with their families before me were allowed to receive a food parcel as well, just this once. When my turn came we were informed that there was a typhus epidemic outside and so it was forbidden to have foodstuffs brought to the prison.

Paula put the delicacies—including the chocolate my friends had

---

[1] In Russian, both Yiddish and Hebrew are called *pa-yevreyskye*, except that Hebrew is called *drevnye-yevreyskye*, the " ancient " Hebrew language. I had not added the word " ancient ", hence the " misunderstanding ".

sent me—back in the bag. There were tears in her eyes. That wonderful girl had displayed complete calm when she impersonated my wife and gave me forbidden messages, even a note-in-the-soap. She was in the hands of the N.K.V.D., inside the lion's jaws, in the most serious danger that she could possibly have been in. What if they had found the note on her? She had carried out everything that she was told to do without any sign of emotion. But when she had to take back the " good things ", she simply could not overcome her disappointment and her eyes filled with tears.

She begged the warder : " Let me at least leave the sugar."

" Forbidden! " answered the warder. " I said it was forbidden and that's enough."

He inspected the linen, and then began to cut the soap. Paula and I looked on, from either side of the grille. The warder held the halves of the soap up to his eyes—and handed them to me, together with the linen.

" Au revoir, Paulinka! "

" Au revoir, keep well! "

" I'll be back."

" I know. Keep well! "

For a long time I dreamed that I might once again see this girl, braver than any soldier at the front, and shake her hand and thank her for the service she had done me, at such grave risk to herself. But I never did. Paula, little sister of Shlomi who was murdered in Eretz Israel, not by strangers but by the hand of Cain, was well worthy of her brother. She was a fighter. When the German barbarians held sway in Vilna she joined the armed underground, which was formed in the ghetto by Joseph Glazman, and became one of his chief aides. But Paula, wonderful Paula, the courageous Hebrew girl, bearer of tidings in the darkness, fell into the hands of the German murderers. She lived like a fighter and like a fighter she died.

14

SPITTOONS

WHEN I came back from the interview I had in my hands four half-pieces of soap. One of them had the note in it. But which? I told Sheskin everything that Paula had told me. I revealed our secret about the note to one of my pupils as well, a sergeant in the Polish army, who had become my loyal and devoted friend. The three of us went over to the window-corner and stood in a small circle. The sergeant, who was an expert at any job, took the pieces of soap in his hands, and examined them from all angles. He wanted to find the note without having to " operate ", for a piece of soap was very precious in prison. But he, too, could not see anything. We had no alternative ; we decided to " operate ". The sergeant had a metal spoon with a handle sharpened like a knife. He took it down from the shelf and began to cut the soap. The note was not in the first piece. Nor in the second. When he had just about cut away the third piece as well, layer by layer, something protruded from one end. His face glowing with happiness, the happiness of success, the sergeant finally handed me a small, folded piece of paper. The note had arrived! My friends had not inserted it deep into the soap, but in an outer layer. Even the all-knowing, all-powerful N.K.V.D. does not always get the better of—common sense!

The " note-in-the-soap " was from my friend Joseph Glazman. It confirmed all the good news, all the happy, consoling tidings that Paulinka had brought me, and it also contained an additional piece of information. Our friends in Eretz Israel and America, the letter informed me, were working for our release. There were good prospects that their efforts would succeed.

We believed.

Once again the composition of our cell was broken up. Prisoners were taken out, and others put in. Among the outgoing prisoners was Sheskin ; among the newcomers was cheerful David Kroll.

Kroll was a middle-aged man. The many wrinkles that covered his face made him look older than his years. Everyone called him by the pet name of " Kotka ". He was really young in spirit, and would laugh even in prison like a carefree child. But good-hearted Kroll did have cares. He had left two women behind ; an old mother, for many years a widow, who was dependent on her Kotka just as he had once been dependent on her, and a young wife whom he had married just a few months before his arrest.

Kroll was also one of those who kept on demanding " Daiosh Kotlas! "—" We want Kotlas! "

At the end of May there was considerable activity in Lukishki. The cells grew fuller and fuller. There is no such thing as " No room! " for the N.K.V.D. They maintain that room will always be found for prisoners—and it is! There were not enough bowls for all the prisoners. Those we had we shared with our new neighbours. It is not a pleasant thing, but we got used to that, too. In prison, do as is done in prison. In any case, we had the consolation of Kotlas before our eyes. There we would eat at decked tables. There we would work, and breathe fresh air. There life would be different. . . .

The prison officials, among them N.K.V.D. officers, began to pay us more frequent visits. One man would come in, write something, and go out again. Another would enter, and make some more notes. We asked them when we were going. " There are no ' sastav ' ", was the reply, " but you'll be leaving soon." We wondered what " sastav " were. Those who knew Russian interpreted the word in different ways. Some said it meant that they did not have enough staff. The others said " sastav " referred to railway-trucks. Everyone was amazed. Not enough officials ? No railway-trucks ?

At last the day came.

N.K.V.D. officers stood in the doorway and read out the names. Those whose names were called, answered like soldiers : " Here! "

" You will each pack your belongings into one bundle. The bowls, cups and spoons you will leave behind. When you are ready we will come for you."

" Has the ' sastav ' come ? " one of the prisoners asked.

" Yes. You are leaving for the labour camp."

" Where will we be going ? "

" That I don't know. The man in charge of the transport will know."

The door closed. The cell was like a railway station. There was a din and an uproar. The prisoners were in high spirits. " We are going, we are leaving the stench! " The sergeant helped me pack my belongings, gifts from my friends. We both helped the old colonel. He kept on muttering: " We're going hunting! Hunting! "

" Ready ? " asked the warder, after a while.

" Ready, ready! " we answered in chorus.

With our bundles on our backs we went out into the prison courtyard. There we found other groups of prisoners. We were ordered to sit and wait. We knew how to do both those things. We waited patiently. The time went by, and so did lunch-time. Prison officials scurried to and fro. We began to shout: " How much longer ? "

Towards evening an N.K.V.D. officer appeared and announced that an alteration had been made in the time-table, and we had to return—though not for long—to the prison wing. He told us we would not go back to our cells, but to temporary ones. We were hungry. We cursed. And, cursing, we were taken to our temporary cells.

They were very " temporary ", and situated in the cellar. They differed from the solitary confinement cell only in respect of the small window that they had, a little above the ground. The cell had no beds and no mattresses. Four walls and a cement floor— such were the " furnishings " of the cell into which we were put. It was about the same size as the cell which I had occupied during the interrogation. But there were twenty people in our group. All the same, we managed to squeeze into the cell.

Morning came. The door opened. Two warders counted the prisoners, who were standing, sitting, half-lying in the cramped space. The warders made no comment. In the cell in which it was impossible to lie down, we were permitted to do so—even after the reveille, even in the daytime. They made a mistake in the count. It was no wonder. In this cell the calculation would have been difficult for a professor of mathematics ; how much more so for a Soviet warder. Eventually the exact figure was ascertained. The warder noted it down. " In a little while you'll get bread," he said. That was something!

Through the hatch we were handed our bread ration. " What will we drink the coffee in ? " we asked in chorus. " They told us to leave our bowls and mugs upstairs. What will we drink in ? "

"You'll get other utensils," said the warder, closing the hatch.
A little while later the hatch was opened again.

"Take!" shouted the warder.

"What's this?" asked the prisoners who stood at the door.

"Utensils for coffee and lunch."

"What?"

They were—spittoons!

With a grating noise the dixie was pushed to the door of our cell.

"Coffee!" the warder announced through the hatch. We refused
to take it.

"We don't drink from spittoons," we said, all together.

"We have no other utensils," said the warder.

"We will not drink from spittoons. We are human beings. Call
the duty officer. We are not going to drink."

The hatch closed. The dixie was pushed to the next cell.

We ate dry bread. Breakfast-time went by. Lunch-time was
approaching. Again the hatch opened.

"What's the matter?" asked the duty officer.

"They gave us spittoons," we shouted, "How can we drink from
them?"

"Don't all speak together," he said, standing in the doorway.
"One of you speak."

"Citizen Duty Officer," said our spokesman, "look at the utensils
they gave us for our meals. These are spittoons. They have been
taken from the cells. We ourselves spat into them, and now we
have to eat in them? When we just look at them our stomachs turn
and we want to vomit. How will we be able to eat in them. Why,
we are human beings!"

"We cleaned them," the duty officer replied tranquilly. "They
have been disinfected thoroughly. They are quite clean."

"Look, Citizen Duty Officer," said another prisoner, "look at
this spittoon. The enamel at the bottom is completely broken. Look
at the holes. What disinfection can cleanse it?"

"It was disinfected," the duty officer replied, "and it is clean."

"We will not eat from spittoons," the chorus of indignant
prisoners stormed. "We demand that the Prison Superintendent
come here. We won't eat!"

"Listen," said the duty officer, "the Superintendent won't be
able to help you. We don't want to make things more difficult for

you. I understand that conditions here are hard, but it will only be for a day or two. You know that you are leaving for a labour camp. Conditions will be different there. What can we do ? There are many prisoners and there are not enough utensils to go round."

" Then why did you arrest so many people ? " asked one of the prisoners, forgetting himself for the moment.

Without replying, the officer left the cell. We were left with our grievances and our spittoons.

Came lunch-time. The dixie was brought up to the door of our cell.

" Lunch! " cried the warder, through the hatch.

" We will not eat out of spittoons."

The hatch closed.

In the afternoon the warder ordered us to collect up all the spittoons and pass them through the hatch. A little while later the duty officer came into our cell. He had put himself out and brought— new spittoons.

" You see," he said, " they are brand new. They've come straight from stores. They have not been used. They are clean. Now you will be able to eat."

We could not. Old or new, spittoons are spittoons. A person cannot eat from a vessel that is made, from the outset, to be spat into. We simply could not. We went to sleep supperless, too.

Only the next day did the warder hand us a number of bowls and mugs.

" You'll have to take turns at eating," he said. " Fix it among yourselves."

The dixie was pushed down the corridor, from cell to cell, backwards and forwards, until everyone had eaten according to his turn. We did not rinse out the dishes. In the temporary cell there was no water, no pail. The few bowls and cups that there were, were passed from hand to hand and from mouth to mouth, with the remains of soup or coffee still in them. But we ate. And we did not eat out of spittoons, even although we were extremely hungry.

That is how the N.K.V.D. treat human beings. But man is not an animal, although . . . although in the place where princes used to go hunting I learnt that there are people who, after a certain period of " education ", are even prepared to eat out of spittoons.

One day in June we were taken out to an enormous field inside the prison walls. The prisoners, who numbered, according to my estimate, some two thousand people, were divided into groups. At a table in the centre of the field sat high N.K.V.D. officers. Hundreds of N.K.V.D. soldiers moved about among the groups of prisoners. They searched the prisoners' bundles more thoroughly than I have ever seen anyone searched in my life. Even in searching the prisoners' persons they were most punctilious. They made us strip naked. We were not unused to that : in all the night searches in the cells we were ordered to strip. But on the field there was an innovation : we were ordered to " squat ", a number of times. The N.K.V.D. searched everywhere. One of the prisoners in my group had an upset stomach. The searcher's curses were ear-splitting. We smiled.

"*Davai, davai, davai paskareya!*—Hurry! Hurry up!" was the shout that could be heard unceasingly, from one end of the field to the other. The scene was reminiscent of a slave-market.

Fifteen men and their bundles were crammed into a small prison van. One of the prisoners, whom I saw for the first time, started to scream that he was suffocating. He was exaggerating. Man does not suffocate so easily. The car moved off. It came to a halt in front of the prison gate. The gate opened. The car, with its living, silent load, glided into the deserted street. We were off! Where to ? To Kotlas.

I heard a voice within me say : The journey has begun—to Eretz Israel.

15

INTO THE WHITE NIGHTS

On a siding intended for loading freight a long train awaited us. The freight-cars had been converted into prison-cells. The small windows were barred. A double tier of bunks made of wooden planks lined the sides. In the middle of the floor of each truck a wide, open pipe protruded ; this substituted for a pail. N.K.V.D. soldiers carrying bayoneted rifles and bloodhounds straining at the leash supervised the embarkation. We were loaded into the mobile prison.

As we clambered into our coach, some army people among us told us that its normal capacity was forty men, or eight horses. We wondered why it was proving so difficult to fit ourselves in, with our bundles, until we did a rough count and found that we were close on seventy people. The congestion on the upper bunks was terrific. The suffocation in the lower berths was frightful. I very much doubt whether the N.K.V.D., applying the same proportion, could have succeeded in piling fourteen horses into our truck. But prisoners are not horses.

The coach-door, which was reinforced with iron, was closed on us and bolted. We shouted that we had no air. The soldiers of the guard shouted back that enough air was coming in through the two hatches. It was forbidden to open the door ; forbidden, and that's all there was to it. A short while later the occupants of the upper tier announced that the soldiers had gone. There was no longer anyone to whom to address ourselves.

The day drew to a close. We were tired and hungry. Because of our exhaustion, or through force of habit acquired in Lukishki, we fell asleep. I woke to find the mobile prison fully under way.

We travelled on, for days and nights. We also halted for days on end. Every morning and every evening we were afforded some slight contact with the guardians of the revolution : they counted us twice a day, and unless they actually touched each one of us they were never sure of their total. Once a day they brought us our food. In that way we managed to get some extra air three times a day, whenever the coach-door was opened.

Our food was brought to us by prisoners wearing special arm-bands. It consisted of bread and salted fish. During the entire journey, which lasted for weeks, we were not once given any kind of cooked food. We used to slake our thirst with unboiled water.

We were, of course, very much troubled by thirst. The cry " Water, water! " could be heard constantly, from one end of the train to the other; not only at stations but in the course of our travelling. There was only one drinking vessel which everyone had to use—a pail. We took it in turns to drink. In this respect the N.K.V.D. does treat men like horses.

One day, when we had already travelled quite a long way, we experienced a particularly nasty shock. The train stopped in a wooded area. At the sides of the lines were puddles of water, covered with green slime. They were not far from the train; we could hear the croaking of frogs emanating from their haunts, the puddles. We shouted, or to be more exact, went on shouting: " Water, water! " And there, through the hatch, we saw the order-lies with the arm-bands go up to the puddles and scoop up water for us. One big cry of protest burst from the mobile prison: " You'll give us that to drink? " The reply of the N.K.V.D. men was quiet and leisurely, even reasonable : " The next station is still far away. You wanted water, and this is the water we can give you. If you don't want to drink, don't. But you won't be able to get any other water until tomorrow."

We drank.

At one station our train came to a halt alongside a " sister-train ", another mobile prison. From where I was sitting, from my bunk on the upper tier, next to the barred window, I caught sight of a pair of eyes, the eyes of a woman with greying hair. Her large, sad eyes met mine through the bars. We gazed at each other in silence. Her eyes seemed to ask : " Where to? Why? " Her train moved off; and, almost simultaneously, our train moved off too. For days and nights after that the rhythmic clicking of the wheels over the rails seemed to be repeating the questions : " Where? Why? Why? Where? . . ."

Similar trains continued to pass our train. We began to wonder how many such " sastav " the authorities had, and whether Russia had as many mobile prisons as she had stationary ones.

In the past, a movement of masses on such a scale might have been called a " migration of peoples ", or even—slave traffic. In the days of progress, it is called " organised travel to social re-education ".

In the course of our journey we began to see trains of another type as well. Because of them we were often compelled to stop for hours ; sometimes whole days or nights. Train after train flashed by, all going in the direction opposite to the one in which we were travelling ; they were rushing westward.

" What's going on ? " we asked one another, when we saw the trainloads of troops and military equipment. Had general mobilisation been proclaimed in Russia ? Were we imprisoned eye-witnesses to direct preparations for war ? We all remembered the announcement of the Soviet Telegraphic Agency, which was picked up from the loudspeaker and transmitted to us through our " telegraph service " in Lukishki. The announcement said that TASS had been authorised to deny the information that had appeared in the foreign Press concerning a concentration of German military forces along the frontiers of the Soviet Union. Such German troop movements as there were, the announcement went on to say, were nothing more than a routine regrouping, necessitated by the termination of the fighting in Greece and Crete. We began to wonder whether events were giving the lie to the official Soviet denials.

One day the news burst into our locked coach. It burst in with the force of a storm. War! No one knew how the news had penetrated to the prison-train. Perhaps one of the people handing out the food had whispered something to the duty prisoner who received it. Perhaps one of the Russian railway workers, tapping the wheels with his long hammer, whispered something to someone. We could not ascertain the sources of the information. It transpired that for days already we had been drawing farther and farther away from the advancing German forces who were pressing forward in spite of the Blood Covenant, in spite of the denials of TASS.

The news of the German attack gave rise not only to excitement, but also to heated arguments in our coach, where there were three nationalities : Poles, Lithuanians and one Jew. Even the common prison did not succeed in overcoming the mutual hatred—principally because of Vilna—between the Poles and the Lithuanians. There were endless clashes between them, both at Lukishki and in the train. But Poles and Lithuanians alike thought that their friends who had remained at Lukishki were lucky, while they, on their way to Kotlas, had missed the chance of being freed. " If only we had remained in Vilna a few more weeks," they all sighed. But the heaviest sighs came from the Lithuanians. They had not fought against the Germans. They had been waiting for them.

The Germans were fighting against Poland's ally, Britain ; it was natural that the news of the war between Russia and Germany should give encouragement to the Polish prisoners. One of them (in another coach) even went too far in giving expression to his renewed self-confidence. He was being taken, for some reason or other, to the solitary confinement coach, and we heard him cry out :

" I am a Polish officer. Whom are you taking to ' solitary ' ? "

The reply of the N.K.V.D. soldier also reached our ears :

" Polish officer ? We put Polish officers in the lavatory! "

Neither could have known that a new Soviet-Polish Pact was in the making.

One day the train slowed down to a snail's pace. On both sides of the line men dressed in rags were digging trenches. We did not know who they were, but suddenly we heard a whisper in a familiar tongue : " From Poland ? "

" Yes, yes," some of the Polish prisoners replied, also in a whisper. It was strictly forbidden to speak to anyone from the outside world. The punishment for breaking this regulation was " solitary ".

" Vilna's in his hands already. He's moving like a knife through butter," the Pole managed to whisper from the trench before our coach passed.

And there was rejoicing among the Lithuanians. And there was lamentation among the Poles.

Excited over the stupendous events that had occurred since we left Vilna, hungrier than we had ever been in Lukishki, thirstier and dirtier than we had ever been in our lives, we arrived at Kotlas. Throughout all the weeks that we were travelling the guards who brought us our food would not reveal the names of the stations where we stopped. But they did not conceal from us the fact that we had arrived at Kotlas—the place that every Lukishki prisoner was talking about. We had, therefore, additional grounds for thinking that we had arrived at the end of our journey, and would begin our new lives here.

We were mistaken. The only passenger who was taken off at Kotlas was the old colonel. He died there.

We continued on our way. The train rocked us about like a ship pitching and tossing in a stormy sea. We had not been shaken like this before. Many of us became train-sick and vomited continuously. Our strength was exhausted. We dozed. No one spoke any longer. But one solitary question hovered in the air of the coach : " Where to ? Where are they taking us to ? "

At the close of one of the days of our journey—which one, I cannot say, as we had lost count by then—we began, as usual, to prepare for the night's sleep. Of course, we did not know what the time was, but we knew it was bedtime from force of habit. But night did not fall. It was never fully light in the sealed goods-truck, but those who were lying beside the hatches could see that it was daylight outside, not even twilight yet. So we went on dozing, without saying goodnight to one another. After a while I awoke from my nap and looked out. It was still day. What a long day! Again I dozed off. When I awoke this time there was still no sign of night. *What a long day!*

That same day (or was it the next day ?) the riddle was solved. One of the food-orderlies told us, simply : " We've come to the white nights."

" Are we so far north ? " we asked, in mingled amazement and anxiety.

" Yes," he said tranquilly, " we are in the north."

The north! Where the sun rises the moment it sets in the summer; and the northern dawn lights up the nights in the winter. What a miraculous phenomenon! How stunningly beautiful it is! And how awe-inspiring in its beauty!

Involuntarily, one of the prisoners exclaimed : " What a paradox! Our days are black, and our nights are white! "

After travelling for a number of these " double-days ", we were finally ordered to get out of the prison-train. We stood in an open field. All around us we saw swamps. Here and there low bushes were to be seen. We were in the *taiga*, or northern tundra. The name of the railway station where we stopped was Koshva. Over the little wooden hut which served, evidently, as a railway station, ran the inscription " The People's Ministry for Internal Affairs ". Apparently the railway line from Kotlas northwards " belonged " to the N.K.V.D., and not to the Soviet Ministry of Communications.

With our bundles on our backs, and surrounded by soldiers with bayoneted rifles and bloodhounds with bared fangs, we walked a short distance, away from the railway lines, and were then ordered to sit down and rest. Immediately, each one began to hunt for people he knew, and the air rang with enthusiastic greetings. I caught sight of my friends Shechter, Sheskin and Kroll. Although we had been warned not to leave our places, we began to edge towards one another, following the example of other prisoners. In special conditions which I had better not describe, I stole a hurried conversation with Dr. Shechter. An N.K.V.D. soldier caught us and ordered us, in a threatening voice, to return to our own places. But before he separated us—I did not know then that it was to be a separation for nine whole years—I managed to convey to Shechter the contents of the note that was in the soap, and assure him that we would meet again in Eretz Israel.

Suddenly the sound of a whistle split the air. We were ordered to get up and line up in fours. An N.K.V.D. officer informed us curtly : " You are going to a transit camp. Keep in line. One step to the right or to the left will be taken as an attempt to escape, and the soldier on guard is entitled to shoot without prior warning."

We began to march, dragging our bundles and our legs. The procession was a long one, and the way to the transit camp was long. We went by a muddy route, sometimes crossing bridges the width of a wooden plank. It was not always possible to keep in line. The people on the outside were unfortunate. They remembered the officer's warning, and every time the line broke up because of its twisted length they had to shout to the soldier on guard : " I have to diverge to the right . . . I have to diverge to the left. . . ."

From time to time I looked back. Row upon row, the candidates for re-education pressed forward. A mighty horde. All of them bent under their bundles, their legs unsteady with long disuse and because of the difficult route. All around them, men with rifles, fingers on the triggers. The blood-hounds growled. One step to the right . . . One step to the left! . . . Among the marchers, doctors, engineers, lawyers, professors, labourers, judges, officers . . . Such a procession in the twentieth century! A procession of slaves.

An N.K.V.D. soldier opened the conversation, and asked me : " What did you get ? "

" Eight years."

" What for ? "

" Section 58."

" That's bad."

" They told us in Vilna that if we work well we'll get out sooner."

" People don't get out of here."

" What do you mean ? The judge-interrogators told us that if we worked well we'd get out sooner, before the time."

The soldier burst out laughing.

" The judge-interrogators," he said, " remained in Vilna, and you people will remain here. You listen to what I tell you : people don't get out of here."

" Don't talk to him," said my friend, the sergeant, who marched next to me and helped me carry my bundle. " We'll still see whether we get out of here or not."

I took his advice. But silently I cursed the " silent " Lukishki barbers.

After walking for hours, we finally reached the transit camp. A barbed-wire fence surrounded the whole area. Watch-towers dominated it. The camp was enormous. The prisoners were divided into groups of one hundred each. In my group were Sheskin and Kroll. Shechter went to another camp. We were put into large, wooden hutments, which had bunks made of wooden planks, in several tiers. For the first time in many weeks, we were given a hot, thick soup. Then we were led to the " shower ", to have a pail of lukewarm water thrown over us. Group by group, we were summoned to the office.

The office staff were also prisoners. They wrote down personal details concerning each of the newcomers.

The prisoner-clerk asked me : " When were you arrested ? "

" On the 20th of September, 1940."

" What did you get ? "

" Eight years."

He wrote it down, murmuring as he wrote : " Date of arrest : 20th September, 1940 ; date of release : 20th September, 1948."

" That means that the period of re-education in the N.K.V.D. begins from the day of arrest, and not from the day when sentence is given. Evidently the interrogation is also part of the education," I thought to myself. But there was no time to ponder over the generosity of the N.K.V.D. The second date rang in my ears, its full significance penetrated my consciousness : 20th of September, 1948! Day of release, 20th of September, 1948! . . .

" What were you convicted of ? " the official went on to ask.

" I don't know exactly. The judge-interrogator told me that I was being charged under Section 58."

" What did they say when they sentenced you ? "

" They said : ' *sozialno-opasni element* '—Element dangerous to society."

He wrote the letters " S.O.E.", and as he handed me the index card to sign he whispered : " Never say Section 58. Say what was in the sentence : S.O.E."

This was the advice of an N.K.V.D. prisoner to a novice, and the " veteran " knew what he was saying.

The nights continued to be white. The rest in the transit camp was brief. A few days later we again formed ranks, we were again warned about taking one step to the right or one step to the left, and we were led away. For hours we plodded through swampy land, until we came to the banks of a big river.

A number of prisoners who were bustling about on the bank hailed us with a chorus of Russian curses, but it was clear from their intonation that they were actually greeting us.

" What river is this ? " we called out.

" What ? Don't you know ? " the prisoners yelled back, with more curses. " This is the Pechora River, and you're going to the *Pechor-Lag*, the Pechora camp."

Together with a quantity of long, iron rails, we were loaded into a river barge which was towed by a small steam-tug.

" She's old, still from the days of the Czar," said one of the Russian prisoners, pointing to the tug, " but the—old lady is a jolly good——"

" You've got nothing," jeered one of the Polish prisoners. " In Russia the highest manager eats and dresses worse than any concièrge in Poland before the war."

A torrent of filthy curses burst from the Russian, the likes of which I had never heard. The main innovation in his blasphemy, as against the " traditional " curses that were known in the days when the tug-boat was built, lay in the substitution of " mother-of-God " for the word " mother ".

" We're getting on," said the old major, utterly shocked. " Here you have another of the achievements of the revolution."

" But there is something characteristic in his outburst," I replied.
" This man is himself a prisoner, a victim of the regime, and see
with what vigour he defends the regime against the criticism of an
outsider."

Before nightfall we were on our way. I sat in the stern of the
boat. For hours we sailed along the broad, greenish river. The
white night revealed itself before our eyes in all its splendour. One
moment a flame glows on the horizon—the sun is setting into the
Pechora. The next moment the sun has risen in the heavens, and
shines over the surface of the Pechora. And there is light at night.

At my side there was a soldier of the guard. He looked at me,
transferred his glance to my bundle, and said : " What have you got
in this ? "

" Clothes, underwear, top-boots."

" Leather top-boots ? "

" Yes, leather ones."

" They'll take them away from you," he said with a smile.

" Who will ? " I asked in astonishment.

" You'll see. They'll take it all."

" They'll take it all ? " I repeated. " Why, these things are mine!
I would understand it if they were to take part of it and share the
things out among prisoners who have nothing, but why take
everything ? "

One of the Polish prisoners intervened and said to me crossly :
" What ? Are you already surrendering part of your belongings ? "

The N.K.V.D. soldier went on smiling, and said : " Don't argue
about it. They'll take it all, they'll take everything from you people.
You'll see."

We did not know whom he meant when he said " they ", until
we arrived at the camp.

But before I got to the labour camp I was put into another
transit camp where, to my delight, I again met Sheskin and Kroll.
We went together to our first medical examination. We sat outside
the hut in which the general examination was to take place. Sheskin
or Kroll, or both of them, got talking to one of the office staff. He
asked them if they had any shirts with collars. They answered in
the affirmative, and he informed them that in return for half a dozen
such shirts he would have them transferred to the hospital " for
further examination ", and there they would be well off. My friends
told him that there were three of us, not two. In exchange for another

three shirts with collars he agreed to transfer me to hospital as well.

I was not sick, and I did not want to go to hospital. But I was grateful to my friends for thinking of me, and I did not want to get separated from them as long as the N.K.V.D. did not compel me to. So I paid my shirt contribution and the three of us, together with another group of prisoners, some sick, some shirt-owners, were taken to hospital.

When I got there I was taken really ill. I ran a temperature, though not a very high one. I soon recovered. I was in hospital for less than a fortnight. But in this short time I learnt more about the Soviet Union than it is possible to learn in years from thick books. A world I did not know unfolded itself before me. I came to know it only too well. . . .

16

SOVIET PRISONERS' TALES

THE wooden hospital-huts were almost buried in the ground. Only a small part of the wall jutted above the surface. This type of building suited the climate that prevailed in the Pechora area, near the shores of the Barends Sea. The veteran inhabitants of the place told us, with a bitter smile on their lips : " You want to know about the climate ? It's ideal! The winter only lasts nine months, and after that you have summer ' *skolko ogodno* '—to your heart's content." And the cold in the winter, which lasts " only " nine months, reaches seventy-six degrees (Fahrenheit) below zero.

All the same, the N.K.V.D. engineers' building methods are strange. It is true that, taking into account the climate in the north, they gave instructions that the boards of which the hospital huts were constructed should be inserted deep into the ground, and the spaces between the planks filled with sawdust to insulate the walls, as far as possible, against the fearful cold ; but the bath-house for the patients was erected on a little hill more than a kilometre away from the hospital! The sick were taken to the bath-house in their underwear, with nothing but a thin blanket over them. The new-comers wanted to know whether the patients went like that to the bath-house in the winter, too. It was, to them, inconceivable that sick people should be made to run such a distance in the frightful frost, half naked, particularly after a hot shower. Only a miracle could prevent them from getting pneumonia.

The reply they received to their questions was the answer to all questions and problems in the correctional labour camp : " You'll get used to it, and if you don't you'll die."

It takes time to get used to it. The first night I experienced in the N.K.V.D. health-institute was a positive nightmare. It was not a white night, nor even a black one : it was a *red* night. I was attacked by a corps of bugs which emerged from the sawdust, column upon column. I was attacked without cease. No counter-attack was of any avail. The terrible enemy, out for my blood, kept on increasing in number. I even tried evasive tactics and lay the other way round in my bed, but the manœuvre did me no good. The enemy had me and held on. I did not close an eye that night. It was the same with all the other novices. But not so the veterans. They slept the sleep of the just. They had managed to get used to it.

In due course we also grew used to it. Nevertheless, we asked the old-timers whether it was not possible to get rid of the bugs. " Sure! " they replied with philosophical calm, " you can get rid of them easily if you burn the hut down." The " sub-tenants " of the Soviet prison-hospital could increase *skolko ogodno*. The law against sabotaging State property safeguarded them.

In hospital I made the acquaintance of a number of other sick prisoners. One of them surprised me by asking : " Are you not the head of the Betar in Poland ? "

" Yes," I replied. " How did you recognise me ? "

" I am also a Betar member," he said, moved. " My name is Marmelstein. I saw your name on your knapsack but I was not sure that it was you. Now, alas, I am sure."

Tears glistened in his eyes ; he was grieved to find me like this ; but he soon regained his composure and rejoiced at having met me. From then on we were together in various places in Russia. He was a greater help to me than I to him.

The other prisoners, with whom I struck up a brief acquaintance-ship, were Soviet citizens. But it took a few days before we grew used to one another, before we became close enough (thanks to our common fate) for them to unburden themselves and tell me their life stories, pouring out their hearts in the typical Russian way.

I found there a soul-poisoning doctor, a woman spy, an industrial saboteur, an agricultural saboteur, and the assistant-editor of *Pravda*, and these are the stories they told me :

THE SOVIET DOCTOR'S TRIANGLE

" I was a happy man," the doctor began, " and it still seems to me that what I have been through lately is only a bad dream. I lived in Moscow. I was a surgeon. In my profession I went from strength to strength. I loved my work. I met my wife while I was still a student at the university. We had two children. My family life was happy. Every day I thanked God for all the good things he had bestowed on me, both at home and in my work. But suddenly my life was shattered. My wife fell in love with another man. He was an officer in the N.K.V.D. My wife wanted a divorce by mutual agreement. I didn't want to do it. I loved her. And I was also worried about the children. I hoped that her infatuation would pass. After all, we had loved each other since we were boy and girl. But my wife stuck to her demands. In the past she might have left me and gone to live with her lover. But in these times such things are forbidden. It's a difficult thing to get a divorce. Abandoning one's family is considered an anti-revolutionary deed, according to an ukase of the Praesidium of the Supreme Soviet. The authorities maintain that people who leave their families do so on instructions from counter-revolutionary headquarters, in order to stir up mass dissatisfaction in the Soviet Union. So my wife did not leave home and continued to demand a divorce. And I kept on hoping that things would change.

"One fine day I was arrested. The interrogator told me that I was charged with grave anti-Soviet crimes, and demanded that I confess. 'If you confess,' he said, 'perhaps we will be lenient with you.' I could not make head or tail of it. I told him that I had been interested in nothing but medical science all my life, and had no interest in politics. The interrogator told me to stop pretending to be a simpleton. In any case, he said, he knew all about it. He knew that I used to take advantage of my job as a doctor and inculcate religious beliefs into the patients I treated. He also knew, he said, that before operating I used to make the sign of the cross over the patient. 'And now,' he asked, 'are you ready to confess?' I replied that I had done nothing of the sort. The interrogator began to abuse me, and shouted: 'You won't succeed in bluffing us! You yourself told all this to your wife, and now you deny it!'

"The interrogator brought my wife face to face with me. In my presence she confirmed that I used to make the sign of the cross over my patients and that I myself had told her about it. I got ten years for counter-revolutionary activity. Of course, after I was arrested, my wife could divorce me without impediment. In fact, it was her patriotic duty to leave an enemy of the people, and she was no doubt commended for her loyalty to the Soviet mother-country. Now I am here, and she is there—with him. I don't know what has become of my children. Maybe my wife took them, and she and her new husband are telling them that their father was a traitor and a criminal. I pray for their safety, and I also pray that God will forgive my wife. The truth is that I believe in God, and no one can take my faith away from me. But I did not make the sign of the cross over my patients. My wife lied, may God forgive her. . . ."

" S.E."

" My husband was the manager of a large factory in Moscow," said the woman with the beautiful Grecian features. " He was much older than me. I was his second wife. He loved me very much and did everything to make my life pleasant. Do you see this fur ? It looks worn already. It is no wonder. I knocked about in it in prison and in the train that brought me here from Moscow. But when I received this fur coat it was absolutely new. In Russia it is not an easy thing to get a fur, but my husband managed to get one. He was getting a high salary, and on several occasions he was given bonuses because his factory output exceeded the quota. He went to a lot of trouble to get me the fur for our wedding day. It was supposed to be a surprise, and it was indeed a pleasant one! How happy I was over this fur!

" Suddenly everything was shattered. My husband was arrested. I did not know why. I could not know why. My husband treated me like a child and never told me about his worries. I began to go from office to office. Wherever I went I asked: ' Why did you arrest him ? ' No one wanted to tell me the reason. They all gave me the same reply : ' He was arrested : that means he has done something. If he is found not guilty, he will be released. We don't arrest people here without reason.'

" One day, I was summoned to the N.K.V.D. offices. I thought I was going to be told the reason for my husband's arrest. And, indeed, I was. ' We have discovered,' the judge-interrogator said, ' that your husband was in the British Secret Service, and we want you to tell us everything you know about his espionage activities.' I couldn't control myself, and cried out : ' How dare you say things like that about my husband ? He was in charge of one of the biggest factories in Moscow, and did his best for our country. He was given special awards for his work. What has he got to do with espionage ? ' The interrogator replied : ' Calm yourself. We know everything about your husband. He managed to disguise himself for years, but we know everything. We have uncovered his criminal activities.

157

You are his wife. He loved you. He must have told you many details. As a loyal Soviet citizen, you have to tell us the truth.'

" ' But I am sure that my husband is innocent,' I said. ' What can I add for you ? ' ' Well, then,' said the interrogator, ' it is clear to me that you were your husband's criminal collaborator. In the cell you'll have plenty of time to consider whether it would not be better for you to tell us the whole truth.'

" I was under arrest. I sat in the cell for several weeks and no one called me. I demanded that I be brought before the judge-interrogator. They transferred me to another part of the prison and put me in another cell. Again a few weeks went by. Eventually I was summoned for interrogation. As I passed the next-door cell, I had the impression that I heard my husband's voice on the other side of the door. It was terrible. The interrogator asked me if I was ready to tell the truth. Again I told him that my husband was innocent and I had done nothing wrong, and asked him to release us both and let us live our lives in peace. ' Your husband has confessed,' said the interrogator, 'and you are still obstinate.' 'What did he confess ? ' I asked fearfully. ' He confessed to many crimes, but he has not yet confessed to all of them. I am sure you know everything but you don't want to tell. Why are you covering him ? Where is your loyalty to your country that has done so much for you ? Come on, tell us everything. Your husband, in any event, has told us everything about you.' ' What did he tell you ? ' I asked. ' Is it true that you began to take English lessons lately ? ' he asked. ' Yes,' I said, ' that's correct. And what's wrong with that ? ' ' What's wrong with that ! ' he shouted. ' You know that your teacher is a professional British spy. She has already got her deserts. And you learnt English in order to be the liaison between your husband and the British Embassy. You were all in one spy ring, but we will wipe it out. We will wipe out the whole thing.'

" I felt as if the ground was giving way beneath me. I was dazed. ' What is he talking about ? ' I asked myself. ' What spy ring ? What liaison with the British Embassy ? What woman spy ? ' I said to the interrogator : ' It's all a mistake, Citizen-Interrogator, a terrible mistake. My teacher, I am sure, could not do anything bad. She was an old woman. True, she was a little old-fashioned, but she was very loyal. She used to give English lessons to high Soviet officials. My husband knew her well. Sometimes she used to visit us, and on one of those occasions my husband happened to say, jokingly, that if she would teach me English, I would be less bored waiting for him to return from the factory. That's how the idea of my taking lessons came up. I only managed to have a few lessons with her. Afterwards my husband was arrested, and I didn't see her again. I swear, Citizen-Interrogator, that there was nothing else in my English lessons.'

"The interrogator sneered at me and my oath. 'We know everything,' he repeated. 'Now go to your cell and think it over for a bit. You'll still tell the truth.' When I passed the cell next to mine, again I seemed to hear my husband's voice. I could not sleep a wink. I heard my husband call me by name, and moan, and call to me for help. He was much older than me, in fact he was almost an old man. He was like a father to me, and here he was asking for my help. And I, how could I help? To this day I do not know if it was really he on the other side of the wall, or if I only thought I heard him moan.

"One day the interrogator called me and informed me that my husband had died. I cried like a baby. I was so grieved for the old man, the good suffering man. The interrogator let me cry for a while, but did not give me very long to lament the death of my husband. 'Calm down,' he said. 'Your husband was a spy and an enemy of the people. In any event he would have got the death sentence. And now you can tell me everything you know. Tell me what your duties were in that spy ring of yours."

"The interrogation went on for a long time. I told the interrogator that I demanded to be brought before a court, and there I would prove my innocence. 'I believe,' I said, 'in Soviet justice!' 'For such as you,' said the interrogator, 'no court is required. The proof is very clear. The Advisory Commission will judge you.' And it did. It judged me on the strength of the proof that I had received a few English lessons and was the wife of a man who had been accused of espionage and had died in prison. I got five years. If I were really a spy I would be happy. Five years for espionage is a very minor punishment. I am S.E."

"What is S.E.?" Kroll and I asked.

"Haven't you heard that before? That is also a 'Section': 'Suspected of Espionage'. Nevertheless, there is justice in the N.K.V.D. They did not sentence me as a spy, but as a suspected spy. Apparently they took into account the fact that I had not managed to learn much English. . . ."

THE LOT OF A "LAGERNI"

" I am a mechanical engineer by profession," the saboteur began his story. " I worked in a factory, in various managerial positions. I rose to the position of director. I became a member of the Party. I had everything a man could wish for. I was commended for my work and given prizes. In 1937 I was arrested. They accused me of sabotage as the factory lagged behind its quota. It is actually true that we did not fulfil the plan that year. But why was it my fault ? I did not get raw materials in time. A number of machines broke down and I could not, in spite of all my demands, get spare parts. All my explanations were of no avail. Another engineer who worked with me confirmed, to my face, that he had warned me of the possibility of a breakdown in the machines and that I had told him that there was nothing to worry about . . . That meant that I purposely wanted to sabotage the machines. As for the letters I wrote, before the machines broke down, demanding that I be provided with spare parts, those—the interrogator maintained—had been written to camouflage my sabotage activities. I got ten years. This is my fourth year in the north, in the camp.

" Ah! What do you novices know about the north ? What do you know about the *lager* ? Here, in hospital, you are not badly off. You have a bed covered with a sheet. You have a blanket to cover your bodies. Of course, there are the bugs : but you get used to them. But can you lie down during the day ?—You can! Do they bring your soup to your bed ?—They do! What more can a man ask ? But when you come to the camp, when you go out to the construction field at the crack of dawn, *then* you will know what it is to be a camp-man, a *lagerni*.

" Now it's summer. The weather is pleasant, is it not ? But when you go out to work you will see that even in the summer the north is no joke. We have little flies here in the north, tiny little flies that you can hardly see. And those cursed things love the *lagerni* ; they love him very much, the cursed blighters! They settle on your face, on your hands, get into your ears, your nostrils, and under your skin. Try to drive them away. By all means try! There are millions of them, billions. And they sting, the blighters. Ugh! How they sting! No, they are not mosquitoes. Mosquitoes are delightful creatures. These are north flies, and they guard the prisoner better than all the *strelki*,[1]

---

[1] Plural of *strilok*—sentry.

160

better than all the guards with their rifles. How ? Once a prisoner got out of the camp and ran away. The *strelki* fired after him, chased him, hunted for him with bloodhounds, in vain. The prisoner had vanished. And the *strilok* who had been guarding him was already preparing to take his place as a prisoner. Three days later the escapee returned of his own accord, of his own free will. He was unrecognisable. They took him to ' solitary '. But he swore he would never again try to escape. The north-flies had taught him a lesson. I warn you people, too, to look out for them. Remember, before you go to work, cover your hands and your faces. Cover them with whatever you can, otherwise it will be bad. And don't try to escape. It's not worth it. You'll come back of your own accord.

" But actually," the veteran continued, initiating the novices into the inner mysteries of camp life, " you have come to a prepared place. You have a hospital already standing. On every side of it there are camps. You will work in one of them. There you will find a hut waiting for you, you will be given a bunk to sleep on. I know that when you get there you will wish you were back in your prison, and long for this hospital like I long for a few extra teeth. But still, you will have a roof over your heads. When *I* came here there was no camp and no hut. We came in the winter. There were days when the temperature was seventy-two degrees below zero, and even lower. But in the winter the days are not days, just as in the summer the nights are not nights. In the winter there are only a few hours of daylight, it is dark most of the time. But what of it ? You work at night, too. The white snow gives you light.

" We used to sleep in the snow. The guards had the one and only tent there was. First we had to put up the four sides of the barbed-wire fence. After that we built four watch-towers. And only after we had imprisoned ourselves within the barbed wire and ensured for ourselves effective supervision against escape were we permitted to begin constructing huts for ourselves. A camp isn't built in a day. After twelve, or fourteen, or sixteen hours of work, we had to dig ourselves deep into the snow and go to sleep. Yes, we had a very white bed. But not everyone could rise from it. Every day, some or other prisoner would find, on awakening, that one of his neighbours was fast asleep. The *strekli* would shout at the sleeping man : ' *Vstavai*—get up and work! ' They'd shake him, curse him, kick him, but it would be no use. In the course of time the number of prisoners who fell asleep and were buried in the snow was greater than the number of people left working in the camp. But the work went on. In place of those who had fallen asleep, new prisoners came.

"What did we build? We built the railway-line that brought you to Koshva, and you will go on building it when you go to the nearby camp. Were you well shaken up when you travelled along it? Ha! She's a bit crooked, this bitch of a line . . . Oh, well, that's how they built. They were in a hurry, although they didn't complete it according to plan in any case.

"For a while I was one of the foremen in my camp. One day a big shot came from Moscow and shouted: 'The Party and the Government have set us a job which we have to complete by a certain date. The train must move, even if there is a man buried under every metre of the line!' He was speaking of a line seven hundred kilometres long. Now, work out how many people would have had to lie under the rails for the work to be completed by the time stipulated by the Party and the Government. Well, I don't know if seven hundred thousand men are lying beneath the rails, but thousands certainly found their graves there. Actually, we were late in finishing, but the train moved all the same. Yes, the line's a little crooked. . . .

"And have you heard about '*tsinga*'?" The engineer opened his mouth and showed us pallid, almost white gums. Only two teeth were stuck in them. "Yes, they'll also fall out soon," he said. "This is *tsinga* and you can't escape it in the north. Your teeth will fall out, too, but don't think that *tsinga* will leave it at that. It turns your whole body into a mass of suppurating sores that ooze pus and blood. Look!" He rolled down his long underpants and revealed legs covered with large black blotches. "These," he said, "are just scars. It's healed up a bit. But when I get back to the camp I'll get sores all over again and my body will ooze pus and blood again. The *tsinga* is a common disease in the north. No prisoner is immune from it, so it is not considered an illness. People with *tsinga* work as usual.

"Another thing you'll get is '*panos*' (almost unceasing diarrhoea). But you must know that ordinary *panos* is not considered a sickness. Only acute *panos*, with blood, warrants exemption from work, and, if you are lucky, transfer to hospital. If you say you have diarrhoea, someone will go along and check how often you function. If you say there's blood in it, someone will go along and watch that too. Ah! We have a 'norm' here even for *panos*, and whoever does not conform to that norm has not got *panos* ; he is healthy and has to go to work.

" And have you heard about ' *Etap* ' ? When you finish your job in your camp they will transfer you to another place. Maybe they will transfer you even before you finish. That is *Etap*. In the new place there may be a camp already erected, or there may be nothing but an open field—as I found when I came to the north. It's all a matter of luck. But don't think that where you are going is the thing that matters most ; there is something to be said about the journey. The *Etaps* take place both in summer and in winter, over-land and by water, in transports or on foot. If you are ever in an *Etap* ship, you'll know what a ship can be. I remember an *Etap* that started out from our camp. The prisoners were bundled into trucks. The frozen river served as their road, an excellent road. But it was freezing cold. The trucks broke down, apparently because of the frost. The prisoner-drivers tried to repair them, but it was useless. Their frozen hands could do nothing, or else the trouble was too serious. From the *Etap* they returned on foot to the camp. But only the *strelki* came back. The man in charge was duly punished for the waste of *rab-sila*, that is to say, manpower, working hands, but his punishment did not bring back to life those who were left on the frozen Pechora.

" And have you heard of the limb-hewers, the ' *chleno-rubi* ' ? Yes, they are people who operate on themselves, who amputate a finger, or several fingers, or even a foot. How do they do that ? In various ways. There are *chleno-rubi* who put the palm of their hand on the tree-trunk, raise the axe, say ' Huh! '—and the fingers are dangling in mid-air! Those who don't work with an axe, or can't stand the sight of blood, use another method. The cold is their axe. They wet their thumb in urine, hold it in the air for a few seconds, in air more than 100 degrees below zero. In a flash, the finger turns completely white. Third-degree freezing. Hospital. Operation. Disablement.

" You ask why they do that ? How a man can cripple himself? When you are in the camp you will understand. Every morning at dawn you will hear the gong. Every morning they will tug you by the legs and yell at you to get up. You'll get up. In the clothes, the rags, in which you slept, you'll go outside. You'll stand in the yard. They'll number you off. Once, twice, three times. . . . Half an hour. . . . An hour. . . . After that you'll get your bread. You'll eat it, all of it at once. After that you'll be taken to work. At night you'll be brought back to the hut, you'll throw yourselves down on your bunks. Your bones, oh! your weary bones! You'll wipe the pus from your *tsinga* sores. You'll fall asleep and sleep like the dead. And in the morning, at four o'clock in the morning, again the gong, and again ' Hey you! Get up! '. And so every day, every morning, every night. . . . When you are in the camp you will understand how a man can want to fall sick. Yes, to be sick, not to have to go out to the construction field, not to have to get up, to lie down a little, just a little. When you're in the camp you'll understand what joy it is to be sent to hospital. Yes, that is how the *lagerni* gets to mutilating himself. You will, of course, find people in the camp without fingers, or without toes, without ears, even without a nose, who are not *chleno-rubi*. *Their* members froze, froze while they were working. One of the usual work-accidents. They are, of course, unfortunate, but don't you believe they were miserable when they were taken to hospital to be operated on. On the contrary, they were happy then! The happiness of a *lagerni*—to be sick in hospital.

" And don't think that the *chleno-rubi* are considered to have punished themselves sufficiently. The authorities also punish them. They add an extra month to their term of imprisonment. After all, what they have done is a form of sabotage of State property. But what do they care? Have they any hope of ever getting out of the *lager*?

" Well, that is the lot of man in the *lager*. Can you understand how he feels? "—asked the engineer.

I was beginning to understand. Again I cursed the barbers of Lukishki.

THE CONTENTED *LAGERNI*

" You ask what I was arrested for," said the old peasant who lay next to my bunk on the top tier. " For sabotage they arrested me. I was in a kolkhoze, of course. But they said I neglect the work for the commune and work too much for myself. Well, you know, the Soviet authorities give the kolkhoznik a piece of land which he can work for himself. What the kolkhoznik produces from it, he can sell in the open commune market. That's very good, of course. But they said I work too much for my own land and will soon become a kulak. What kind of kulak am I? Tell me, please, what sort of kulak I am if there was nothing to eat in my house. But they said I was sabotaging the commune and gave me ten years. Now I am here. Don't think I am complaining against the Soviet regime, God preserve it! I am not complaining, I am well off here. At home I never had such a clean, comfortable bed. And the food I get is better than what I had at home, and how much better! And they bring the food to my bed. I am well off here, better off than at home. I am not complaining against the Soviet regime, God preserve it! Let them only allow me to remain here. I'm well off here."

THE STORY OF THE ASSISTANT EDITOR
OF *PRAVDA*

At first Garin was unfriendly. About himself he did not speak. Our conversations centred mainly on the war, anti-Semitism, Zionism and Communism. When I heard him speak I heard an echo of what my interrogator at Lukishki had said. Zionism and anti-Semitism, Garin explained, are but two sides of the same coin. Anti-Semitism is the expression of a racialist, nationalistic prejudice ; and so is Zionism. In fact, Garin said, Zionism says exactly what the anti-Semites say : " Jews to Palestine "—and plays right into their hands. And the contention that Zionism is the agent of imperialism was, for Garin, positively axiomatic. Our conversations developed into arguments, and the arguments were very stormy.

Once Garin attacked me for what he called my shameful self-effacement before the anti-Semites. He heard me talking with the Polish prisoners and noticed that they, as well as I, used the word " *zhid* " for " Jew ". " ' *Zhid* ' is an insulting name commonly used by anti-Semites," said Garin, " and it is forbidden in the Soviet Union." And I, a Zionist, who claimed to be proud of my Jewishness, was not only letting these Poles says " *zhid* " and " *zhidavski* ", but was even using these anti-Semitic words of opprobrium myself, without shame. " Is that not proof," Garin asked hotly, " that anti-Semitism and Zionism are in fact allies ? "

I tried to explain to him that the ways of anti-Semites differ. It is true that in Russian the accepted word for Jew is " *yevrei* ", while the word " *zhid* " has in it an implication of hatred and contempt. In Polish, on the other hand, the usual word for Jew is " *zhid* ", and when the anti-Semite wants to show his contempt for the detested Jew, he calls him a " *yevrei* ". Garin heard me out, but refused to accept my view. " That is Talmudism," he said. " The word ' *zhid* ' is an anti-Semitic word in every language, and you let it be used and use it yourself because of the partnership between anti-Semitism and Zionism."

Garin also had stormy arguments with the saboteur engineer, although on different grounds. The *lagerni* said he did not care if the Germans got as far as the Pechora. In any event he had nothing to lose. Garin stormed and raved. " Look here," he said, " I am also a prisoner, I am also suffering, but my personal tribulations have not made me lose my mind! I want the Soviet Union to win. Fascism is a deadly danger to humanity. If the Soviet Union falls, all the achievements of the revolution will be cancelled. You have forgotten how much the mother country has done for you. Now, when your country is in danger, are you going to betray her ? "

The engineer had no desire to continue the discussion. He took fright, apparently, at what he had said. Although the prisoners are not particularly careful what they say in the camp (for, after all, what more can they do to them ?), there is sometimes—even in the *lager*—practical importance in the Russian saying : " My tongue— my enemy ". The engineer said that Garin had not understood what he said, and, flinging the epithets " viper " and " parasite " at him, walked out of the hut. These epithets are very common not only in the *lager* but in the Soviet Union as a whole.

One day an Inspection Commission turned up at the hospital. The engineer told us that the surprise visit was the result of an informing letter sent to the authorities concerned complaining against the doctor appointed to our hut. Our doctor was a prisoner of Esthonian origin, a tall, middle-aged woman with a certain sad charm. The rumour got about among the sick that the doctor was discriminating in favour of the Esthonian prisoners who had arrived together with us, and was keeping them in hospital ostensibly for further tests. To what extent the engineer's story was true, it was, of course, difficult to establish. Garin and I, in any event, did not manage to get to the bottom of it in the time that we were in hospital.

With the Commission came the superintendent of the labour camp. He asked the patients whether they were prepared, of their own free will, to go to work, because there was urgent construction work to be done and they were short-handed. The patients' reply was silence. The superintendent left us. We, the novices, could not conceal our astonishment at this odd call for volunteers from among sick people. The engineer laughed at us, and cursed. " You'll still see the result," he said.

Next day Garin unbent and told me the story of his life up to the time that he came to the Pechora.

"Don't think, Menachem Wolfovitch, that you are the first person with whom I have argued about Zionism and Socialism. You remind me of the days of my youth in Odessa. What arguments I had with the Zionists! Do you know how old I was when I joined the Party? I was not more than seventeen when I became a Bolshevik and began to work for the Revolution.

"During the Civil War, I was in the Red Guard and took part in many battles against the Whites. I was taken prisoner. The Whites beat me and tortured me horribly, but they did not succeed in getting anything out of me. They threatened that they would shoot me like a dog. They would certainly have killed me had they not had to retreat in confusion before a Red counter-attack. When the Civil War was over I was given various duties in the Party in the Ukraine. I was still young, but I worked hard and devoted myself heart and soul to the Party. What days those were! I worked in the Party and studied at the university. When I had finished my studies I was given even higher positions. I moved to Kharkov, and after that to Kiev. I worked for a few years in the Secretariat of the Party in the Ukraine. Eventually I became its General Secretary. From this position I was transferred to an even higher post. I was summoned to Moscow and put on the editorial staff of *Pravda*. I became assistant editor of the Party newspaper.

"In 1937, the year they went crazy, my wife was arrested. I haven't told you about my wife. We met when we were both students. My wife was also a member of the Party, and a very active one. My wife isn't Jewish, but what's the difference? Our family life was wonderful. We had a son and a daughter. My wife helped me in my work, and I helped her. Her main interest was science. In her scientific work she went from success to success. She became a lecturer at the University, and, after that, a lecturer at the ' Institut Krasni Professori '. Oh! You don't know what the Institute of Red Professorship is? I'll explain it. In the Soviet Union it is not like in the capitalistic countries. We have special institutes in which future university professors study, and they are called Institutes of Red Professorship. My wife was so outstanding in her scientific work that she rose to the position of professor in this Institute. And all of a sudden, in 1937, she was arrested.

"I did not know what to do. I was certain that my wife would soon be released. She was such a loyal member of the Party. They didn't touch me. I went on working on *Pravda*. One day I was summoned to the Ministry of the Interior. I thought it meant that I was going to be arrested, too, but I was mistaken. A high official told me that he had orders to take me straight to the Kremlin hospital to see my wife.

"I found my wife very pale, but smiling happily. She told me that the interrogator had accused her of Trotskyism and demanded a confession. She did not confess. She never had been a Trotskyist. The interrogator told her she would rot in jail. She was in despair and decided to commit suicide. But before making the attempt on her life she wrote a personal letter to Stalin, asking him to order her release and give her back her Party membership card, for she had always been and would always remain a loyal member.

"By some miracle the letter reached Stalin. I know that during that period many people wrote personal letters to Kalinin, Stalin, Molotov, Ordzhonikidze, or Voroshilov, but none of them ever received a reply. My wife's letter arrived, and even achieved immediate results. Stalin gave orders for her to be removed from the prison hospital to the Kremlin hospital. The best doctors tended her and saved her life. Stalin also gave orders that her Party membership card be returned to her immediately. A few days went by but the card did not arrive. She waited patiently. The General Secretariat of the Party enquired whether the card had already been received. My wife replied in the negative. Next day the secretary of the Organisation Department handed her her membership card with profuse apologies, 'in accordance with the personal instructions of Comrade Stalin'.

"You can't imagine how happy we were during the days that followed. Just imagine! My wife is arrested and accused of being a Trotskyist, our whole lives are on the verge of being ruined, and suddenly the sun comes out for us once more. Stalin himself set my wife free and granted her full rehabilitation. I assure you that I am not exaggerating when I say that those were the happiest days of our lives.

"A few weeks later my wife left hospital and went back to her work at the Institute. I went on working on the paper. Our future seemed to be shining and secure. Who would dare bother my wife again after what had happened? But a few months later my wife was arrested for a second time by the N.K.V.D. It's hard to believe, isn',t it ? But it's a fact. My wife was re-arrested in spite of the fact that the first order of arrest had been cancelled by Stalin himself. This goes to show that a fundamental change has taken place in the rulership in the Soviet Union, a change that only we know about. You people abroad think to this day, no doubt, that the Party is the ruling power over here. That was so during Lenin's life-time and for a few years after his death. In those days a Communist's membership card could be taken away from him only after he had been sentenced. As long as he had not yet been found guilty he did not forfeit his rights, even though he was under arrest. But today the position is different. The centre of gravity in the rulership has been transferred from the Party to the N.K.V.D. A Party member has his membership card taken away from him the moment he is arrested, and loses all his rights. The Party no longer rules in the Soviet Union. The N.K.V.D. rules—even over the Party. You see that the N.K.V.D. re-arrested my wife and had no doubt already seen to it that her letters would not reach Stalin again. And I—I was power-less to do anything.

" A short while after my wife's second arrest I too was arrested. The interrogator demanded that I tell him of my connections with Trotskyist headquarters. This was a terrible accusation, without any foundation. I told that to the interrogator and brought him proof of my innocence. I thought I had the best possible proof and would succeed in clearing my name. I told the interrogator about an article of mine that had appeared in *Pravda* the day previous to my arrest. The article was called : ' A rapid retreat to Menshevism ', and in it I showed that Trotskyism is really a return to treacherous Menshevism.

" ' And you accuse me today of connections with Trotskyist headquarters,' I said to the interrogator, confidently, in conclusion. The interrogator answered me derisively : ' You want to be smart, eh, Garin ? People can't be smart with us. We know everything. Yes, we know all about your article in yesterday's *Pravda* and all your other articles against Trotsky. But whom are you trying to bluff ? Us ? Trotskyist headquarters instructed you to write all those articles, to enable you to camouflage yourself better within the Party, to enable you to go on with your criminal activities.'

" These accusations were pure figments of the imagination with-out any substance. I am saying this, not to a representative of the Soviet authorities, but to you, Menachem Wolfovitch, in a private conversation, here on the banks of the Pechora. If I were a Trotskyist I would not deny it to you. But I am telling you the whole truth. I had no connections with Trotskyist headquarters. On the contrary, I fought them in my articles and in speeches I made on behalf of the Central Committee. Yes, it is correct that in the 'twenties, before the death of Lenin, when I was a student at the university I was inclined towards Trotsky's way of thinking. A big argument was going on then inside the Party between Lenin and Trotsky. The whole thing was public, everyone knew about it. Because of the scathing tone of Trotsky's articles Lenin once threatened to resign from the leadership of the Party and the State. Then there was still internal democracy in the Party. No one was afraid to express his opinion, whether in favour of Trotsky or in favour of Lenin. The university students were at the time practically all in favour of Trotsky's line. Everybody in the Soviet Union knows that. Many of the people who are today working in the Z.K.V.K.P., Central Committee of the All U.S.S.R. Communist Party, studied together with me at the university and, like the rest of the students, supported Trotsky's views. The whole thing was perfectly legal. But since then—since my student days—I have had nothing to do with either Trotsky's views or with his supporters. On the contrary, I fought them hard.

" But the proof didn't help me. The interrogators—and I had many interrogators—went on demanding that I reveal connections that I did not have, and confess to things that I did not do. Do you know how long my interrogation lasted ? Work it out for yourself. I told you I was arrested in 1937, and I left Tomsk three months ago, after I had been informed that the Special Advisory Commission had sentenced me to eight years in a labour camp. The interrogation went on for nearly four years. Most of the time I was in the Tomsk prison, in Siberia. But until I got there I was pushed around from prison to prison. I sat in jail with some of the biggest party leaders, some of the finest officers of the Red Army ; with veteran Bolsheviks who led the proletariat to revolution and were victorious in the Civil War. I have seen terrible things ; and I have experienced terrible things.

" Don't think that there were no genuine saboteurs among those who were arrested at that time. Of course there were. I myself met some of them. They used to go to the interrogation without a care, and come back highly satisfied with themselves and the interrogator.

They used to do propaganda openly in the cell. 'Yes,' they used to say, 'we give away names. One should give names. Let others go to jail, too. The more prisoners there are from among the active workers in the Party, the greater the confusion will be. We will break the Party. The more names we give the better it will be for us.'

" I am sure that thousands of the best Party people were arrested and liquidated because of the deliberate saboteurs who cast innocent people into the whirlpool. And the interrogators wanted only one thing : confess, tell us your connections ; who else was a Trotskyist ? Who else was against the Central Committee ?

" Perhaps it is because of this deliberate sabotage that most of the interrogators of those days were, in the end, themselves liquidated. I tell you, that year, the year 1937, they went stark crazy. One day the prisoners are interrogated by a cruel interrogator who hits them, abuses them, demands a full confession, and a few days later that same interrogator enters the cell—as a prisoner. And he, in his turn, would return bleeding from the interrogation, he would be asked to confess that he was connected with Trotskyist headquarters, and that everything he did against Trotskyism was nothing but a blind. Sometimes the interrogator was told to confess that, on instructions from sabotage-headquarters, he had arrested loyal members of the Party in order to weaken the active cadres, in order to break the Party. Before many days had passed the interrogator of that interrogator was also arrested and required to confess to all the crimes he had attributed to his former victims. I tell you it seemed to all of us, then, that we were living in one vast mad-house. We began to wonder how far this would go. When would an end be put to this madness ?

" For four years I was under interrogation, and I passed from one interrogator to another. The worst of them all was my interrogator at Tomsk. He was notorious in the whole prison for his cruelty. They used to give him the 'special cases'. He excelled in breaking the stubborn cases and used to boast openly that no prisoner had yet withstood his system of interrogation. And this man, devoid of all human feelings, was sent to interrogate me. I was already then a sick man. I had made two attempts at suicide. I had tried to open my veins because I simply could not stand it any more. But in Russia they don't let a prisoner die so quickly. In both cases I was spotted before I had lost too much blood. As a result of all I had gone through, I developed a heart disease. I had a temperature every day—just as I have now—and in that state I was brought before the expert in breaking obstinate prisoners.

" He did not ' converse ' with me, as the other interrogators did. He asked me if I was prepared to confess, and I replied that I had told them all I knew. He thereupon pulled off a leg of the chair— he was as strong as a bull—and began to rain blows on my head, my shoulders, my whole body, shouting as he did so ' Will you confess or not ? ' over and over again. Instinctively, I should have covered my head with my hands, but I felt a pain in my heart. I put my hands over my chest and begged him only not to hit me over the heart, but he paid no heed. After that night I tried again and again to do away with myself, but those attempts also failed. And here I am, Menachem Wolfovitch, on the banks of the Pechora. There was no trial. After four years of interrogation they informed me that I had been sentenced administratively to eight years' detention in a correctional labour camp. Tomorrow we go to work together."

The day Garin told me all this, the doctor had read out the names of the patients who, it had been decided, would be sent from the hospital to the labour camp next day. Among them was Garin, too. The doctor explained to him that she had asked the Inspection Commission to leave him in hospital as he had a serious heart ailment and a persistent temperature of about 100. But the Commission had rejected all her explanations, warning her to stop and think what responsibility she was taking upon herself.

In Garin's file there was an inscription consisting of four letters : K.R.T.D., which meant : " Counter-revolutionary Trotskyist activity." And that is one of *the* Sections, the worst that there is in the Soviet Union.

That day, Garin and I had gone out to the garden patch in front of our hut. A tall, Russian *Urki* prisoner, who was standing there, smiled, and said, half to himself : " Oh, *zhidi, zhidi*! What's going to happen to you ? Hitler knocked you about, and here you're kept in a *lager*. I'm sorry for you poor Jews. They've got it in for you everywhere. What's going to happen to you, *zhidi* ? "

The assistant editor of *Pravda*, who was expelled, sick, from the hospital, heard the word *zhid* in Russian and hung his head.

It was after that that he told me his story.

17

WITH ORCHESTRAL ACCOMPANIMENT

" MEN," said the Camp Superintendent, a short, fat fellow, in a voice charged with enthusiasm, " you are now in our camp. You are going out to work for the first time. Remember that you are working for the Soviet Mother-country. Over there, far away from us, a terrible war is being fought. Blood is mingling with mud. You are far from the front, and you must be grateful to those who are defending you from the German cannibals. Therefore it is your duty to work with the greatest application, so that we should fill our quota and more, to help the front. Today you are wielding a spade, tomorrow you may be summoned to wield a rifle. To work! Forward! Hurrah! "

The prisoners, who were listening to this exhortation, stood in groups on a hillock which gave a view of both banks of the Pechora for a considerable distance. Below, on the left bank of the river, were railway lines, and a large number of goods-trucks. On the river, freighters. The superintendent pointed first to the ships, then to the trucks : " The Party and the Government," he said, " have given us the job of off-loading the ships and loading the trucks by a certain date."

The prisoners were a very cosmopolitan collection. I noticed among them Russians, Poles, Lithuanians, Latvians, Esthonians, Rumanians (from Bessarabia) and Jews. " Vertically", the prisoners were grouped according to language and origin; but " horizontally " they were divided into two groups only : political prisoners and criminal prisoners. It is the horizontal division that really matters.

The patriotic call of the fat superintendent was addressed to all the prisoners, but only the criminal prisoners answered "Hurrah!" to his "Hurrah!" and, with this, began to run down the slope towards the river. The political prisoners also arrived at the boats at a breathless run, and our day's work began. We were to construct the Kotlas-Varkuta railway, by order of the Party and the Government.

All of a sudden the sound of music reached my ears, just as I was about to go down into the hold of the ship. I, and the other new prisoners, turned and looked back to the hillock: There was no mistake about it. On the rise sat a band—wind instruments, drum and cymbals—to make our work pleasanter. They played the tune of a song in praise of Soviet liberating toil.

We off-loaded sleepers that support the railway lines. The Russian railways are of particularly wide gauge. The rails are also longer than is customary in the countries of Western Europe. The length of the sleepers and their weight are in proportion to the rails. The minimum unloading quota for a prisoner was two sleepers for every trip from the boat to the trucks. Anyone who did more was a candidate for special mention for excelling at work.

We carried the iron sleepers on our shoulders from the ship, along a narrow plank, on to the shore and to the railway truck—a distance of about three hundred metres. After a few hours of this I felt a burning pain in my shoulders every time I hoisted the sleepers on to them. All the skin had been scraped off. The same thing happened to many of the other new prisoners. The criminal prisoners sneered at us and made fun of what they called our delicate, white hands. "You don't know how to work," they shouted. "Watch us." They really did know what to do. They put pads made of rags on their shoulders to protect the skin.

"*Zakurka!*" shouted one of the criminal prisoners suddenly. Work stopped. Some of the prisoners took strips of old Soviet newspaper from their pockets, made boats out of them, and put in a little *machorka* (tobacco). Then they rolled the paper, spat on it well to make it stick because the paper was very thick, and produced a "cigarette", thick and long like Havana cigars. From the look on the smokers' faces, it was evident that they were getting no less pleasure out of them than a man who smokes Havanas, although—or perhaps just because—the "cigarettes" passed from mouth to mouth. Three or four puffs was the maximum smoking quota.

"The *zakurka* is over," shouted the group-leader. "Back to work!"

"—— Brigadier, damned viper," said the criminal prisoners loudly, though half to themselves, adding a "camp" rank to the group-leader's government rank.

The group-leader is not insulted. Work is resumed.

A Polish captain who worked beside me recalled Adam Mieczkiewicz's poem on the fall of the fortress of Granada, and the revenge

of its defender, Almanzur, on its Spanish conqueror
recited :

> " They shattered the night of the Moors, and they gave
> A burden of iron, without pity,
> But there in Granada the fortress still rallies,
> Though pestilence stalks in the city . . ."

And he added : " We're hauling iron ; plague we've got ; but we
have no Almanzur! "

" *Zakurka!* " came the cry again.

" But you've just smoked," shouted the group-leader. " You've
got to work."

" Don't hiss, snake," answered the chorus of criminals. " Try
working a bit yourself! Parasite! " This was followed by the usual
curses and vituperation.

The *ʒakurka* is not just a matter of columns of smoke issuing from
what was once *Pravda* ; it is an integral part of the battle of life of
those sentenced to hard labour.

In spite of the smoking recess, in spite of the moments of
work-sabotaging rest snatched under the wheels, the truck fills
up with iron sleepers, while the band plays the Labour March.

From the rise, a cart, harnessed to a horse with all its bones
showing, slowly descends. It reminds one of the cooking-water
carts of the past. The midday meal has arrived.

A few of the prisoners have a little of their bread ration left
over. But most of them are compelled to make do with the miserable
fish-soup. The Lukishki prisoners drink it and sigh : " There, they
gave us food! "

In the afternoon the band departs. But the little flies increase
and hum a new song of praise : to the hungry prisoner's blood. They
sing and sting, drink and buzz. There is no escaping them. And
again the criminals jeer at our " white hands ". The criminals are
experienced. On their faces they put masks made of netting, or
rags punched with holes. They covered their hands with rags
which served as gloves. We, the novices, were utterly at the mercy
of the tiny parasites. The engineer-saboteur had warned us, but
we paid no heed to his warning. We reckoned we would be able
to stand up to mosquitoes!

Fourteen hours had passed since we had risen from our bunks.

Twelve hours since we heard the criminals shout "Hurrah!" to the fat superintendent. The day's work was over. We lined up in fives and numbered off. "I warn you, one step to the left, one step to the right means an attempt at escape and I shoot without warning."

The criminal prisoners mumble their curses. It is a wonder that the Pechora does not blush.

At the gate of the camp they searched our persons.

"We lugged iron all day," shouted the criminals. "What are they searching for?"

In the yard a parade. A mistake in the count. A re-count. Still the number does not tally. And we stand weary, hungry, bent. Our legs are unsteady, our aching shoulders are peeled raw. But we have to stand. The number must be right.

Eventually it is. We are free. We wait for the evening meal ; for more soup, the taste of which makes us homesick for the gruel that once revolted us.

Suddenly a shout is heard :

"Hi! Brigadier! Parasite! Have you fed them?" He used the Russian word "*nakormil*", which means "feeding the brutes". We were no longer human beings that eat. In a day we had become animals that had to be fed ; the *rab-sila* of the Soviet Union.

The Soviet Union has a weakness—perhaps because of a tendency to Talmudism ?—for initial-abbreviations. *Rab-sila* is the abbreviation for *rabotchia-sila*, which means man-power or working-hands. But the three letters R—A—B also constitute a Russian term on their own, which means a slave. That, no doubt, the N.K.V.D. philologists overlooked.

With this thought, I climbed into my bunk. Until I fell asleep I kept on hearing the echo of the question : "Have you fed the brutes?" in all its revolutionary significance.

In order to understand how the *rab-sila* of the Soviet Union lived, and how they were used, one should know the essential terms and the principal functions that are to be found in a correctional labour camp. They are :

Brigade—a hard-labour gang, numbering 20 to 30 people. A group.

Brigadier—group-leader, responsible for the work of his group.

Pro-rab—*proizvoditel rabot*—foreman or overseer over a number of groups.

Nariadschik—work-distributor in the camp.

Norm—daily quota of work for each prisoner.

Normerovishchik—clerk who keeps the quota-accounts.

Katiol—Dixie—daily food ration, which includes the bread ration, and is dependent on the output percentage recorded to the prisoner's credit, in relation to his fixed work-quota. In our camp there were four dixies. A prisoner who did less than thirty per cent of the norm would get the penalty-dixie. That is to say, two hundred grams of bread, soup once a day. A prisoner whose percentage reached sixty, would get dixie No. 1 : four hundred grams of bread, soup twice a day. Sixty to eighty per cent entitled the prisoner to dixie No. 2 : five hundred grams of bread, and a spoonful of cereals added to the soup. Over eighty per cent : seven hundred grams of bread, better soup with cereals added, sometimes dried potatoes, and occasionally a dry, unsweetened biscuit, thick and as hard as a stone, but quite tasty. Whoever exceeded the quota would get, in our camp, dixie No. 12(!) : eight to nine-hundred grams of bread, good soups with all kinds of things in them, the taste and quality of which I shall never know, because I never had the pleasure of partaking of this dixie, and never saw any one who did in the actual process of eating. Why they jumped from dixie No. 3 to No. 12, no one was ever able to explain to us. That's how it was. The guardians of the Revolution can also be very conservative.

Padiom—getting-up time, the most hated word in the camp.

Element—There is S.O.E.—*sotzialno opasni element*—element dangerous to society, and S.V.E.—*sotzialno vredni element*—element harmful to society. The political prisoners who were sentenced by the Advisory Commission usually belonged to the first category. The criminals, also sentenced administratively, generally belonged to the second category. But in camp they were both called " element ". " *Ti element ?* " (Are you an " Element "?) —was the question the veterans used to ask newcomers. Sometimes, but not always, they would also ask : " Which ? "

Urki or *Zhuliki*—a general name for Soviet criminal prisoners.

Vospitatiel—Instructor. A man who delivers speeches together with the Camp Superintendent on Soviet holidays and festivals. His main job is to spur the prisoners on to greater efforts. Organiser of " socialistic competitions "(!) between two labour camps.

Lek-pom—*Larkarski pomoshnik*—medical assistant, or orderly. There is no doctor in the labour camp. Such doctors as there are among the prisoners are put to work in the hospital—if they work at their profession at all. In the camp they have a *lek-pom*, a layman, who knows how to take a temperature, give an aspirin for every ache, and distinguish between *panos* with blood, and diarrhoea without blood. The *lek-pom* is important to the prisoners, not because of the way he takes care of their health but because he can recommend transfers to hospital. There are *lek-poms* who have no human feelings ; there are others who adopt an unfeeling attitude towards the prisoners out of fear. Many a *lek-pom* had his sentence extended for sabotage, because he exempted too many people from work " with the express purpose of harming the socialistic construction work and preventing the plan from being carried out ".

Dochodiaga—a prisoner on the decline, unable to work. His end is drawing near.

Commandant—caretaker of a prison hut, responsible for keeping it clean.

Punkt—" Point ", labour camp. The term " Camp "—*Lager*, or, in short,

Lag—applies to a large administrative unit composed of a number (sometimes hundreds) of " Points ". Hence " *Pechor-Lag* ", which extended over an enormous area of labour-camps.

Blat, Pa-Blato, Blatnoi—bribery, wangling, ability to " fix " things.

In the camp curse-words are legion. There never has been such obscenity since the day when man first opened his mouth. The curses are not always an expression of hatred, anger or aggressiveness. There are times when they are merely a form of greeting, or serve to express gratitude, or friendliness. The *Urki* know how to talk ; one just has to be able to understand them.

Of all the terms, the curse-words are the most useful, but the most important are : Norm, dixie and *blat*.

I once saw a book of norms. It looked like a collection of logarithmic tables. In thickness it looked like an encyclopaedia. On the basis of these tables all work in the Soviet Union is—or should be—done, whether it be manufacturing tanks or digging the soil, in the factory or in the kolkhoze. The norms in the labour camp have been calculated on the basis of a twelve-hour day.

It would certainly be a healthy idea for those who calculated the norms to try working according to their own figures ; just as it would be beneficial to society as a whole if every judge—not only in the Soviet Union—were required to spend some time in jail as part of his training. In the latter case there would be less injustice in the world ; in the former, less bluff in Russia.

The daily quota imposed on the *rab-sila* in the labour camps could not be fulfilled—and certainly not every day!—even by people accustomed to manual labour. That applied even more so to the political prisoners who were, for the most part, intellectuals unused to any form of physical work. But the norm is linked with the dixie, and the dixie determines how quickly a man will turn into a *dochodiaga* without the strength to work any longer, a declining shadow waiting for the end. The Soviet Tantalus has to give the last ounce of his strength in order to get—an extra hundred grams of bread, a spoonful of *kasha*, or a little *machorka*. That is his reward for a physical effort which is in itself fatal. There is no other reward. Not even for those who work by the rule that "Every two workers will achieve three hundred per cent", which was printed on a big signboard prominently displayed in our camp.

The reward for completing the quota, or even surpassing it, is not satiety, but less hunger, and the hunger in the camp defies comparison with anything we experienced in prison. In Lukishki we sat closed up in a cell ; in the camp we were out in the open for sixteen hours a day. The work is back-breaking. The body demands some recompense, but the compensation we were given was smaller than that we received in confinement. We saw what hunger did to people in Lukishki. It is not difficult to imagine, although hard to assess, what hunger did to those living in the labour camps. In Lukishki I saw "telephonists", on the banks of the Pechora I found animals walking on two legs. Hunger. . . .

For the sake of getting enough to eat a hungry man is prepared to do more than a man who is replete is prepared to do for the sake of getting rich. For the sake of being less hungry a man is prepared to do more than for the sake of repletion. It is the desire to live that determines these degrees of effort. And the desire to live is very strong in the correctional labour camp. It keeps on growing. It does not decrease. In proportion to the extent that he has been weaned from civilisation, the imprisoned Tantalus is prepared to do anything to graduate from dixie No. 1 to dixie No. 2, not to be demoted from the second dixie to the first. But not every prisoner is capable of the physical effort this involves. The patriotic speeches of the Camp Superintendent and the instructor leave the prisoners unmoved. They all know that the norm is beyond the powers of the average man. The result is—*blat.*

How does *blat* fix the relations between the norm in the book and the percentage entered to the prisoner's account, and between these two and the dixie ? The norm is always dependent on a number of factors. For example, the norm for the off-loading that we were employed on, depended on weight and distance. If, in reckoning up the day's work, a few metres were added to the real distance between the point of off-loading and the point of re-loading, the output percentages went up. The same applied if the weight of the load we transported from the vessel to the train was put down in round figures.

Our brigade was not one that particularly excelled itself. Its average dixie was No. 2. We worked hard. If we set aside the " romantic, reactionary " contention that every prisoner is entitled to eat even if he does not work at all ; and if we accept for the moment, for the sake of argument, the great revolutionary slogan that he who does not work does not eat, then we earned our dixie, with the toil of our hands and the sweat of our brow. But as far as the norm was concerned we would certainly have been pounded between the millstones of the penalty-dixie and No. 1. But we went up to dixie No. 2—occasionally even dixie No. 3—on the ladder of *blat.*

This ladder has many steps. The prisoner tries to keep on good terms with the brigadier ; the brigadier tries to curry favour with the overseer. Both of them will do anything to get around the quota-clerk. A shirt with a fixed collar will pass from hand to hand, from one official to another. Sometimes a bit of *machorka* helps, sometimes a stolen article does the trick. Sometimes mutual fear adjusts the difference between the norm laid down by the " party and the Government", and the actual work that is done. There are people in the group that the group-leader is afraid of ; there are brigadiers who are afraid of the *pro-rab* ; the quota-clerk, who is himself a prisoner, is also afraid of certain people in the camp, people below him. The result is : general perpetual *blat.* And Soviet statistics record the output percentages of the *rab-sila*, together with the results of the *blat.*

Is the Soviet Government not capable of putting down this mass conspiracy ? No, it cannot. Actually, the *blat* does get discovered in the end, and they learn about square metres of ground that were dug on paper, and iron sleepers that were loaded on paper, or about a railway line that is " a little crooked ". Then the labour foremen are sent to a labour camp and the *pro-rab* gets his sentence extended. But the *blat* continues, for it is discovered only in the end, and a man has to live in the meantime. And the desire to live waxes stronger. This is one of the internal contradictions of the N.K.V.D. regime. It has reduced man to a *lagerni*, to the status of a beast of burden, but has thereby given him a greater desire to live, which sabotages the plans and calculations of the authors of the "State Construction Plan".

The N.K.V.D. entrusted the direct " autonomous " supervision of the *rab-sila* to the criminals, of all people, who were given practically all the managerial posts in the camp. The result was that the political prisoner who did not have, or no longer had, shirts with attached collars, was at the complete mercy of the criminal prisoners who had a traditional hatred for the intellectuals, and used to get an intense satisfaction out of humiliating them.

Throughout the world Communists have fought for the special rights of the political prisoner. In the Soviet Union the political-prisoner class has been liquidated, but there is no equality between different classes of prisoners. The political prisoner in the land of Communism has only this special right : to be hungrier than the hungry, more debased than the lowliest.

" Hey, Commandant, somebody's taken my things."

" Who has ? "

" I don't know, my things have disappeared."

" So what do you want of me ? Why don't you look after your things ? "

" I was asleep. I knew nothing."

" So whose fault is it ? You should have looked after them."

" You are the caretaker, it's your job to take care of things."

" I didn't see anything. Let me alone."

This exchange took place between me and the commandant the day after I began work in the correctional labour camp. That morning I did not hear the gong. Shouts of " Get up! *Podiom!* " woke me. I opened my eyes and glanced over to my bundle of clothes which lay at my head. I got the impression that it had shrunk somewhat. I felt it, I opened it. There was no doubt about it: the greater part of my belongings had gone.

The sentry who had escorted me in the ship on the Pechora had warned me that " they " would take everything. But he had been proved wrong. They had not taken everything. Not yet. . . .

We went on hauling iron. We had finished off-loading the sleepers and began to draw the long train-lines out of the ship. This work was harder, but it was collective. There was rhythm in it, and even a certain amount of hilarity.

We made a bridge of rails from the water-line up on to the bank, and connected two steel cables to the lines. At a given signal, six people on either side would grab the cables and move forward towards the trucks. " Together," shouted the overseer. " Together! " we shouted. But with the very first heave traditional Russian curses began to fill the air, with the addition of revolutionary amendments and unheard-of abominations. " Heave," someone would shout. " Why aren't you pulling, parasite ? " " You're not pulling," the other would answer, "you parasite, you viper! " One of the people harnessed to the cable slipped. The others laughed, like they do all over the world. Together we go on heaving ; and the rails are placed on the ground, in spite of the " internal sabotage " . The dumb iron also comes in for a curse.

Among those heaving the rails was the assistant editor of *Pravda*. A bad heart, constant high temperature and rapid pulse are no deterrent—certainly not for the K.R.T.D.—against participating in the construction work. " He who does not work does not eat." Garin tugged at the cable, but almost doubled up under it. The *Urki* would ask him : " How many people did you manage to send to their death before you came here, hey ? There you were strong enough, but not here, hey ? " Garin would say nothing. The *Urki* went on abusing him. Day after day, on Soviet territory, the assistant editor of *Pravda* would hear the word " *zhid* ". Not in Polish, but in Russian.

Every ten days we were given—not a day of rest, but ten night-shifts. Night work enfeebled us even more. During the smoking interval many of the prisoners would fall asleep sitting. If the brigadier or the *pro-rab* could not waken them, the sentry's rifle butt would make them go back to work. During the nights— including the white nights—the *blat* was greater than by day.

One night I began to feel alternately hot and cold. Next day I was sent to the *lek-pom*. Garin was with me. We both took our temperatures under the supervision of the orderly. My temperature was almost 103. " Go to your hut," said the medical assistant. " Today you will be let off work." " Today ? " I asked in amazement. " Only today ? " " What else did you think ? " he replied. " That I'd send you to hospital ? Come tomorrow and we'll take your temperature again."

" And you, what are you doing there with the thermometer ? " The *lek-pom* shouted at Garin. " Are you trying to bluff *me* ? Don't be a crazy ——, you ——! "

Garin removed the thermometer from his armpit.

" It slipped," he said. " I'm not playing any tricks. He can testify," he said, pointing at me, " that I had a temperature all the time in hospital, and came out of there with a temperature."

Garin did not need to use any trickery to make the thermometer register 100. Even a layman, looking at the man's large, overbright eyes, would know that it was a sick man standing before him. But just as there is a " childish " sentence (three years), so there is a " childish " temperature ; what is a few points more or less than 100 ? What sort of temperature is that!

" You go to work," said the *lek-pom* to Garin.

For three days I lay on the lice-infested bunk, burning. For the first time since my arrest, I felt, to my annoyance, that I was beginning to be sorry for myself. No one will even know where I am buried, I thought miserably. On the fourth day I went to the *lek-pom* again. I was feeling better. The thermometer showed that my temperature was just over 98.

" Tonight you'll go to work," said the orderly.

" Tonight ? Why, I had a high temperature for three days! I'm still very weak. Surely you will let me stay in bed another day ? "

" Can't be done. You'll go to work."

I kept on protesting. The *lek-pom* burst out (although without cursing and without invective) : " Do you think I like sending you to work ? I know you are weak, but I have been imprisoned for four years and I still have another four years to go. I don't want to get another eight years because of you. The Camp Superintendent has already remarked that I let off too many people. Do you know what that means ? Tomorrow they can accuse me of sabotage. You won't die, and I don't want to get a new ' date ' because of you."

I went to work. I wondered how often the human body can stand up to such medical treatment. But the *lek-pom* is also a *lagerni* ; one has to understand how he feels.

18

RE-EDUCATION

"LAVATORY"

"HI! 'Lavatory!' Move away!"

The first time I heard this said to one of the men in my group, I was astounded. The *Urki* are always giving people nicknames, mostly according to some external feature. They called me "*Otchki*" because I wore spectacles. Someone else they called "*Spragi*" because of his top-boots. But "Lavatory"! I soon learnt that the name was not accidental.

The owner of this nickname was a young man of twenty, who had been a prisoner for four years already. When he was a boy he went to work at the railway station. At the age of sixteen he was arrested and accused of sabotage.

"Did you confess?" I asked him, when he told me his story.

"How can you *not* confess?" he replied in astonishment.

The period of re-education gave him an illness which made him urinate without being aware of it. They made no attempt to cure him. He had no temperature. And the fact that he no longer needed a lavatory in no way interfered with the construction work.

The poor fellow was shunned. Everyone despised him. It was really difficult to stand next to him. The tatters that passed as trousers, and even the rags that covered his feet instead of boots, were always wet; and a frightful smell emanated from them. The others thought he was dull-witted. I remember the smile with which he accepted all the insults and the buffetings. It really looked like the smile of an imbecile.

I had many talks with him. I used to give him part of the *machorka* which I did not smoke. He told me about himself. He told me long stories of the great famine in his birthplace, the Ukraine, during the collectivisation period. He was not a fool at all. He was simply reconciled to his condition and his fate.

Before my eyes stood a symbol of " re-education " : a man who became a lavatory.

LIVING DECAY

" Have you seen this ? " asked the man who shared my bunk.

He uncovered his legs up to the loins. I took a look and quickly turned my head away. There was not an unaffected spot on them. They were covered with sores from which a yellowish-red matter oozed.

" Aren't they doing anything about curing you ? " I asked.

" This is *tsinga*," he replied. " The *lek-pom* gives me some sort of ointment, but it doesn't help. That's why they don't send me to hospital."

I had seen a man whose body had begun to decay before it was even put into the grave.

HE DID NOT MANAGE TO DIE

In my hut was a Red Army captain, a gay young fellow. He had served in one of the units that constituted the Soviet " base " in Lithuania, before the June Revolution.

"They gave me five years," he told me, " for extending my leave. I really extended my leave, for twenty-four hours. I was with friends. Every evening we went to a different restaurant in Kovno and in Vilna. We were enjoying ourselves. All the restaurants there are so clean and attractive! The waiter serves you politely and pleasantly. Well, we had a bit to drink, of course. . . . I was late in getting back, and I got it! You people, from there, can't understand how much a Soviet man longs for a little private life. *We* can never be alone. Food?—We eat in the ' *stolovka* ' which turns the food out like a factory. There are always hundreds of people in the hall. They sit at long tables, always in a hurry. . . . ' Finished ? Make place for others.' Sleep?—In a large dormitory, always with strangers. Even in one's family life there is no privacy. Most of the apartments are shared by several families. You can't imagine how a Soviet man wants to be alone a little, with himself, or with his family. But how does one get to it ? So, believe me, those days in Kovno and Vilna were the best days of my life. And I would be prepared to make an agreement with the authorities : when I've completed my five years let them allow me to live over again the five months I spent among your people; and for each such month I am prepared to sit another year in jail. Yes, another five years for five months of that kind of life!"

"What happened to your family?" I asked him, in the course of one of our many talks.

"I got married before I went to the front in the war against Finland. I have no children. I don't worry. My wife won't be wasted. She'll marry someone else. Our women don't go to waste."

On another occasion we spoke about the Soviet war against the Finns.

"They told us," the captain said, "that we would draw rings around the Finns, but it turned out to be not so simple. The official communiqués said that it was a war between the military district of Leningrad and the Finnish State, but it had an effect on life in the whole Soviet Union. Because of it, even the bread ration was reduced. The Finns knew how to fight. Those white devils used to appear suddenly on the line, rain fire down on us from all sides and scare our men out of their wits. Many of us were taken prisoner. It was not easy, not at all easy. But I am sure we would eventually have broken the Finns. The Red Army is no laughing matter. We are strong. . . . Do you know what happened to our prisoners? The Finns released them, but *we* arrested them. Not all remained in jail, that is true, but all were interrogated as to why they had fallen into the enemy's hands, how they had fallen into captivity. Many of them got another long term of imprisonment for treason, although whole battalions used to surrender there at the front. I was told about such an investigation by a soldier who served, afterwards, in my company in Lithuania. When he got back from captivity after the agreement with Finland, the soldier was brought before an interrogator and asked to explain how he was taken prisoner.

"'Very simply, Citizen-Judge,' the soldier replied. 'The Finns surrounded us completely and threatened to kill us all. Our Commanding Officer gave the order to surrender. We put up our hands and surrendered!'

"'You gave in like that?' the interrogator shouted. 'You should have died for your country!'

"'I didn't manage to, sir,' the soldier replied."

THE STAKES ARE HEADS

They called him Redbeard. He was in jail for murder. He was head of the *Urki* and was held in genuine high esteem by the criminal prisoners. He had a nose for locating in which boxes the good things were, which were sent to us for off-loading for the " *sastav* ", the N.K.V.D. officers and officials. And when Redbeard " smelt out " a despatch of delicacies, he promptly did what Communism said should be done, in the early days : Take from the few that have much, and give to the many that have little or nothing. The N.K.V.D., however, does not agree with such anti-revolutionary distribution in its day and in its country. But Redbeard knew how to get away with it in spite of the Soviet's laws of distribution. Even the sentries were afraid of him.

One night Redbeard managed to break open a number of cases containing smoked ham. There was great rejoicing in the *Urki* camp. In spite of all the threats and entreaties of the *pro-rab*, the *ʒakurka* turned into a feast around a bonfire. The *Urki* had more pork than bread. How much pork they would have given that night for one loaf of bread ! But they had eaten bread without pork for so long, that they felt no revulsion at the pork without bread. Of course, only the *Urki* enjoyed the booty. There is no hospitality in a labour camp.

When the *Urki* had eaten their fill, Redbeard told them a story about one of the camp superintendents.

" He was a —— sonofabitch," he began. " He stuck his nose into everything. He was a Party man, y'know, very loyal to the Soviet mother-country, y'know. He always used to remind us how grateful we ought to be to the Government. He said we should all have got the death sentence, but our kind Government let us live and even gave us food, and that's why we ought to be grateful. Let me tell you chaps, you couldn't do any *blat* with him. And for every little thing he used to dish out ' solitary ' or have you brought to trial. That cursed dog used to invent new punishments every time. He used to send you to ' solitary ' only in the winter. In the summer he had you stripped naked and turned out into the forest. You can imagine what the mosquitoes and little flies did to you. That's how he used to maltreat us, and we decided that our Russian soil doesn't need to put up with that kind of —— vermin. So what did we do ? We did a very simple thing. We took cards, and agreed that the loser would do the job. Well, one of us lost, of course, and the jolly old superintendent disappeared. He simply vanished. How, or where, doesn't matter. The main thing is—he was gone. They hunted for him high and low. Well, there was an awful row, of course. They threatened to shoot every tenth man, they transferred people to a punishment camp, but the super-intendent was nowhere to be found." (His narrative was very liberally and graphically interspersed with curses and swear-words.)

A number of political prisoners, among them Garin and myself, were warming ourselves by the bonfire, and heard about the game of cards that was played not to win, but to lose ; not for money, but for a man's head.

19

ETAP

" ARE you a Pollak ? " the sentry asked me one day, as he was taking me to work.

" I am a Jew, but a Polish citizen."

" I don't understand. 'Polish citizen' means you're a Pollak! "

" So what of it? " I asked, abandoning the attempt to explain the difference between nationality and citizenship.

" All the Pollaks are being set free."

" Who said so ? " I asked, suddenly getting weak at the knees.

" I say so, and if I say so it means it's true."

" But who told you ? " I persisted.

" He doesn't want to believe, hey ? All right, I'll tell you where I heard it : on the radio. Yes, our radio announced that all the Poles are being amnestied and will come and help us against the Germans. . . . Well, now do you believe me ? The Soviet radio would only say what's true."

The rumour of our impending release spread like wildfire through the camp. We wanted to believe it ; we could not help doubting it. We were afraid to ask the Camp Superintendent. We refrained from showing our joy at the prospect of getting away from the camp. Perhaps it was a trap, we thought. And even if the news were true it was better to be careful. Moscow was far away, the Pechora was near by, and our fate, for the time being, was in the hands of the superintendent of the *Pechor-Lag.* . . . We continued to haul iron. We participated in the " socialistic competition " between our camp and the neighbouring prison-camp, which the instructor, in the presence of the Camp Superintendent, had announced in a stirring, flowery speech. " Demosthenes," we observed to one another, " could have learnt the art of public speaking from our instructor, but from him we had to learn to work like helots."

One day the instructor informed us, not so enthusiastically, that we were required to come to a meeting of Polish citizens, at which the Poles from the neighbouring points would also participate.

" What's up ? What's happened ? " we asked the instructor, who was a prisoner like ourselves. " I have no authority," he said portentously, " to give any information. Some high representatives of the authorities will be at this meeting and they will tell you what it is all about."

Among those who came from the surrounding camps to the meeting there was also a woman. The Camp Superintendent, coming across her, stopped dumbfounded, and said : " Are you also one of the Poles ? "

" Of course I am," the woman replied. " I was born in Poland. I am a Polish national."

" We'll see about that," said the Superintendent. " But it seems to me you don't belong at this meeting."

The woman was a former fellow-student of mine at the university. I did not know her personally, but I had heard about her. She was the daughter of a rich Jewish merchant in Warsaw. An ardent Communist, known for her ability as a speaker and for her beauty. And now I found our *"La Passionara"* on the banks of the Pechora.

Before the meeting began she managed to tell me her story briefly. Yes, she ran away from Warsaw and left Poland. By way of Danzig she succeeded in getting to Russia. Was she happy ? How can anyone ask such a question! Can I know what happiness is ? Only she knows, she knows what true happiness is. She settled in Moscow. She studied and worked. She married a young engineer. No, he wasn't a Jew, but I must know that she has no time for the prejudices that our parents tried to inculcate in us. He, her husband, was a Russian. A wonderful man, very popular, and he made her happy. Life was so lovely, so lovely. Soviet university, Soviet surroundings, Soviet soil, Soviet skies, Soviet everything. How wonderful it was to breathe Soviet air!

What happened ? How did she get here ? Why was she arrested ? Better not to ask. What does it matter ? They arrested her in 1937. She doesn't know what happened to her husband. Perhaps he was arrested, too. That is a terrible thought for her. It means he was arrested because of her. But who knows ? Perhaps he was not arrested. She has had no news of him. No, not since her arrest. Who knows where he is! And would he still like me, Comrade ?...

Is this Naomi? The question hovered on my lips. This is almost an old woman, greying hair, eyes dulled. Is this the lovely girl-student about whom I had heard so much when I was young?

Of course, I did not ask any such questions. I asked how life was in the camp, and what work she did. At first, she said, it was difficult, but now her position was much easier. She was working in the kitchen and managed somehow. . . . But she wanted to get out, now that there was a hope. She was a Polish citizen, she maintained, and everyone was saying that Polish citizens were going to be pardoned.

In the course of the next few days I found out from one of the veteran camp-inmates how she " managed ". . . .

At the meeting of Poles, where I sat next to my unfortunate colleague, the *Pechor-Lag* representative said it was true that a pact had been signed between the Soviet and Polish Governments, and the Russian Government had decided to grant an amnesty to all imprisoned Polish citizens. He himself had read the text of the pact in *Pravda*, but the management of the *Pechor-Lag* had not yet received any instructions concerning the release of Polish citizens. Until such instructions were received they had to go on working shoulder to shoulder with the rest of the prisoners. He had summoned us specially to explain the position to us. He wanted no misunderstandings. He was confident that we would, in the meantime, intensify our efforts at work, for the Soviet Union and Poland were now allies in a war against a common enemy, the German cannibals. " And our work "—the authorised envoy concluded—" is our contribution to victory."

After him, the Superintendent of our camp made a patriotic speech, and after him, our instructor made an even more patriotic one, calling on us to be a shining example to the other prisoners in the socialist competition between the two neighbouring camps.

" Are there any questions? " the Superintendent asked, finally.

The woman got up and asked if the pardon applied to all Polish prisoners, or only those who were arrested after 1939.

" You're not Polish," the Superintendent replied, curtly, " and the whole thing does not concern you."

The poor thing fell silent. No one wanted to ask any questions. The meeting was closed. We had now heard three Demosthenes speak and, despite the amnesty, back we went to work.

A few weeks later a new rumour broke out in the camp. Some

of the prisoners, rumour said, would be transferred by *Etap* to another camp. This rumour evoked dread in the hearts of all the prisoners. The *Urki* gave it expression, as was their wont, in curses. " They are sending us to our death," they lamented. In their despair they began to get impudent, even with the sentry. " Why don't you go to the front ? " they would ask him. " Here you're a hero, hey ? You know how to torture people, but to the front others go, hey ? " The sentry would answer with surprising imperturbability : " Quiet! Keep quiet! " The *Urki* continued to belabour him verbally. I had never seen them so nervous. Even Redbeard lost his sang-froid. The word *Etap* had cast a shadow over the whole camp.

The medical examination which preceded the new mass-deportation was astonishingly brief. What was equally astonishing was the large number of people that were passed as fit, for purposes of *Etap*. Garin was passed as " healthy ". So was " Lavatory " The man who oozed matter from his rotting body was also given a clean bill of health.

Among those examined were the Polish citizens too. One of us asked the Superintendent why we had been put on to the list of Etapists. The officer replied that it did not depend on him. He had received instructions to prepare an *Etap*, and had no instructions to leave Polish citizens behind. If we wished to lodge a complaint, he was prepared to take our delegation to the authority who, as it happened, had just arrived from Moscow. By all means, he said. He would be glad if we went free.

The Polish citizens among us demanded that I go with one of the army officers to the authority. I refused. Safeguarding one's personal and national dignity was one thing : to demean oneself before the N.K.V.D. as spokesman was an altogether different matter. But the Polish prisoners kept on pressing me and insisting that I be the one to bring their contentions before the authorities. " It may be a question of life or death for us," they declared. " Others will go free and we'll die in the new camp." I gave in, and went with the Polish officer to the Competent Authority.

He was seated in a small hut on the hillock from which the orchestral strains of the Labour March had wafted down to us as we worked. Next to him sat a middle-aged woman.

" What's it all about ? " he asked, after the Camp Superintendent had introduced us.

I told him that we Polish citizens were asking that we should not be sent on *Etap*. Our pardon was a fact. In a short while we would be released and would go to fight. What was the logic of sending us north, if we were soon going to travel south in any event?

" And how do you know you are going north ? " he asked.

" I don't know ; that's what they are saying in the camp."

The woman began to talk about the necessity for construction work, and how Soviet construction could be benefited everywhere. She also spoke like Demosthenes. Her companion suddenly cut off her flow of words.

" I have been authorised on behalf of the Party ; don't interfere and don't talk such a lot."

Addressing himself to us, he said :

" The *Etap* is essential. There is not enough productive work for all the prisoners in this camp. But the construction requirements of the Soviet Union are considerable. We need many people in other places. I know about the agreement between the Soviet Union and the Polish Government. Yes, the Soviet Government has granted you a pardon. But I have not yet received any concrete instructions —you understand, *concrete* instructions—to release the Polish citizens. Therefore I have to treat you the same as the rest of the prisoners. You are required for the construction work elsewhere. But don't worry. If the order to release you arrives we'll even take you off the ship and send you where you have to go, according to the instructions of the Soviet Government."

He asked my name, and with my reply the interview came to an end. It was clear that we had to prepare to go on *Etap*.

But my friend Kroll did not give up yet. He had come to the labour camp from the hospital a few weeks after I began to work. He soon became a group-leader. For a while he was at the head of my group. He had " professional connections " with the *pro-rab*, with the quota-clerk, and other office-holders in the camp. Thanks to these contacts, he was not included in the list of candidates for deportation, and he tried to get me out of it too. I still had some shirts with collars, but even these did not help. Some acquaintances of Kroll's told him that the Superintendent had told them that I would certainly go on *Etap*. Kroll reckoned that I had cooked my own goose when I appeared before the " Competent Authority " in the name of the Polish citizens. Perhaps he was right. But it was no use lamenting over something that was already done. I consoled Kroll as best I could. His joy at having succeeded in remaining was overclouded by his distress at my going. But I was sadder at the thought of leaving him than at the actual fact of being sent away.

We could not have known then that Kroll's seeming good fortune was ultimately to prove to be his misfortune, as so often happened. He did not go on *Etap*. He remained in the camp—but he remained forever. Had his aquaintances not favoured him, had he sailed in the *Etap* ship, he might have been alive today. . . . Jolly, kindly Kotka, staunch friend. I still see the sadness in his eyes as he watched me embark on the slave-ship of the *Etap*.

Somewhere in the frozen north, his bones lie buried. My people will remember the name of David Kroll among the rest of its martyrs who died for Zion and for Jerusalem.

They counted us over and over again. Eventually we were constituted into a group of labourers required by the Soviet Construction Plan at another place of work. But the norm in preparing an *Etap* is also just so much theory. After we had already been taken out of the camp, it transpired that the ship in which we were to sail down the Pechora, northwards, was not yet ready to receive its passengers. For three days and three nights we lay on the ground, and all the food we received was a reduced ration of bread —after all, we were not working!—and cold water. We were like outcasts. Our new " home " could not receive us, and our old home no longer wanted us. Winter was setting in. The white nights were over. The damp of the cold, dark night penetrated to the very marrow of our bones, and over our heads the northern dawn would rise, the most breath-taking of the wonders of the universe, and illuminate the hell on earth.

The last night before we set out they took pity on us. They brought us back into the camp and put us into huts which were standing almost empty. We climbed into the bunks, which seemed like the most comfortable of beds to us. The stench was nauseating ; the heat over-powering. Learning from experience, I tied what was left of my clothing bundle to my wrist. Having thus secured the last remnants of my property, I fell asleep.

Morning came. My first waking glance turned instinctively to my bundle—but it was gone! Only the severed string remained on my wrist, a souvenir of the work of the *Urki*. I had nothing left besides what I was wearing. The sentry in the tug-boat knew what he was talking about when he said : "They'll take everything, you'll see! " He knew. It is true that they took it in two instalments : but they took it all. The Soviet guardian of the law knows all about the law of robbery that prevails in the labour camp. They take everything, and there is no protection from it and no escaping it.

The day the *Urki* relieved me of my entire burden we were taken down into the hold of the ship, which lay at anchor with its prow in the direction of the current of the Pechora. We were about eight hundred men, some from our camp, some from the neighbouring camp. The vast majority were *Urki*. Among the politicals were Poles, Lithuanians and Esthonians. Including Garin, we were six Jews in the ship. That was the human composition of the *carcer*[1], in comparison with which the solitary confinement cell at Lukishki was a holiday-resort.

How they packed eight hundred men into the small capacity of the freighter is something that only the N.K.V.D. science of loading can explain. Three tiers of bunks were built along the dank walls of the hold, for the Soviet *rab-sila*. It was impossible to stand, impossible to move, impossible to sit. We had to lie, day and night. But who could tell the difference between day and night in the eternal darkness that prevailed below deck ? Thus we sailed along the Pechora for nearly three weeks. Northwards, to build a new world.

We drank cold river-water. Most of the prisoners went down with *panos*. But the N.K.V.D. engineers had built only two lavatories for the needs of eight hundred people. These lavatories, two boards placed at an angle in the stern of the ship, were on deck. To get to them, we had to climb up a ladder, two at a time, according to our turn. There was a queue day and night. Some prisoners, as they came down, were immediately compelled to join the end of the queue again. The sentry on deck, his finger on the trigger of his bayoneted rifle, kept the queue in order and kept us moving. "*Davai, davai*, quick, hurry! " he would shout. "Others also need to. . . ."

But the worst thing of all was the *Urki* domination in the floating communal dungeon. In the camp, too, the *Urki* had had the upper hand. They had a finger in the norm, in the tasks, in the stores, in

---

[1] Russian for " solitary confinement cell."

the sleeping berths, in everything. But, below deck in the *Etap* ship, the last barrier in the way of *Urki* domination fell away. It was no longer *Urki* autonomy, but *Urki* independence : rule by criminals without restraint, absolute rule.

The sentry stood on deck, his hand on his rifle. His job was to guard the *rab-sila*, to prevent anyone from jumping to a get-away, or jumping to suicide in the greenish waters of the Pechora. He did not venture down below ; he would never go down, he himself was afraid, and rightly too. In the murky depths of the ship it would not be difficult for Redbeard's men to surround the sentry, give him a blow on the head, take away his rifle, and finish him off. It was useless, therefore, complaining to the sentry that you were being beaten or robbed below deck, or that your bread ration was stolen, or that you had been maltreated. He would not intervene. He could not, nor would he want to. He is up top ; the *Urki* are down below. If you complain against them, your troubles increase sevenfold. In the *Etap* ship the rule of Soviet law comes to an end on the second rung of the ladder that leads to the independent realm of the *Urki*.

On *Etap* there is no work and plenty of time. The Etapists while away the time playing games. The main game is the one forbidden by Soviet law but permitted by the higher *Urki* law : cards. The *Urki* play for everything under the sun : for money (they always have money) : for stolen goods (once when I was going on deck I saw my fur-lined gloves on the upturned barrel which served as their card table ; I saw and kept quiet); for shoes (not of *Urki* players, but shoes still on the feet of some unfortunate " intellectual ") ; at times they even staked their bread ration.

But card-playing is not always amusing. Someone loses. Someone claims that he has been cheated. Someone is accused of trying to cheat. Someone gets hit. *Urki* against *Urki*. Gang against gang. Curses, blows, with murder in their eyes. And immediately afterwards, friends again. Embraces, hand-shakes. Greeting curses, friendly curses. The quarrel is forgotten. The feud is over. Preparations begin for a new, concerted robbery.

The *Urki* also had amusing games. The most entertaining of all was playing with lice. In the labour camp we had forgotten about clean shirts and had grown used to a shirt that swarmed with lice. Yes, it is only a question of getting used to it. The saying : " You'll get used to it! " which passes from prisoner to prisoner in the Soviet camps is not a futile one. What is futile is the attempt to cling to the habits of civilisation. If you have no toothbrush—(the *Urki* have stolen it, not for their personal use, of course, but for their card-game)—you will get used to not cleaning your teeth. If there is no soap, not even any water, you will get used to that, and you will eat with hands that grow grimier every day. And if you find lice on your body you will feel revulsion only at the first one, in it you will see the symbol of your downfall. Only the first louse will shake you out of your apathy, and move you to ask fearfully : " To what have I been brought ? " As their numbers increase, as they go from bunk to bunk and multiply from day to day, they will no longer bring you gloomy thoughts. You will fight them ; they will win. You will get used to them. They will get used to you. You will live with them ; and you will want to live, even with them.

But even a man who has lice, who has grown accustomed to the sub-tenants of his shirt and the eaters of his flesh, will be thoroughly revolted at someone else's lice, " foreign " lice. Is this revulsion irrational ? Perhaps. Perhaps the whole thing is beyond the grasp of rational man. It is not beyond the grasp of the *Urki*. They made fun of our revulsion. They used to collect their lice, sometimes in handfuls, and put them through the gaps between the boards on to our bodies, heads and faces. " Did you receive the presents ? " they would shout from above, and bellow with uproarious laughter, hellish laughter. An even lustier laugh would echo in the thick air of the hold, when the *Urki* succeeded in putting their gifts under the shirts of the detested intellectuals as they passed them on their way up to the deck. " Ha, ha, ha! Let the poor things get warm in the bosom of the intellectuals, let them warm up a bit." . . .

In this atmosphere of stench and darkness, of suffering and mal-treatment, of threats and horror, the crisis of the assistant editor of *Pravda*, who had fallen from the ruling heights to the realm of the *Urki* in the hold of a ship of hungry, sick, humiliated, wretched slaves, reached its climax. Garin was still suffering from the nights of interrogation in Tomsk, from the blows of the expert at breaking stubborn cases, from his attempts on his own life. His suffering was increased by his expulsion from hospital, in spite of his temperature, in spite of his defective heart. And he suffered still more, every time he heard the word " *zhid* " spoken under the Soviet sky, openly, insolently, with mocking scorn and hatred ; unpunished, and without fear of punishment. This tortured man, the entire world of his dreams and his strivings crushed beneath the blows of reality, was no longer able to stand up to a new test, the test of *Etap*.

One day, Garin, who was lying some distance away from the Jewish prisoners, asked if he might lie next to me. My neighbour moved up a bit. We made room for him. Garin lay down beside me.

" They want to kill me," he suddenly whispered in my ear.

" Who want to kill you ? What are you talking about ? " I asked in amazement.

" They want to kill me. I am lost. The *Urki* want to kill me. You don't know what happened. I'll tell you. Yesterday I went up on deck to the lavatory. At the entrance the *Urki* got hold of me. I think they were of Redbeard's gang. They dragged me into a corner and demanded that I give them my money. I said I had no money, and they searched me. They found nothing. They hit me and kicked me. They said they know I've got money, and that I've hidden it. If I did not bring them all the money next time, they would kill me. I actually had three hundred roubles. I had it still from Tomsk ; I told you, remember ? I lay all day, I didn't go out. But in the evening I simply had to go. I couldn't contain myself any longer. I was afraid to pass the entrance. I knew they were lying in wait for me. I had no alternative. I took with me the little bag with money. I fastened it round my neck, as usual. I thought maybe they would not start with me again. But if they did, it was better that I should have the money with me. I can't stand being hit. I didn't want them to kill me. They were waiting for me. ' Did you bring it ? ' they asked. I opened the little bag and took out the money and handed it to them. They pulled at the bag with all their might, the cord broke on my neck. It hurt. They searched inside the bag. It was empty. I didn't even leave one rouble for myself. ' Is that all ? ' they asked. ' Haven't you got any more ? ' I told them I hadn't. and that they could search my bunk if they didn't believe me. They laughed and let me go on deck. I could hardly get there.

" When I came down," Garin continued in a feverish whisper, " I found them playing cards. One of them shouted at me : ' You told the *strilok*, hey ? Communist parasite, vermin ! You informed on us, hey ? How many people have you sent to their deaths in your time ? Do you think you'll make trouble for people here too ? We'll still fix you. . . .' Complete with all the usual curses, you know . . . I told them I hadn't said a word to the *strilok*, I swore I hadn't. But they didn't believe me. ' You informed,' they said, ' and we'll still show you.' Then they let me go and went on playing. I am certain, Menachem Wolfovitch, that they were playing for my head. Do you remember Redbeard's story? They were playing for my head, I'm certain of it. I am lost. They will kill me."

I tried to calm him down.

" Don't talk nonsense," I chided him. " They weren't playing for your head, they were playing for your money. They only wanted to frighten you. They wanted to warn you not to tell the *strilok*. Don't be afraid, they won't do you any harm."

" No, no," Garin whispered, " they were playing for my head. I know them better than you do. They'll kill me! "

" Do you know what? " I tried again. " I'll have a talk with Redbeard. You know I spoke to him about my stolen belongings and he said he would look into the matter. Actually, I am sure he himself has part of my things, but all the same his attitude towards me is not bad. He told me several times that ' the boys ' told him I helped them, and particularly ' Lavatory '. Do you remember how he defended me from the foreign *Urki*? I promise to speak to him and explain that you haven't told the sentry anything at all."

" No, that won't be good," Garin replied. " Better not to speak to him. If you speak to him he will say that I am telling everyone about the money, and if so I must have told the sentry too. No, don't talk to him. It won't help. It will only make matters worse.

" Look! " Garin screamed suddenly, grabbing my arm and clinging to me like a frightened child. " Look, he's coming with a knife."

I looked. From the top tier of bunks one of the *Urki* got down slowly. His body cast a shadow in the semi-darkness of the hold. He held something in his hand. From far, in the dark, it was hard to make out what it was. It could have been a knife.

The *Urki* passed close to us. He did not even glance at Garin. In his hand he held a spoon. But in the meantime Garin went through abysmal agony. I did everything I could to calm him. I used his mistake as proof that he was wrong, to try to dispel his terror. I changed the subject. We talked about literature. From then on he never left me. He brought his meagre bundle over to where I lay, and lay beside me day and night. He used to try and go up on deck at the same time as I did, or he would ask me to go with him when he had to go. The *Urki* did not do anything to him, but they continued to pester him with their mockery, curses and threats. He was convinced that his doom was sealed.

One day—it might have been night—Garin's voice aroused me from the semi-sleeping state that we were in perpetually, because of the dark, hunger, weakness, and the stench.

" Menachem! Menachem! " he called in a whisper.

It was the first time he had addressed me intimately, without adding my patronymic. " Do you remember the song ' *Loshuv* ' ? " He spoke to me in Yiddish for the first time.

" What song ? " I asked, also in Yiddish.

He had said " *Lo-shuv* ", and at first I did not understand him, perhaps because of his pronunciation, or perhaps because I was still half asleep.

" How is it that you don't know ? " he asked rather crossly. " It's the song the Zionists sing, it's the song the Zionists used to sing in Odessa when I was still a boy. *Lo-shuv, Lo-shuv*—don't you know that song ? "

" Ah! You mean Hatikvah," I said, using his pronunciation.

" Perhaps it is Hatikvah. What I remember is the word *Lo-shuv*."

" Yes, it is Hatikvah. You mean the song ' *Lashuv Le'Eretz Avotenu* ' (the song of hope to return to the land of our fathers). Of course I remember it."

" Well, then," said Garin, " sing it to me. You see, Menachem, I won't get out of here alive. Feel this . . ." He took my hand and placed it on his breast. His heart fluttered rapidly against my hand.

" You see," he went on, " I am a lost man. The *Urki* were playing cards for my head, they'll kill me. I am certain of it. But even if you were right, even if it is true that they were only trying to frighten me, how much longer can I live with a heart like this ? I won't get out of here alive. You are healthy. You are with other Jews. They've given you an amnesty. Perhaps you'll get out. Perhaps you will one day come across my children. Who knows ? Tell them about their father, tell them everything. Tell them I always used to think of them. But now I want you please to sing me *Loshuv*, sing me *Loshuv*."

Together with Marmelstein I began to sing Hatikvah. Three other Jews, lying near us, joined in. We sang with the Ashkenazic pronunciation, the version in use in the lands of the dispersion. Garin listened in silence to the words : " To return to the land, the land of our fathers . . ."

The *Urki* woke up.

" What are the Jews singing there ? "

" They're praying, they're praying to their God to help them."
Unruly laughter from the *Urki*.

We went on singing : " Hearken my brothers in the lands of my
wanderings ... To return to the Land, the Land of our Fathers ..."
The *Urki* were right. It was a prayer, not a song.

I felt as if I were saying the confessional prayer with a Jew who,
like a kidnapped child, has pastured in strange fields and, on the
threshold of death, after many tribulations, returns to his people and
his faith. Life does, indeed, create situations more fantastic than any
in fiction. We are lying here, in the Valley of the Shadow of Death,
among *Urki*, half-men, half-beasts. And with us lies Garin, former
assistant editor of *Pravda*, a Communist from his earliest youth,
estranged from his people, enemy of Zion, persecutor of Zionists.
When last did he hear the strains of Hatikvah in Odessa ? When
last did he scoff at the *Lo-shuv* ? What did he not do to destroy the
" hope to return " ? What did he not do, what was he not ready to
do, so that the other " hope " should be attained ! Almost twenty-
five years had passed since his life's dream had become a reality,
since the triumph of the Revolution, for which he suffered, for
which he was ready to give his life, for which he toiled and fought.
Twenty-five years. . . . And here was the reward of the Revolution
to one who had been loyal to it, to one of its fighters, its leaders :
traitor—enemy of humanity—spy—prison in Tomsk—expulsion
from hospital—" *ʒhid* "—hauling iron—" *ʒhid* "—*Etap*—" *ʒhid* "
—kicks—robbers—*Urki* threats—entreaties to the robbers—card
games—lice games—parasite—vermin—sick heart—fear—" *ʒhid* "!
And when the time comes, after infinite trials and tribulations, what
does the assistant editor of *Pravda*, General Secretary of the
Ukrainian Communist Party, remind himself of ? He reminds himself of *Loshuv*. " To return to the land of our fathers," that is his
consolation.

And, perhaps for the first time since it began to flow northwards,
the Pechora heard the prayer of confession and thanksgiving :
" And out of the depths we cried unto the Lord : Lashuv Le'Eretz
Avotenu."

Our ship had been lying in harbour for several days. Around us
other ships were anchored. A slave fleet. We had come a long way,

and still had a long way to go, always northwards. The port workers, prisoners like ourselves, were preparing the ship for the resumption of her voyage.

One day, the sentry shouted down into the hold : " Be—gin! " The *Urki* who stood beside the entrance took up the shout : " Be—gin! "

" Here I am," I shouted back.

" Name and father's name ? "

" Menachem Wolfovitch."

" Correct! Danavsky! " The *strilok* went on calling name after name, in alphabetical order. When he had finished he said : " All those whose names I have called, collect your belongings. An order has come to release the Poles. You are going free."

I said goodbye to Garin and dashed for the entrance. I had no belongings. As I went, I tried to put my arm into the sleeve of my jacket. One of the foreign *Urki* seized me by the sleeve as if he wanted to rid me of my coat, too, or as if he wanted to hold me back. I jerked away from him and began to climb up the ladder.

" But he's a ' *ʒhid* ', not a Pollak! " one of the *Urki* shouted. I could not explain to him, either, the difference between nationality and citizenship. But I could appreciate how he felt. There is no envy like the envy of a prisoner who sees the next man go free. I went on to the deck. In no time, Marmelstein and the rest of the Jews stood beside me. A number of Poles were crowded together with us. The group of prisoners to be released was not big.

A boat drew up from the shore.

" Ready ? " shouted one of the men in it. " Are the Poles ready ? "

" Ready, ready! " the sentry shouted back, and we shouted with him.

We were taken off the ship just as the " competent authority " in the *Pechor-Lag* had said. We went down into the boat which carried us to the shore, to a transit camp. From there we would travel south.

I was travelling light, without any luggage.

I felt very light. I could hear the whirring of the wings of freedom.

20

THE END AND THE MEANS

BEFORE I tell the story of how I left Russia, I shall summarise what I learnt, from my own experience and from the experience of others, about the correctional labour camps—the Soviet concentration camps.

Soviet political writers give particular praise to two features of these camps. " In Russia," they write, " the prisoner does not rot in idleness like in the capitalistic countries. Here the prisoner works and builds, and it is this construction work that reforms his character. Secondly," the Soviet propagandists maintain, " prisoners are given ' internal autonomy ' in the Soviet Union. They arrange their affairs among themselves. The authorities only supervise the process of their education towards lives of honest labour." But it is impossible to get the Soviet writers to reveal to the world what the conditions of labour are in the correctional camps, what sort of climate the prisoners work in, what sort of housing, food and clothing they are given. Nor do the N.K.V.D. spokesmen tell that the autonomy which exists in the TIL[1] actually means *Urki* autonomy ; the turning loose of criminal prisoners of the worst type in the world, constantly maltreating one another, perpetually maltreating the victims common to the N.K.V.D. and themselves—the political prisoners. The authors of the descriptions of " work and autonomy " in the Soviet camps should be consigned to the place to which we, when we reached the Pechora, wanted to consign the Lukishki barbers.

Political writers outside of the Soviet Union have suggested that there is no difference between the correctional labour camps and the Nazi concentration and extermination camps. This comparison arises out of a natural tendency to simplify, but it is not true. For the sake of truth, one must distinguish between the Nazi

---

[1] Correctional Labour Camp—abbreviation.

concentration camps which existed up to 1939 and the death-camps they set up during the Second World War.

The concentration camps in Germany, Austria, Bohemia, Moravia and Slovakia until the outbreak of the Second World War were more comfortable than the Soviet labour camps. That is what I heard from a Jewish doctor whom I met on the banks of the Pechora after he had been in Dachau for several years. This doctor had been released from the notorious German concentration camp and decided to leave Nazi Germany at all costs. After the outbreak of war and the collapse and subsequent partition of Poland the doctor crossed the demarcation line between the German and Soviet areas of occupation and arrived in the Soviet Union as a persecuted person seeking sanctuary. But, like thousands of other persecuted Jews who stole across the frontier, he was arrested on the other side, told to own up and confess what job the German Secret Service had sent him to do, and sentenced to five years' imprisonment as a suspected spy. Thus the fates—or the N.K.V.D.—brought us both to the same correctional labour camp. And this is what the Jewish doctor told me :

᾿" I was in Dachau. We worked at road-making. The work was hard, but we worked eight hours a day. Yes, sometimes the Nazi overseer used to slap my face and say : ' Jewish swine.' That was terrible. But don't the *Urki* say ' lousy Jew ' to me here, almost every day ? Don't they kick me ? Do you think there is much difference if the jailer hits and abuses me, or if the criminal prisoners do it ? There I had a clean bed. I had soap to wash with, a toothbrush, clean underwear, warm clothes for the winter. All the time I was confined I had contact with my family. I was sent letters and parcels. I was not hungry. I do not have to tell you how much I hate the accursed Nazis. But when I lie here in the muck and the stink, when I scratch my body, when I long for an extra piece of bread, a terrible thought sometimes comes into my head. I admit it is a terrible thought, but I will not conceal it from you. At times I think that if I had to choose between *Pechor-Lag* and the Dachau concentration camp, I would choose Dachau."

It was indeed a terrible thought ; but his admission is no less damning—for the Soviet Union.

But in the 'thirties the Germans showed only the tips of their claws. In the 'forties they dug their teeth and their talons into the body of the Jewish people. With German thoroughness they erected the gas-chambers and the crematoria. They put into them millions of men and women, among them a million and a half little children. The factory of Topf & Sons, of the town of Erfurt, had pleasure in announcing to the German Press and to its government that it had invented an important technical device for putting the bodies into the furnaces automatically. Another German factory produced a machine for grinding human bones to flour and estimated, with German exactitude, that it could grind four cubic metres of human bones per hour. From Jewish bones the Germans made flour ; from Jewish bodies they made soap and sent it as gifts to their wives ; with the hair of the heads of Jewish mothers and daughters they stuffed their armchairs. In this way six million Jews died. Such scientific extermination has never before been seen, not since man first came into the world ; atrocities like these have no counterpart, from Caligula to Tamerlane and Genghis-Khan, to Torquemada and Dzherzhinsky. For the sake of the truth, and the memory of our six million dead, the German extermination camps must not be compared to any other kind of concentration camp, including the Soviet Labour Camps.

The German extermination camps and the Russian labour camps were, the one as much as the other, works of the devil. But even the devil's works are various. The difference between the German death camps and the Soviet concentration camps lies in one small word, and a whole world of difference lies in it : *hope*. The German exterminators gave their victims no prospect of living ; the prisoners in the Soviet labour camps have such a chance. In most cases it is a very slight chance, but even a slight prospect is still a chance.

Of all the hunting stories that my cell-mate, the officer, told me in the little cell in Lukishki, the one about the " law of chance " which applies to all hunters impressed me most. The hunter will walk miles through jungle ; he will sink up to his knees and his chest in mud ; he will get drenched to the skin in the pouring rain ; he will shiver with cold—there are people who like this kind of sport—until he gets to the place where the fowl of the sky gather— his prey. Then the hunter will take aim. He will keep on aiming, but he will not yet press the trigger. He has come a long, tiring way ; his prize is before him ; if he does not shoot he may not have another opportunity of getting it. But the hunter waits, he does not shoot. Because the bird is stationary—on the ground, on the waters of the lake, on the branch of a tree. Only when the bird is on the wing, when it has its " chance ", will the hunter press the trigger and fire. If he hits his prey—he gets it ; if he misses—he will return empty-handed and the bird goes free. That is the law of the hunt.

Let it not be said that even if there is a difference between man-hunters who put their victims to death immediately, while " stationary ", and hunters who give their victims some chance of being saved, there is no difference from the point of view of the victims themselves, once the cruel hunter has caught up with them. Nor let it be said that those who are killed at once are better off. Himmler's camps were camps of immediate, or one-time, extermination ; Beria's camps are, on the whole, slow-death camps. It might seem that death after brief torture is preferable to death after years of torture. But that is not the case. The chance of being saved is the thing that counts. If the six million Jews in Europe had all been sent to the forests of Archangel, or the coal mines of Varkuta, or the gold mines of Kolima, or the copper mines in the Urals, perhaps a quarter, or a third, or even half of them would not have come back again. But even in that event, our people would have numbered today not eleven million, but fourteen million, or fifteen or sixteen million. The luckless Jewish doctor who had fallen out of the hands of one tyrant into the hands of another, was prepared— so, at least, he said—to exchange the *Pechor-Lag* for Dachau ; he certainly would not have been prepared to exchange Varkuta for Auschwitz.

Does the difference between the German and Russian camps lie in the fact that the N.K.V.D. officers are less cruel and more humane than the S.S. officers were ? One cannot assume such a thing. The former and the latter, alike, struck out of their dictionary the word " mercy ", or put before it the word " without ". Pick up the *Angriff* and you will find in almost every issue, sometimes several times, the expression " *rücksichtlos* ". Pick up *Pravda* and you will find, time and time again, the expression " *bez-poshchadno* ". Both are one and the same word. It means " without mercy ".

It is not by chance that the rulers of both Germany and Russia, upholders of the slogan " without mercy ", tried to put an end to the belief in God after they had eradicated it from their own hearts. Every religious faith preaches mercy, although not all of them act in accordance with what they preach. The Jesuits spoke about mercy and created the Inquisition. But the mere fact of preaching mercy restrains the beast that is in man, and limits, if it does not prevent, acts of cruelty. However, when there is no preaching of mercy, no belief in the God of mercy, and the cry " without mercy " is heard day and night, the result is man-hunt with or without a chance ; camps of one-time extermination, or slow-death camps.

The difference between them is decided not by the word " mercy ", but by the abbreviation *rab-sila*. The correctional labour camps furnish man-power.

The hordes of prisoners in the Soviet Union have built the greatest of its enterprises in its most isolated areas. The Kotlas-Varkuta railway was completed (without me) in about 1945. Its importance lies in the fact that at Varkuta the frozen ground has enormous coal resources, greater, it is estimated, than those in the Don Basin. They were not discovered by the Soviets ; the Czarist Government already knew about them and had even begun to exploit them. In the days of the Czar the Varkuta coal used to be transported by ship to Archangel and from there by train to the heart of Russia. But the coastal waters of the Barends Sea freeze over nine months of the year ; the transportation of the coal was therefore possible only in the few days of summer. Most days of the year the coal deposits in the north were hidden under the snow. With the construction of the northern railway-line, the despatch of coal to all parts of Russia, especially the northern parts, was assured for every day of the year. In that area oil was also discovered. I do not know if the oil there was more plentiful than in the Caucasus, but oil there certainly was. When I travelled through that area in the unsteady train, going southwards, I saw oil-derricks midway, approximately, between Koshva and Kotlas, around Uchta.

Twenty or thirty years ago the whole area was a white desert in the winter and a slushy tundra in the summer. There were " natives " living there. They were very few in number and were called *Zarianye*, or People of the Dawn, a name no doubt derived from the Aurora Borealis. They dressed in furs from top to toe. Only their eyes peeped out from their clothing. They lived like Eskimos.

Today the railway-line traverses the entire area, a distance of nearly two thousand kilometres. From the south, the train brings people, machinery, building materials ; from the north it brings coal and oil, and perhaps other riches. The area is no longer desolate ; it is " populated ". From where I left the *Etap* ship in the north, to Koshva in the south, I saw on both sides of the river watch-towers that announce the existence of a correctional labour camp. Among the camps I saw, as I travelled southwards, there were some without any signs of life. They had been abandoned. The work was completed. The people who had remained alive there had been transferred to other construction zones. But in most of the camps signs of a life familiar to me were discernible. On that journey, by river and by train, I counted hundreds of labour camps. In my " point " there were almost a thousand people. It was only a medium-sized camp, by no means one of the large ones. It was not difficult to calculate how many people there were in the camps I passed on my way. There is hardly any part of Russia where the Soviet watch-towers are not in evidence. What I passed through was only one construction zone.

The construction zone falls under the N.K.V.D. from the administration point of view, from the point of view of supplies and planning, even from the accounting point of view. The Soviet secret police force is the sole proprietor of the mighty construction works and their output. There are no employers in the Soviet Union ; there is *an* employer : the Government. But the sole employer " leases " the vast construction works to a sub-contractor, a single sub-contractor : the N.K.V.D. The N.K.V.D. is one of the biggest contractors in the world, perhaps the biggest. It employs cheap labour, perhaps the cheapest in the world.

The construction tasks get bigger and bigger, and with them the available labour has to increase. If there isn't any, it has to be created. It must be brought up to the required strength. And so it can happen—as happened, I was told, in Tashkent—that people will suddenly be arrested in their hundreds for . . . not buying a ticket in the tram! A tram journey in Tashkent costs, or used to cost, a few kopeks. This sum is not considered money in the Soviet Union. But it sometimes happens that a passenger does not manage to pay. There are occasionally people who do not like to pay, even kopeks. But usually people do pay. Usually no notice is taken of an occasional omission to pay. But, at certain times, the " crooks " in the tram are suddenly arrested and sent, usually for a year, to correctional labour camps. It sometimes happens that they come out after a year. Sometimes their sentence is extended. In the meantime, they construct. Garin once said to me : " In Russia we are short of everything." There is one notable exception to this rule. There is never a shortage of man-power.

The head of the cattle-supply department in Leningrad told a friend what he had heard with his own ears. He had been arrested for squandering public funds, according to the notorious special ukase of the Praesidium of the Supreme Council. He was accused of having agreed to too high prices, and receiving inferior heads of cattle for his money. An N.K.V.D. officer who had once been his friend interrogated him. The investigation took place in a room next to that of the interrogator's superior officer. During a short break the interrogator went into the other room and left the door open by accident when he returned. From the room came the angry voice of the high N.K.V.D. officer. He was speaking on the telephone. He was asking what the results of some investigation were. The man he was speaking to replied, apparently, that he was gathering material. The officer thundered : " I don't need material. I ⁻eed *men*. Give me men! " And they gave them men. The interrogators see to that. They are responsible for seeing to that.

But if the N.K.V.D. contractor needs so many people, why does he waste them the way he does ? Why does he not create labour conditions for his workers that will not kill them, but enable them to live so that they can work ? The reply to that is twofold. Labour has to be as cheap as possible. That is a law of economy. Secondly, one must not forget that there is in the N.K.V.D. not only a " law of construction ", but also a " law of revenge ". The *rab-sila* are enemies of the people. The *rab-sila* have to work ; enemies of the people have to die. There will never be a shortage of enemies of the people. There will never be a shortage of *rab-sila*. The contradiction between the two laws is reconciled with the aid of the cry " without mercy! "

There are people who say that the source of this cry, and of the activities of the Kremlin, lies in the saying : " The end justifies the means." I think this is a mistake.

Actually, it is true that many a tyrant used this maxim, which is attributed to the Jesuits, to justify his crafty deeds, his trickery and his cruelty. But it is also an historical fact that this very precept lighted the way for fighters for justice and freedom. The Hasmonaeans, and the men who stormed the Bastille, Bar-Kochba and Spartacus, Washington and Garibaldi rose against tyranny in the belief that their ultimate aim justified the resort to weapons, armed revolt, bloodshed. The one truth cannot obscure the other. Whether in the sphere of ideas or in the sphere of action, both are bound up with man's fate. Iron brought humanity progress; but it brought terrible catastrophes. It enriched life and increased death. The same applies to the iron maxim : the end justifies the means.

If we say that, to the rulers of the Kremlin, this adage seems naïve, romantic, petty-bourgeois ; if we say that in their eyes the end justifies *all* the means, an important step forward has been made towards understanding the philosophy that guides their actions, but we will still not have got to the bottom of it. The Kremlin philosophy, in its complete form, is : Every end justifies all the means.

The proclaimed " end " of the Communists is to build a class-free society and set up—a non-existent State. This end, in their opinion, naturally justifies all the means that are likely to bring it about, *all* the means. But on the long journey towards setting up the " non-existent State ", the means—which begin by appearing to be the means of attainment—become ends in themselves. And again : every end-in-itself justifies all the means.

Collectivisation was considered one of the means of achieving Communism. But if collectivisation becomes the end, then all means are permissible in order to carry it out. Lenin promised land to the peasants in order to form the " Brotherhood of Workers and Peasants ". It was not original. Lenin copied his agricultural programme, as he himself admitted, almost word for word from the programme of the rivals of Bolshevism, the Socialist Revolutionaries. The latter did not promise the Russian peasants collective farms, but private ownership over tracts of land after the estates had been broken up. But when they launched collectivisation, it was permissible to throw to the winds the programme which had become not just Lenin's programme but a law of the Revolution. Similarly it was permissible not to have any regard for suffering, whether of the land-labourers or the factory-workers. Millions of land-labourers are taken away to correctional labour camps as enemies of the people ; and millions of workers are starving, even in the Ukraine. For the soil has been abandoned, its tillers have been uprooted. If the Party and the Government decide that the order of the hour, or the intermediate aim, is to turn farmers into farm-labourers, that is an end that justifies all means, even the destruction of millions of people.

If the intermediate aim is to bring about a clash between " B " and " L " so that " M " should be able to " restore order in Europe ", that is an end that justifies a Blood Covenant with Nazi Germany to safeguard her rear in the east while she attacks France.

And even if the aim is as limited—from the point of view of the ultimate aim—as building railway-lines in the north, this aim too justifies all the means : " The railway will be constructed if a human being has to lie under every metre of the line."

It was from this philosophy that the investigation systems of the N.K.V.D. evolved. This philosophy produced the N.K.V.D. " economy ", the labour and slow-death camps.

And the generation that has seen the watch-towers of the Soviet labour-camp, and witnessed the repudiation of God, and heard the cry " without mercy " ; the generation that has seen Bolshevism and Fascism, Nazism and Stalinism ; the generation that has witnessed two climaxes—the climax of cruelty in tyranny, and the climax of self-sacrifice and heroism of those who love freedom—must draw these conclusions :

The end justifies the means ?—If you are faced with tyranny, do not hesitate to say : Yes!

Every end justifies the means ?—No!

The end justifies all the means ?—No!

Every end justifies all the means ?—No, never!

21

WANDERER AND SOLDIER

AFTER leaving the concentration camp and the Northern Zone, I wandered through Russia for several months. I traversed the whole vast area from the Barends Sea to the shores of the Caspian. I passed through large cities and small towns, and out-of-the-way villages. I slept in railway stations, in parks, in yards next to dirty hovels. Hunger and homelessness were the lot of wanderers like myself. We covered hundreds of kilometres, standing on the steps of railway coaches, clinging to the door handle or to each other. We had no money for train tickets. More than once we were pushed off the moving train by the conductors, who reminded me of the stories of the early days of the railways in America. I was heading south. I was looking for my sister and her husband who had been deported before I was arrested in Vilna. I was looking for the Polish Army which was about to be formed on Russian soil, as provided for by the Soviet-Polish Agreement.

It is difficult to know how to set about finding two people on an immense continent, among millions of released internees, streaming from the north and from the east, and among millions of war-refugees, fleeing from the west. But chance came to my aid.

At one of the squalid railway stations of Central Asia, I was lying with a group of wanderers and waiting for an opportunity of getting into a train without a ticket. It was night. I dozed off. As I dozed I could hear a woman telling about the copper-mines in the area of the Ural Mountains. I had heard many similar stories and scarcely paid any attention to what she was saying. Suddenly I heard her say the name "Halperin". Without even having seen her face I promptly said:

"Pardon me, Madam. This Halperin that you were talking about, is he by any chance a lawyer?"

"Yes."

"From Warsaw, perhaps?"

"Yes."

" He was at the deportation-point with his wife ? "

" Yes."

" Was her name Rachel ? "

" Yes, that's right! Do you know them ? "

With this woman's assistance I eventually found my family. At that time I did not know that they were the only survivors of my father's house.

In a wretched mud-hut in a little Uzbeki town, at Dzhizak, between Tashkent and Samarkand, I settled down together with my sister's family and a friend of theirs from the time of the deportation. Her name was Leah Vitkovska.

Vitkovska, a kind-hearted woman, was an active worker in the Bund. A few years after leaving Russia she appeared before one of the Committees of the United Nations Organisation and gave evidence on the labour conditions in the Soviet copper mines. She told the international committee what she told me in Dzhizak, by the light of a smoky, unprotected wick dipped in kerosene. She told of the perpetual danger to the life and health of the miners who descend deep into the bowels of the earth by means of ladders lashed together. The rungs are too far apart. The miners have to grope in the dark to find, in the yawning abyss, the step beneath their feet. Sometimes the rung of a ladder breaks because it is rotten, or because of the weight of the person descending, and the man is left suspended in the air by his hands. The result is disablement or death—not only for the one who has fallen but for others, too, if warning is not given in time. She told them that the miners worked twelve hours a day. She spoke of the meagre food they received, while N.K.V.D. officials were given everything of the best.

When she finished, one of the representatives of the international organisation got up and said : " We know that this woman is a professional spy."

Through Leah Vitkovska and her friends, I learnt of the re-arrest of Alter and Ehrlich, the two well-known Bundist leaders. These two leaders of a party against which Vladimir Ilyitch Lenin had already fought with all his characteristic fire were arrested by the N.K.V.D. when Poland fell and were given the usual sentence: eight years in a correctional labour camp. They benefited by the amnesty granted to Polish citizens, came to Kuibishev and came into contact with the Polish Legation and members of the Soviet Government. One day they were invited to come and see the head of the N.K.V.D., Beria.

They never returned from this "friendly" meeting. The other active Bundists wrote to Vitkovska that "Victor and his friend have been taken seriously ill". A few months later it was made known to the world, through an official communiqué, that the two Bundist leaders had been executed for having "helped the German armies".

If I say that Alter and Erlich fell victims to the Japanese attack on Pearl Harbour I shall no doubt be accused of indulging in paradoxes. But I am convinced that it is the truth, and not at all paradoxical. More than once the fate of individuals has been decided by distant international events, without their even being aware of it.

The Soviet Union needed Alter and Ehrlich as long as the United States did not join the world conflict as a belligerent. Although the German columns were halted at the gates of Leningrad and Moscow in the winter of 1941, the plight of the Soviet Union continued to be very grave. It was so grave that Stalin found it necessary, on the anniversary of the Revolution, to console his people with a statement which would have sounded very strange coming from a realist were it not for the necessity of raising their morale. "The war," said Stalin, speaking in the Red Square on November 7th, 1941, "will continue for another six months, or perhaps a year." Russia, in her serious situation, looked to the Western powers for assistance, particularly the United States. But while aid from Britain began to arrive shortly after the outbreak of the war between Russia and Germany, aid from America was tardy in coming. At any rate, it was not forthcoming to the extent required to meet the demands of the Soviet Union. In her desire to increase the measure of American assistance without delay, the Soviet Government sought ways of influencing American public opinion. For that purpose, Russia formed the Anti-Fascist Jewish Committee, which called Jews the world over "brothers". For that purpose, Beria was prepared to send Alter and Ehrlich to America, together with a delegation of the Anti-Fascist Committee.

But on December 7th, 1941, the Mikado's bombers sent the American Pacific Fleet to the bottom of the ocean. America came in as a belligerent against both Japan and Germany. An increasing stream of American equipment was now assured to Russia, who was halting the columns of the German foe and preventing them from linking up with the Japanese enemy columns. So Alter and Ehrlich were no longer needed to mobilise American public opinion. For that, Soviet anti-Fascists like Michaelis and Pfeffer now sufficed. Alter and Ehrlich had been opposed to Bolshevism from the earliest days, so the law of revenge applied to them. In addition to this, they were Polish patriots and insisted that Poland's right to the areas East of the River Bug, or Curzon Line, should be recognised. People who are needed are allowed to live in Russia even if they are " dangerous " ; but for dangerous people who are no longer needed there is but one law in the realm of the N.K.V.D. : they must disappear. When America entered the war Alter and Ehrlich were doomed men, condemned to die as German spies, of all things!

The news of the re-arrest of the Bundist leaders, which was carried out verily under the nose of the Polish Ambassador, influenced me to make another attempt to join the Polish Army. I had tried to do so before I discovered my sister's whereabouts, but without success. Although I, in my wanderings, was looking for the Polish Army, it soon became manifestly clear to me that the Polish Army was not looking for me. " Jews are not wanted," said the Poles. And a rumour was bruited from city to city, from mouth to mouth, to the effect that Stalin himself had told General Sikorski and General Anders (Commander-in-Chief of the Polish Army in Russia) that although the Jews were good engineers and doctors, and were good at administrative army jobs, they did not know how to fight. We refused to believe this rumour. We thought the Poles were spreading it to justify their own discrimination against the Jewish citizens of Poland.

Many years later I learnt that the rumour was essentially true. But I also learnt how strong anti-Jewish solidarity can be. It can put people like Stalin and Molotov, Sikorski and General Anders, on one and the same side.

In his memoirs General Anders reproduces in full Stalin's talks with the Polish representatives. Among others the author reports the following conversation :

ANDERS: I reckon I shall have at my disposal one hundred and fifty thousand men, but there are among them many Jews, who do not want to be in the army.
STALIN : The Jews are poor fighters.
SIKORSKI: Many of the Jews who reported for military service are black marketeers or people who have been punished for smuggling. They will never make good soldiers. I do not want people of this sort in the Polish army.
ANDERS: Two hundred and fifty Jews deserted from the army camp at Buzuluk after the unfounded rumour reached them of the bom-

bardment of Kuibishev. More than sixty Jews deserted from the
Fifth Division on the eve of the distribution of the arms.

STALIN: Yes, the Jews are bad fighters.

In another conversation with Stalin, the representatives of the
Polish Government-in-exile expressed concern over Polish citizens
from the Eastern districts, who had been mobilised in the Red Army,
and, in spite of the agreement between the two governments, had
not yet been released and transferred to the Polish Army. This time,
unlike in the previous conversation, they also upheld the rights of
the minorities. What had caused this surprising change? General
Anders's report solves the riddle, and also reveals something of the
diplomatic wisdom of General Sikorski, who was considered to be an
able statesman.

SIKORSKI: I feel strongly about the fact that you are not releasing
from the Red Army and labour battalions the Polish citizens you
mobilised from the occupation zones in 1939.

STALIN: But we *are* releasing them.

ANDERS: The releases from the labour battalions began recently. But
at the moment only Poles are being released. We have been informed
officially that Byelo-Russians, Ukrainians and Jews are not going to
be released. And all of them were (and in fact never ceased to be)
Polish citizens, after you cancelled all the agreements with Germany.

STALIN: What do you want with Byelo-Russians, Ukrainians and
Jews? You need Poles, they are the best soldiers.

SIKORSKI: *I am not thinking of the people; they can be exchanged for
Poles who are Soviet citizens.* But I cannot, in principle, agree to the
instability of the frontiers of the Polish Republic. . . .

These facts, revealed in General Anders's memoirs, were of force
and effect in the winter of 1942, although we, like many other Jews,
felt their effects earlier. It is no wonder that, in the first stage of my
being at liberty in Russia, I was not accepted into the Polish Army.
Sikorski said " speculators " ; Anders said " deserters ", and Stalin
said " poor fighters ". The two Polish Generals were no doubt very
pleased to get Stalin's moral confirmation for their anti-Jewish discrimination. They did not grasp the fact that Stalin would exploit
their babblings in order to strike at Poland!

Many Jews were pounded between the millstones of the Soviet
Generalissimo's dislike for the Jews, and that of the two Polish
Generals. But a few years later all three of them learnt that Jews do

know how to fight. In Stalin's name, this fact was acknowledged by David Zaslavsky, political commentator of *Pravda*, who, at the International Journalists' Convention in Prague, spoke with wonder about the soldiers of the Irgun Zvai Leumi and their deeds. Former commanders of the Polish Army spoke of them with equal wonder, and even a certain measure of pride. In his book General Anders went so far as to promote me, retroactively, to the rank of corporal. The fact of the matter is I was never more than a private in his army ; and even that I became only by a miracle.

After I learnt of the arrest of Alter and Ehrlich I decided to speed up my departure from Dzhizak, where many people had got to know about my Zionist past. I left for Margilan, the second largest city in the famous Fergana Valley, where a Polish Army division was stationed. At headquarters I found my friend Sheskin. He told me that when he got to Kuibishev he had begun negotiations for the creation of a Jewish military unit within the Polish Army, but he did not succeed. So he joined the army, and was drafted to the Supply Corps at Divisional Headquarters in the fertile Fergana Valley. A few weeks after I arrived at Margilan my sister informed me that some " unknown person " had come to her little Tartar shack and asked where he could find me. . . .

At Margilan I found two Betar members from Vilna who more than once saved me from hunger and the debility it brought in its train.

I had a long discussion with Sheskin, as a result of which we decided to send for our friend Dr. Yohanan Bader, whom we all knew to have a brilliant brain, and consult with him about the chances of getting an exit permit for Palestine, after our friends had promised us immigration permits.

Dr. Bader who, together with his family, had been exiled to the heart of Russia, went to live in Mari, the capital of Turkomen, after his release. He travelled thousands of kilometres in order to meet us. He immediately realised that there was no prospect of getting a Soviet exit permit, and advised me to make every effort to get into the Polish Army. I doubt whether in all his judicial and public career he ever gave anyone a better piece of advice.

I did as he suggested, and presented myself before the draft board of the Division. A doctor examined me.

" Sir! " cried the doctor in a startled voice. " What sort of heart have you got ? You are a man with a serious heart ailment, how can you be a soldier ? "

The doctor almost succeeded in frightening me.

Then he examined my eyes, and cried out again : " Sir! Your vision is very faulty. You will never be able to shoot properly."

In short, I was rejected. In view of the disturbing news I had received from my sister I decided to try my luck again and apply direct, by personal letter, to the Chief of Staff. I wrote to him frankly, though at a certain risk, that if I was not accepted into the army I would be re-arrested. Sheskin saw to it that the letter reached the Chief of Staff. A few days afterwards I asked the adjutant whether there was any reply to my letter. He said that the Chief of Staff wanted to see me personally, and at this interview it would be decided whether I was to be accepted into the army or not. The interview had positive results. With a smile on his face, the Chief of Staff warned me that if the Division went abroad, he would keep a special eye on me to see that I did not take it into my head to run off to Palestine. In conclusion, he ordered me to report to the draft board. I told him I had already done so and had been turned down. " Never mind," he said. " There will be a letter from me. Go again."

I presented myself before the same draft board. The doctor who had examined me the first time asked me, in surprise and rather crossly:

" Am I mistaken ? I have the impression you've already been here once."

" Yes," I replied. " I have. But the Chief of Staff ordered me to report again."

" The Chief of Staff ? "

The doctor went up to the major in charge. I saw him hunt among his papers, and heard him say to the doctor :

" Yes, there is. Please examine him."

The doctor examined my chest.

" Heart and lungs," he said in a loud voice, " excellent! Your lungs are like iron."

He then tested my eyes.

" Hmm," he said. " You are actually shortsighted, but in the army you'll learn to shoot properly. If you try, you'll still be one of our best marksmen."

" I'll do my best, sir."

That is how I was accepted into the Polish Army.

But until I donned army uniform and was put into a military camp, I managed to see, as a free wanderer, a number of characteristic features of life in the Soviet Union.

22

GOVERNMENT AND EQUALITY

THE accepted definition of the term " State " contains three elements: territory, population and a single Government. Lenin's definition of a state contains two elements only : the oppressing class and the oppressed class. The State, wrote Lenin, is an instrument by means of which one class oppresses other classes. The aim of the proletarian revolution is, according to him, the elimination of classes and, thereby, the elimination of the State. The process of the " withering-away " of the State would begin after the victory of the Revolution.

But in my wanderings in Russia, I saw no signs of this. On the contrary, I saw the " State " in every town and village, in every place of employment and in every corner of the life of the Soviet citizen. The State not only fixes the work-quota for each one of its millions of citizens, but also chooses for him his place of work, and ties him down to it, under the ever-present threat of " re-education ". Not only does one *see* the Soviet State in everything, everywhere ; one also *hears* it unceasingly. In vain do the Americans try to speak to the Russians through the broadcasting stations of " The Voice of America ". In the Soviet Union the private homes that have a radio set are few and far between. And even such radios as there are, are as a rule capable of picking up only one of the local Russian stations which transmit the news from one centre : Moscow. Even if a Soviet citizen could by chance tune-in to broadcasts from outside the country, he would not be so foolhardy as to risk listening to the " imperialistic radio " in the presence of—his wife and children! The vast majority of the people listen to the radio in the street. The State talks to them night and day, every day, always.

It is clear to any observer that the Soviet State, instead of beginning to wither, has become the sole arbiter and the sole " provider ". The question therefore arises as to which, in the light of Lenin's definition, is the " Oppressing class ", and which the " Oppressed classes " in Russia, now that the pre-revolutionary classes, the factory and estate-owners, have been completely eliminated. Against the background of this question arises the problem of social equality in the land of Communism, in all its seriousness and in all that it embraces.

I think the genuine conquests of Communism—not by physical force, but by means of the Idea—were achieved through the slogan of equality. Although Communism promised land to the peasants, peace to the soldiers, bread to the hungry and improved living conditions for all, these promises—like all human promises—could be (and in fact were) regarded as doubtful. And reality proved that these doubts were not groundless. As against this, there is nothing doubtful about man's striving for equality. It is as natural as the striving for freedom. It can be suppressed, but not destroyed. As long as a large section of the human race really believed that differences of birth are natural differences, the striving for equality was dormant. But since the days of the French Revolution, and the general pyschological revolution that came about as a result of the First World War, there are no longer many people in the world who still believe that there are natural differences between those that dwell in palaces and those that go hungry. Communism exhorted them to rise against these differences. Therein lay, and still lies, its main strength.

It is not by chance that the Communist revolution succeeded —contrary to Marx's well-known prophecy—not in the industrially developed countries, but in the backward countries. For in the developed countries the process of perpetual enrichment on the one hand, and continual impoverishment on the other (the basic assumption of Marx's prognostications) did not occur. It is a process which, according to the author of *Das Kapital*, should have led to the creation of only two classes : the few who have everything, and the many who lack everything. But in the backward countries a wide gulf existed, and persisted. There, the strata of people with means, in their blind egoism, made no attempt to bridge the gulf, to bring the extremities of society closer together. These strata are doomed. For humanity, impelled by the striving for equality, is ever on the march. Whoever reaches the gulf has the choice either of bridging it or of falling down into it. And when a people does not bridge the gulf, instead of development comes explosion ; instead of progress, disaster.

In Russia such an explosion occurred. The privileged strata, those with considerable means, were hurled into the abyss. The Revolution triumphed. Everyone assumed there the great hour had come for equality to rule. Had the time come? And did equality prevail in the land of Communism?

I shall always see before my eyes the woman who was sentenced to five years' imprisonment as a suspected spy. I saw her in her misery, but from her story one could see that she had once been very happy and comparatively wealthy. She brought a fur coat with her from Moscow. Her husband was a factory manager, with a salary considerably higher than that of the workers in his factory. He could, therefore, buy a fine fur coat for his wife. He treated his young wife like a rich old man does in any other country. Out of affection, he lavished on her everything of the best. Which workman, of all the millions of working men in Russia, could afford to give similar expression to his feelings?

Her fur coat was not the only one I saw in the Soviet Union. One day, in the streets of Tashkent, I came across two tall, good-looking women wearing magnificent fur coats. A pleasant perfume emanated from these ladies. They were taking a stroll. Beside the one walked an officer with the rank of general; beside the other, a civilian, he, too, well-dressed. And all round these favoured couples moved Soviet citizens clad in rags; barefooted, hungry, corroded with lice. Only many years later did I see furs anything like those that covered the two Soviet ladies—in the Champs Elysées, in Paris.

But perhaps that is not the thing that really matters. The decisive question is whether privileges—manifested either in fine clothing, or comfortable homes, or good food—are the portion of individuals (who are exceptions to the general rule) or of whole strata of society. When a privilege is given to one particular stratum, and to each of the individuals in it, they become a " class " in the accepted—or, one may say, Marxist—sense of the term. It is not important if the privilege comes to these individuals in the stratum because of their possessions or because of their posts. It is the fact of the existence of the stratum-privilege that matters.

In Tashkent and in Samarkand, in Dzhizak and in Margilan, where I stayed longer than in any other cities, I managed to get to know the differences between the four kinds of " markets " in the Soviet Union. I dare say there are more than four kinds, but these are the principal ones, and the most characteristic in so far as equality, or lack of equality, are concerned. From personal observation, I was able to distinguish between the *spetz-torg*, the *voin-torg*, the Commune market and the General market, including the queue.

Spetz-torg means, literally, "special market". Although the name does emphasise the special nature of this market, it gives no hint as to whom it is intended for, or with whom it is connected. In fact, this is the special market of the N.K.V.D. Corps. In the *spetz-torg* stores, no one outside the ranks of the N.K.V.D., no one other than those who hold the special badge of the Secret Police, can obtain anything. Even members of the Communist Party, or people high up in the Party machine, have no access to the *spetz-torg* shops. Even high Government officials and high-ranking army officers may not benefit by them. The only ones entitled to avail themselves of the special market are the N.K.V.D. people and their families, who do benefit considerably by it. During the war, when the inhabitants of the Soviet Union were verily starving and bore their suffering with mass heroism, N.K.V.D. people, especially the high officers, could be seen taking white bread, butter, meat and everything of the best from the special market shops. Sometimes part of these goods used to pass to another market which I have not mentioned—it is called the black market in Russia, too. Among the guardians of the revolution there are people who like to make a little money on the side—but that is another matter.

Voin-torg means "army market", and, as its name implies, is intended for army people only. In these shops, too, there are goods that ordinary people cannot buy. But they are poorer than the special market shops. The black market is sometimes fed from this market, too.

The "free market of the communes" is open to every Soviet citizen. Certain foodstuffs are available in this market, the produce of the land-allotments worked by the kolkhoze men on their own account. These sometimes include flour, sometimes fruit and vegetables. But the prices in this market are several times higher than those in the regular market. Not every working-man can permit himself much in the way of additional provisions purchased in the kolkhoze market, especially when prices go up, whether because of diminished supply or (as happened when I was in Russia) increased demand on account of the war, mass mobilisation and the flood of refugees.

For the rank and file, for the masses of labourers and professional men, there is a general "distribution market" where, at low official prices, a very limited number of commodities is available, principally bread.

We therefore see that at the head of the social pyramid in Russia stands the secret police with its special market. At the base moves the grey multitude of workers and labourers. The intermediate grades consist of members of the Communist Party and government officials. That is the social division from the point of view of the supply of essential commodities; which is, of course, the decisive one. From the point of view of financial income, which is also important but not always decisive, public entertainers go to the top grades: singers, musicians, actors, writers and artists of various kinds. Every stratum has its market; every class its privileges.

The differences between the various social strata in Russia are unlike the differences found in other countries, where there is private ownership of the means of production. In the first place, the basis of the distinction is different. In the capitalistic countries, the basis is property; in the Soviet Union the basis is a man's function in the governmental structure. Secondly, one does not find, in Russia, the tremendous quantitative differences that exist in other countries, between the shareholders of a large production concern and the hired labourers or white-collar men in the same concern. On the disappearance and non-existence of these differences practically every Russian, even of the previous generation, who has seen other times, prides himself. More than once I had occasion to hear a Russian say:

"Do you see this big factory? It belongs to no factory-owner."

The Russian will not say: "This factory belongs to us." He may say: "This factory belongs to the Government." Generally, he contents himself with the negative fact; and that is what he is proud of.

The most serious differences between the "classes" in Russia are not quantitative, although quantitative differences do exist and are, comparatively speaking, very noticeable. The most serious differences that I saw with my own eyes are qualitative.

The difference between a person who eats luxury meals and one who satisfies his hunger with simple fare—is quantitative; the difference between a satisfied person and a hungry one—is qualitative. The difference between a man who has five suits of clothing and a man who has only one—is quantitative; the difference between a man who wears a proper suit and one who is dressed in rags—is qualitative. The difference between a man who has three pairs of shoes in his cupboard and the man who has only one pair—is quantitative; the difference between a man who has shoes to wear and a man who goes barefoot—is qualitative. It is precisely the qualitative differences in the social-economic sphere that I saw in Russia. I saw surfeited people and hungry ones; properly dressed people and people clad in tatters; people in shoes and barefooted people. There is not much justice in the existence of big quantitative differences; but qualitative differences between one man and another are appalling.

People may remind me of the fact that I was in Russia during the world war, and contend that peace-time conditions must not be judged by war-time conditions. The fact is indeed a fact, but the contention is not just. I did not see only war refugees and released prisoners; I also saw the ordinary way of life of Soviet citizens in their fixed places of abode. They were not always the losers because of the stream of refugees. On the contrary, sometimes they benefited from it and were happy to buy a shirt, or a coat, or a pair of shoes. I asked more than one person whether there was any difference between the food supplies they received before the outbreak of the war and those they received since the war. They replied that there was a difference, but not a big one. They had always known dearth, they said, and they were not ashamed of it. Actually, this statement, which I heard many times from the Russians, was in direct contradiction to what the Soviet soldiers had said in Vilna and in Kovno. These soldiers used to say: " In Russia we have everything—would you like some matches?—we have everything in Russia! " But in Vilna I also heard rosy stories about the labour camps!

The most characteristic and striking feature of the Soviet Social structure is the economic supremacy of the N.K.V.D. people. They are always dressed in smart uniforms or good suits. Their shoes, or their high boots, are always highly polished. Their food they buy from the special market. The change in the hierarchy of the rulership which Garin told me about was evident in the economic sphere, too. In Lenin's time the secret police force was an instrument in the hands of the *ruling* Communist Party. (In those days there was no special market.) In Stalin's time the Communist Party became a tool in the hands of the N.K.V.D. force, the *ruler*. (And the *spetz-torg* came into being.) The ruler became " the rich ", comparatively speaking ; and " the rich " became the absolute ruler.

One might ask : Is there no envy of the privileged people in Russia? And if the differences are the differences between the satisfied and the hungry, the shod and the shoe-less, why does not natural, justifiable envy find expression as it does in other countries, particularly in countries where qualitative economic differences exist between one social stratum and another ?

The N.K.V.D. supplies the answer to this question. It has succeeded in inculcating into the inhabitants of the Soviet Union the absolute recognition of the hopelessness, the futility, of any sort of opposition to the government. It has succeeded in instilling abject fear into the marrow of the bones of its citizens. It is not the ordinary fear of authority and punishment. It is the horror of disaster. Like a man hanging by his hands over a deep, dark, yawning abyss—so does the Soviet citizen dread the sight of the green caps of the state security service.

There is profound " social " envy in Russia, just as there is in other countries ; but in other countries envy is sometimes stronger than fear : in the Soviet Union fear is stronger than envy.

Although there is no economic equality in Russia (in spite of the promises of Communism) there is—in the realm of the N.K.V.D. —another equality : the equality of fear.

23

THE RULES OF THE QUEUE

FROM one end of the Soviet Union to the other you can hear the question : " What are they giving ? " A Soviet citizen does not ask : " What are they selling ?" What he asks is: "*Chto diut?*"— What are they giving ? And having received a reply he takes his place in the queue. If he is lucky, after a long and tiring wait, he is allowed to pay his money for what he has been " given ". I saw people attach themselves to any long queue they happened to see, without even asking the routine question. In the end, they would discover that it was not a bread or soap queue, but a queue for chits authorising disinfection, or at any rate attempted disinfection.

Among our neighbours in Dzhizak I made the acquaintance of a woman of Jewish extraction who was married to a Russian. She had the face of an angel, but life had been very cruel to her. As the result of an accident, she had lost the use of both legs and become an incurable invalid. Her husband, an energetic, tall, good-looking young man, was devoted to her, heart and soul. They had no children. The man had not only his day's work to do, but he also had to stand for hours—sometimes late into the night—in the various queues in order to keep the household provided with the necessities of life.

The woman was sorry for her husband, who used to come home tired and worn out from work and broken after the long hours in the queues. More than once she complained to me about the difficulties of queue-life, which consumed the man's little free time and sapped his energy. I asked her whether there had always been queues in the Soviet Union, or whether they were the result of the war and the big stream of refugees. She laughed and said : " It's impossible that there should not be a queue here. There were queues before the war, too ; we've always had queues. But we are not ashamed of it. We know that you people abroad live better, but we are working for a great ideal. The important things is that Stalin is with us. The difficulties don't matter, they will pass ; only let Stalin always be with us. Now, Menachem Wolfovitch, tell me, please, how it was in your country. How did you get your food supplies ? "

"Very simply," I replied. " My wife used to 'phone the near-by grocer's store, order rolls, butter, cheese or whatever else she wanted, and the delivery boy used to bring the goods to the house."

The woman went into peals of laughter.

"What are you laughing at ? " I asked, astonished.

She controlled her laughter with difficulty. " Look," she said, " we are speaking as friends. I told you frankly about our living conditions, so why are you giving me capitalistic propaganda ? "

"What capitalistic propaganda ? " I asked, with increasing astonishment. "What I said was true. I give you my word, my wife used to have the supplies sent to the house if she did not want to go to the shop herself, or if she had no time to do so. Don't you believe me ? "

"Stop it, stop it. You know I would never insult you, so why should you insult me ? Do you take me for a dolt ? I have heard some of the propaganda about the way people live in the capitalistic countries, but why do you repeat this ludicrous stuff ? I can understand that you people had easier lives than ours. But to ring up and order butter, cheese . . . and on top of it all a boy delivers it all to the house ? Stop it, Menachem Wolfovitch, stop it. Don't try to tell me such yarns again."

It was useless trying to convince her that what I had said was true. The woman kept on laughing at me, and repeating : " Stop it, stop it! " Under no circumstances would she believe that there need not be a queue, that it was possible to order commodities—even such delicacies as butter and Swiss cheese!—and have them sent home. She dismissed it as nothing more than capitalistic propaganda. She and her husband, of the generation of the Revolution, never even dreamt of ordering goods by telephone. Perhaps they hoped that the queue might one day be done away with, but they doubted the feasibility of this ever happening. Had the queue but been shortened, or the hours of waiting cut down, they would have been contented with their lot, and would have repeated after Stalin : " Life in the Soviet Union has been made easier, better . . ."

An entire philosophy has arisen around the queue in Russia. In the queue stand men, women, old people, young people, children.

The various members of the family take it in turns to keep the place in the queue. The big families with many children are the aristocracy of the queue. They are able to keep places in several queues at once. Small families are in a difficult situation. Bachelors are not to be envied at all.

In Sverdlovsk I was standing in a very long bread queue one day. There were almost a thousand people in it. I had already begun to draw nearer to the distribution point. Behind me stood hundreds of people who had come after me. (The length of the queue behind you is always a great consolation. It makes the waiting easier.) Suddenly they announced that the supply of bread had run out. I doubt whether there is any joy in the world to compare with that of the last man to receive the ration. The people behind him were disappointed, but patient. They were promised that a fresh batch of bread would be brought shortly. We had to wait, and keep our places in the queue. Several hours went by and still no bread. Suddenly, one of the people in the queue called out : " Who's got an indelible pencil ? " In the hungry horde they found a man with a tiny stub of copying-pencil. He agreed to hand it over for the public good. The man who had asked for it went along the line pencilling in the palm of each person's hand—which had been well-moistened with spit at his request—a large numeral to indicate his position in the queue. I was also given a number, and left the queue together with the rest. I made a calculation that if they brought the bread immediately it would take two to three hours for my turn to come round. I went into town in the hope of meeting, perchance, Soviet Jews of the previous generation. I wanted to ask if they had a synagogue. I met old Jews, but could find no synagogue. I went into a public reading-room, called in Russian an *agit-punkt*, or propaganda point. I read a few newspapers and browsed through some of Lenin's writings. I became absorbed in my reading and forgot my hunger. When I came back to the queue I had no alternative but to attach myself to its tail-end. I did show the number on the palm of my hand, but I was informed that my turn had already passed. I had lost my place. There is no mercy in the queue.

Nor is there any politeness in the queue. A young man will not give up his place to an old one, nor will a man give preference to a woman, or a child. They cannot. Everyone is hungry. They are all shivering with cold. They all have hungry families waiting for them. The queue is an expression of the fight for existence. Politeness is a concomitant of existence-without-fighting. Although in some queues in which I stood precedence was given to women with babies in their arms, in other queues even these were not allowed to go first. The irritable people in the queue used to claim that mothers brought their babies with the express purpose of arousing pity, and thus stealing to the top of the queue.

The word *priduritsa*, which means to dissimulate, or pretend, became a noun in the language of the queue. Not only women carrying babies were charged with *priduritsa*, but also anyone who tried to chat with a friend standing in the queue. As a matter of fact, the suspicions of the people in the back section were not always groundless. More than once I saw people begin to chat innocently with someone nearer the distribution point and, after a while, when the others had grown used to seeing him, merge into the queue and become one of the first to receive the ration. Heaven help the man who tried this and did not succeed! If he is caught, the man to whom he is talking is also not to be envied. The cry: "Hi, there! Are you trying *priduritsa*?" is to be heard in every queue.

Just as the general and perpetual dearth has wiped out the warm hospitality so characteristic of the Russians, so has the queue eliminated practically all courtesy between man and his fellow men. In Tashkent I said "Thank you" to a charming young woman who was weighing out my bread ration. She turned to her companion and said, jeeringly: "Did you hear that? He stands in the queue, pays money, and says 'Thank you'!"

There is no danger of being infected with politeness in the queue, but there is every danger of typhus infection. Inhabitants of Uzbekistan told me that typhus epidemics were an annual occurrence in their area. Its main carrier is the queue, for the lice go from person to person as they stand crowded together in the queue for hours on end. The Russians fight against this menace principally with the aid of "Disinfectors", enormous vats outside every public bath. The bather puts his clothing and undergarments into these vats so that the great heat may exterminate the lice. The Russians are very proud of this hygienic arrangement. A Soviet soldier, who had been in Lwow until the outbreak of the Germano-Russian war, once remarked: "Ah, yes, Lwow is a beautiful city. It has fine cinemas, big cafés, but the people are uncivilised. . . . In the whole city I did not find one single disinfector." Of course, without the disinfector the situation would have been much worse; but the queue, crowded as it usually is, resurrects what the steaming vat has killed.

Why do the Soviet authorities not do away with the queue? In theory, there is no special difficulty in doing away with this " institution " of the Soviet regime. If, in a town like Dzhizak, the authorities were to open another ten bread shops, bread queues would no longer stretch along its slushy streets. But it is, possibly, not such a simple matter, if we take into account the organisational difficulties involved in distributing from one source and one centre, for two hundred million souls. It is also possible that there is another reason for the existence of the queues in Russia. There are grounds for supposing that the authorities are interested in maintaining the institution of the queue. It is true that the queue is a source of internal dissatisfaction, suppressed and silenced though it may be. Nevertheless, in so far as the people grow accustomed to it, like they do to most other afflictions, it is actually a " pro-revolutionary " factor in that it prevents the citizens from thinking of other things. The man in the queue is completely preoccupied with getting to the top of it, with getting what they are " giving ", with not missing an opportunity, not returning home empty-handed. His entire thoughts are concentrated on getting what is required for mere subsistence.

The State distribution-system, with its single centre, of which the queue is a concomitant, is intended to do away with the necessity for middle-men, " mediators " between the producer and the consumer. There are no merchants in the Soviet Union; the distributors of the merchandise are " commercial workers ", they are government officials. But has *commerce* been done away with in the Soviet Union, with the liquidation of the merchant class?

Garin's remark : " We are always short of everything in Russia", was, I found, particularly true of essentials. For days I hunted for a toothbrush in the big city of Tashkent, without finding one. If the head of a Primus stove breaks, it is most difficult to replace. If the glass of an oil-lamp bursts, it will take weeks to find another. This chronic shortage is not to be wondered at. Being the sole ruler and also the sole provider, it is obvious that the government will not put the consumers' convenience first. Its first concern will be the requirements of the government and the war industry.

Russians to whom I spoke made no attempt to conceal from me the fact that they put the perpetual shortage of essentials down to the disappearance of the stratum of people who concern themselves with the consumers' convenience for their own sakes : that is to say, merchants. They did not deny that it would be a good thing if the Soviet authorities were to permit " petty commerce ". Not one Russian of all those I came in contact with ever said that it would be better if the factories were transferred to private owner-ship. But they all would have liked to see an extension of the free kolkhoze-market : that is to say, an increase in the allotment of lands that are worked privately by the farmers. And practically all of them would have liked to see a little " petty commerce ". The clearest expression of this was given to me by a man who admitted that he was a Trotskyist. Naturally, I did not find him in one of the queues. I met him on the banks of the Pechora. The man was a Russian. He began the conversation by lauding what he called Jewish common-sense. " I was for Trotsky," he said, " and always will be, even if I have to spend the rest of my life here. If Trotsky were in power our situation would have been entirely different. Trotsky knows what is good for the people. He insisted that free petty commerce be permitted. . . ."

Actually, there was never any such clause in Trotsky's programme, but it is characteristic that the Trotskyist should attribute to his leader what he thought the masses wanted.

But in the meantime the masses in Russia are compelled to make do with what they are " given ". That does not mean that there is no commerce in the Soviet Union. On the contrary, commerce in Russia is flourishing, and touches practically every home. One might say that there is hardly a Soviet citizen who does not try his hand, now and then, at buying and selling or at barter. I doubt whether there is another country in the world where there are so many reciprocal commercial transactions as there are in the Soviet Union. This too is one of the paradoxes of the Soviet regime : the merchant class had been liquidated, and every one occupied himself with commerce. The nation of toilers has also become a nation of merchants.

During my stay in Dzhizak I once stood in a queue, off and on, from four in the morning until late at night. My brother-in-law relieved me now and again. We were waiting for bread. Every few hours they would announce that the precious bread would arrive shortly. But it still did not come. Eventually, after waiting a whole day, we were informed that there would not be any bread as the milling machine had broken down and the bakeries had run out of flour. The long queue dispersed. The people went home hungry. Their families had waited in vain for their daily bread. Hungry, they went to bed.

Next day I got into the line again. I gave the bread department eight coupons for the four people living in our hut.

" Why do you give me yesterday's coupons ? " the woman distributor asked.

" What do you mean ? We didn't get bread yesterday, the flour mill was out of order," I replied, surprised.

" Do you think I don't know what happened at the flour mill? I know you didn't get bread yesterday. But *piruzhil?* You lived through the day ? If so, then everything is in order. You don't get bread for yesterday here. Here is bread for four coupons."

I tried to persuade her, but it was no use. She stood by her *piruzhil*—I had lived through it, so it was all right. This too was one of the rules of the queue in the Soviet Union.

But the main thing I learnt from the queue was this : all the Soviet citizens who waited for the bread ration with me were hungry and starved. Bread was actually their only food. Very few of them were lucky enough to be able to get an onion-stalk or a radish in the kolkhoze market as a sole addition to the promised bread ration. For almost an entire day they stood on their feet and waited, without uttering one word of complaint against the so-called arrangements. When, after twenty-four hours of waiting, they heard the terrible announcement " No bread ", again they did not utter one word of complaint, and went quietly home. There is no doubt that in any other country bread riots would have broken out in such circumstances. In the Soviet Union no riot accompanies the mass hunger.

In the queue I learnt that, contrary to accepted theory, it *is* possible to change human nature. The regime in the Soviet Union has, from many points of view, changed the nature of the people who live there. The Soviet regime has shifted the boundaries within which man can stand suffering without rebelling ; a limit which outside the Soviet Union would be regarded as being the ultimate one, or even beyond the ultimate one. Shifting the boundary or limit of suffering is, for absolute rule, a mighty power-factor. How is it done? The queue and the N.K.V.D. know the way—and the price.

In a little town between Samarkand and Bokhara I was told that the bread distributor was a Jew. In the past I had heard that the

Bokharan Jews had retained their attachment to the Hebrew language and used to teach their children the Bible and the Talmud even under the Soviet regime. So I decided to try my luck. When my turn came, I asked the man in Hebrew : " Have you a synagogue here ? "

He looked up and answered in Hebrew : " Are you a Hebrew ? "

There was no synagogue in that town ; I found one in Samarkand. But until the day I left there to go to Samarkand I was not short of bread. Jewish—or Hebrew—solidarity does sometimes function in the Soviet Union.

But, on the whole, I learnt of a different kind of " solidarity " in the queue. There was hardly a day, hardly a queue, in all my peregrinations that I did not hear the following remarks :

" Hi, Abraham! Who are you pushing ? "

" *Chitroi*[1] Abraham, *he* didn't go to the front. His life is more precious than the life of a Russian *muzhik*."[2]

" You know, a certain Abrahka arrived here yesterday as a poor refugee. He had a suitcase full of ten-rouble pieces."

" Jews aren't at the front, we all know that! Why should they be at the front ? Aren't there enough Russians ? "

I never heard the word " zhid " in the queues. In Russia—apart from the concentration camp—I only heard it once. I was walking in the main street of the city of Fergana. In front of me walked a Russian who was shouting at the top of his voice : " All Jews should be slaughtered! " He spoke with dangerous sincerity. He was drunk.

But it is the sober words of the people in the queue, who are in possession of their faculties, that help one to understand how the Jewish problem has been " solved " in the Soviet Union. These words came mainly from youngsters between the ages of fifteen and seventeen, products of the generation of the Revolution, all or most of them members of the Komsomol. Which means that the Soviet Youth had heard about *Chitroi Abraham* at home, or in school, or in both places. These words not only explain why Ilya Ehrenburg tried to prove that many Jews had fallen on the various fronts of the Second World War ; they also explain what has happened in the shadow of the Third World War, when the order was given for a hate-campaign, considered an essential preliminary to every war, placing " wily Abraham " behind the new main enemy, America.

[1] " Abraham is wily . . ."   [2] Peasant.

24

AFTER THE DEATH OF STALIN[1]

MY contemporaries and their children will see an England without Churchill and a Russia without Stalin. No one asks: " What will happen to England after Churchill dies ? " While not for one moment questioning the spiritual greatness of the man who came to power on the threshold of the successful withdrawal from Dunkirk and who, with the turning of the tide in the East and the West, ultimately achieved success, everyone nevertheless knows that when he retires from the scene, the young woman, Elizabeth, will continue to be Queen of Britain, and one of the Conservatives, or one of the Labourites, will be Prime Minister of Her Majesty's Government. It is almost certain that Britain will go on " granting " independence to the peoples over which she still rules directly, and continue to try and rule them indirectly. It is difficult to maintain a pauper State. It is impossible to maintain a pauper Empire. Churchill's political activity is not retarding this process. His death will not speed it up. At any rate, it will not speed it up to any appreciable extent.

Stalin is only three years younger than Churchill. If we are to go by the laws of nature, and what is known to medical science, the Soviet ruler, too, will have no option but to leave the arena in the 'fifties or—if we are to take into account the Georgian propensity for longevity—in the 'sixties.

And everyone is asking: " What will happen in Russia after Stalin goes the way of all flesh ? "

I have heard two answers to this hypothetical but fateful question : the one, as usually happens, the exact opposite of the other. The one says that with the death of Stalin the Soviet regime will collapse. The other says that after Stalin's death another Bolshevik ruler will take his place and nothing will change in Soviet Russia.

[1] This chapter was written more than a month before the news reached the world of Stalin's illness and subsequent death.

Those who give the first reply base themselves on the laws of history. A one-man rulership, they say, collapses with the removal of the sole ruler. Although one finds throughout history that a military defeat from without generally brings about the fall of a dictatorship, it does not follow that the departure of a dictator will always lead to the *automatic* collapse of the dictatorship.

In any event, the one-man rulership in the Soviet Union cannot be likened to the dictatorships known in other periods and in other countries. The Soviet rulership does not stand above the economic structure of the population ; it is the proprietor of that structure. In its capacity as sole " provider ", the Russian one-man rulership has penetrated into every corner of the life of the people, into every cell of the life of the individual. The ordinary laws of history concerning dictatorships, in so far as such laws exist, do not apply to extraordinary one-man rule. Therefore, one cannot accept the view that on the day when a Moscow radio announcer broadcasts the news of the death of Lenin's heir the edifice whose erection began in November, 1917, will collapse.

But are they right, who maintain that after Stalin's death nothing will change in Russia, except that someone else will become the " wisest of all men " ? People of this school of thought draw their inference from the Lenin-Stalin precedent. Lenin, they say, was also a dictator, and what happened after his death ? There was friction among his potential heirs, but one of them got the better of the rest and became sole ruler in his predecessor's place. That, they reckon, is what will happen after Stalin's death as well.

Logic demands that a fundamental distinction be drawn between Lenin's method of ruling and the character of Stalin's rule. Of course, Lenin also stood at the head of a dictatorial regime ; but he was not a dictator over dictators. He was one of them, even if he was at their head. Lenin used to seek compromises with his friends, to try and convince them. Sometimes he accepted their opinion, contrary to his own, as, for example, in the matter of the negotiations with the Germans at Brest-Litovsk. Sometimes he succeeded in proving to his companions that he was right, as happened after the German-Bolshevik talks broke down and the Kaiser's army renewed its offensive against Russia. Lenin was quite capable of censuring his comrades in public, as he did in the case of Zinoviev and Kamenev after they had published a statement, on the threshold of the October Revolution, in which they openly accused him of being on the verge of bringing catastrophe to the working classes by his attempt at armed revolt. But Lenin also knew how to forgive. Even for this statement, which endangered not only his life's work but his life itself, Lenin forgave his comrades who had opposed him.

Lenin never compelled them to retreat from their stand, or renounce their opinions. He never had any of them killed. . . . And Stalin?

It is possible that the differences between Lenin's and Stalin's methods of ruling arose out of the differences in the characters of the two revolutionary leaders. It is certain that the sources from which their rules were nurtured were different. Lenin attained the rulership by conquest. Stalin inherited it. All his life Lenin's influence over his comrades was merely a moral or intellectual one. He continued to use this means of influence in the few years he ruled. Stalin, at the age of thirty-eight, had already concentrated in his hands the instruments of power. When he came to full power he had behind him, for years already, not only mighty governmental power, but also the habitude of using it. He did not begin right away to kill off his rivals, but, as ruler, he tended to resort to liquidation rather than to persuasion. Lenin could threaten to resign, to remove *himself* from the scene. But Stalin removes his rival comrades from this world! Lenin's rule was that of " the first among equals "; Stalin is a dictator over dictators. From the point of view of revolutionary theory, Lenin was a far greater man than Stalin. But because of the differences in their methods of ruling the vacuum in the Soviet leadership after the death of Stalin will be considerably greater than that created after the death of Lenin.

There is a second factor that makes it impossible to judge by the Lenin-Stalin precedent. That is the factor of the heirs. There is a tendency to overlook the historical fact that Trotsky, Stalin's main rival, began his fight not in opposition to Stalin but in bitter opposition to Lenin. This was not a conflict confined to the innermost chambers of the Kremlin. On the contrary, Trotsky's opposition to the methods of the Party Executive under Lenin was known to all the members of the Communist Party, in fact to everyone in the Soviet Union, through the Press and from public meetings. In order to crush the opposition of Trotsky and his supporters, Lenin, at the last Party Congress in which he participated, proposed the establishment of the office of General Secretary, which had hitherto not existed in the Party. And it was Lenin who proposed that Stalin be appointed to this central, decisive position. Trotsky himself confirms this in his book, whose last but not concluding pages were reddened with the blood of his battered brain. Actually, Trotsky maintains that a few weeks before his death Lenin severed his personal relations with Stalin because of an ill-mannered reply which the latter gave Krupskaya, Lenin's wife. But even if this was true, it was not known except to a very few of those who frequented the Kremlin; just as the contents of Lenin's will, in which he demanded that Stalin be removed from office, were known to only a very limited group of men at the top.

In the eyes of the rank and file of the Party, and the people as a whole, Trotsky emerged after the death of Lenin as the opponent of the great revolutionary leader, while Stalin emerged as the man loyal to Lenin, the guardian of his policy, the man who would continue in his footsteps. In a dictatorship, just as in a monarchy, considerable importance is attached to the question of the succession. From the very first moment, therefore, Stalin had an important advantage —the advantage of loyalty and continuity—over his principal rival and over all the rest of his rivals.

None of Stalin's heirs will have this advantage. No one of them will have opposed him, *could* have opposed him. All will have been loyal to him. For all of them he will have been the final authority, the only one to decide. The people, at any rate, have not heard and do not know of any differences of opinion between Molotov and Stalin that Malenkov or Beria could exploit to prove that he, and not Molotov, is the right man to carry on. The same applies to Molotov in relation to Malenkov, or Malenkov in relation to Beria, or Beria in relation to his two comrades. Is, therefore, a triumvirate the solution?

Ever since the time of Julius Caesar, up to the time of Stalin, triumvirates have proved to be arenas of conflict among those who constitute them. While Stalin had an initial advantage as "loyal successor", over Trotsky, the "rebel opponent", the three men who, on the face of it, are destined to take Stalin's place are equal from the point of view of the succession. Accordingly, one may assume that the inevitable clashes within this triumvirate will not just be conflicts at "palace" level, but will be reflected all the way down.

And lower down, even if there are no classes from the point of view of ownership of property or of the means of production, there have developed in the meantime separate governmental bodies, or blocks, which vie with one another unceasingly for greater influence, or complete control. The four main bodies are : the secret police force, the Red Army, the Communist Party and the trade unions. This inter-block competition for key positions and decisive authority in government already exists, while Stalin is still alive. Many purges have taken place as a result of this rivalry. But the shadow of Stalin, the great Liquidator and the great Victor, continues to camouflage the cracks in the wall of Soviet single rulership. When Stalin goes the cracks are likely not only to be exposed, but to widen dangerously.

It is possible that the Communist Party will try—through one of the rulers who will put himself up as its champion—to get back the standing it had in the days of Lenin, which it lost to the N.K.V.D. in Stalin's day. But the most serious conflict, and the one most dangerous to the Soviet regime, is liable to break out between the N.K.V.D. and the army. They both have arms. And they hate each other.

I had an acquaintance in the ancient city of Samarkand, a Jewish refugee from Riga, who became friendly with a colonel in the Red Army and often used to drink with him to the success of their common enterprises and to victory over the Germans. This acquaintance told me that during one of these drinking bouts the high Soviet officer, having befuddled his brain with Arak, began to embrace and kiss his Jewish friend, and cried : " Believe me, let us just finish with Hitler, then we'll fix those bastards, the N.K.V.D. devils. . . ." Incidents that have occurred in the past give credence to the view that what the colonel said was not just the opinion of an individual in the high ranks of the army.

Besides the contending bodies, there are, in the Soviet empire, centrifugal forces. I am not referring to the annexed countries, most—or all—of which are likely to follow in Tito's footsteps after Stalin dies. I am referring to the nationalities within the boundaries of Soviet Russia. The Soviet regime has, indeed, done very much to give " national form " to the " socialist content " of the lives of the national territorial minorities. Both in the north and in Uzbekistan I have seen newspapers in the language of the local inhabitants. Actually, the inhabitants, to the extent that they have learnt to read and write at all, can and do read Russian ; and the local national paper is used more for making cigarettes than for reading. But it continues to appear nonetheless.

That does not mean to say that the Soviet regime has succeeded in overcoming the traditional hatred between the various peoples who have been assembled within the confines of the vast Russian State, or the framework of the Soviet Union. I saw, among other things, conspicuous signs of the hatred of the Uzbeks for the Russians. One of the clearest expressions of this hatred lay in its " reflex " on the part of the Russians. Once, on the outskirts of Dzhizak, I came upon a noisy gathering, an unusual sight in the Soviet Union. I asked the reason for it and a woman told me that they had again arrested an Uzbek with a little Russian boy. " These Uzbeks kidnap our children," she said.

If my analysis of all the factors is correct, the following conclusion may be drawn :

Just as there are no grounds for supposing that when Stalin dies the Soviet regime will immediately collapse, so there is no justification for thinking that nothing will change in Russia after his death. As against this, there are definite grounds for thinking that within a certain period after Stalin's death the conflicts between the heirs and their followers will come to a head, the rivalry among the four " bodies " will be intensified, and the centrifugal tendencies of the national minorities will increase. All these factors can—although not immediately—lead to far-reaching changes in the rulership of the Soviet Union. They can lead to the creation of a State entirely different from that which exists today in the vast area that stretches from Vladivostok to Frankfurt.

The most important of these conclusions, or postulations, affects not only Russia but humanity as a whole. If, during the next five or ten years, the human race is not dragged into a Third World War, there is a good chance that we of this generation and our children will be entirely spared from the danger of total atomic destruction.

25

NONETHELESS . . .

" PEOPLE don't get out of here," said the sentry who escorted me to the transit camp on the banks of the Pechora.

" Date of release : 20th September, 1948," the prison-clerk wrote in the transit-camp office.

What the sentry said was true ; what the clerk wrote was true. It was the truth of the N.K.V.D. whose authorised representative scoffed at the non-existent State, and who said to me with complete conviction :

" No, you will not see the Jewish State."

But——

On the night of May 15th, 1948, I stood behind the microphone of the secret radio station of the Irgun Zvai Leumi and spoke to my people :

"After long years of underground warfare, of persecution and suffering, mental and physical suffering, those who rose against the oppressor stand before you now, with thanksgiving on their lips and a prayer in their hearts. In bloody battle, in a war of liberation, the State of Israel has arisen. . . ."

It cannot be denied that tyranny is a truth, a terrible truth. But there is also another truth. Happy is the man who believes in the truth that repudiates tyranny ; happy is he who rejects the belief that tyranny is all-powerful. Indeed, he will experience dark days and nights of interrogation, nights of hard labour, underground nights, nights of mental suffering—*white nights*. All this will be his portion.

But a day will come, and he will bask in the sunshine of a child's laughter.